AMETHI

Anant Vijay has been active in journalism for nearly twenty-five years. His articles on politics, literature and cinema are read across the country. He did BA (Hons) in history from Bhagalpur University and followed it up with a post graduate degree in journalism from University of Delhi. He also holds a postgraduate diploma in business management. He is the author of eleven books. Among these, *Prasangvash*, *Kolahal Kalah Mein*, *Vidhaaon ka Vinyaas*, *Bollywood Selfie*, *Loktantra ki Kasauti* and *Marxvaad ka Ardhsatya* have been quite well received. Anant Vijay is currently working with *Dainik Jagran* as Associate Editor. He received the National Award (Swarna Kamal) for best writing on cinema in 2018.

Debdutta Bhattacharjee is Assistant Editor at Daily and Online News Network. A product of Hindu College (Delhi University) and Delhi School of Economics, he has varied experience in journalism, having worked for frontline media organisations. He has published nearly 250 articles covering subjects from politics to economy and sports to aviation.

ANANT VIJAY

AMETHI

FROM DYNASTY TO DEMOCRACY

TRANSLATED FROM THE HINDI
BY DEBDUTTA BHATTACHARJEE

Published in Hindi as *Amethi Sangram* in 2020 by Eka, an imprint of Westland Publications Private Limited

Published in English as *Dynasty to Democracy* in 2021 by Westland Publications Private Limited

Published in English as *Amethi: From Dynasty to Democracy* in 2024 by Westland Non-Fiction, an imprint of Westland Books, a division of Nasadiya Technologies Private Limited

No. 269/2B, First Floor, 'Irai Arul', Vimalraj Street, Nethaji Nagar, Alapakkam Main Road, Maduravoyal, Chennai 600095

Westland, the Westland logo, Westland Non-Fiction and the Westland Non-Fiction logo are the trademarks of Nasadiya Technologies Private Limited, or its affiliates.

Copyright © Anant Vijay, 2024

Anant Vijay asserts the moral right to be identified as the author of this work.

ISBN: 9789357769952

10 9 8 7 6 5 4 3 2 1

Typeset by Ashutosh Jha

Printed at Saurabh Printers Pvt. Ltd

*To that will to live, whose triumph deepened
our faith in democracy.*

Contents

Author's Note

After writing political commentaries for a long time, I had virtually given it up for the past four years or so. After this decision, I made politics of culture the subject of my writing, and its various dimensions are what I deal with nowadays. In the meantime, the Lok Sabha election of 2019 came about. This election was witness to several big incidents. Contrary to all estimates, the BJP under Narendra Modi's leadership notched up a historic win. It was during this election that one of the constituencies received a result that nobody could have anticipated. None of the pre-poll surveys could predict this. No poll pundit could catch any signal of the big upset that was in store in Uttar Pradesh's Amethi Lok Sabha seat, let alone so much as predict it. There, the BJP candidate Smriti Irani beat the then Indian National Congress president Rahul Gandhi by more than 55,000 votes. Even noted journalists in Delhi didn't expect the winds of change in Amethi. Not even those who had visited Amethi a number of times and reported from there. They missed the hint even when Rahul Gandhi announced that he would contest from Wayanad as well apart from Amethi. It was beyond their imagination that Rahul Gandhi could even lose from his so-called fortress. A number of journalist friends declared through their articles or on news channels that Rahul Gandhi would win in Amethi. By and large, all the surveys had handed the victory to Congress in two seats of Uttar Pradesh—Raebareli and Amethi. One of the surveys had certainly forecast a close fight, but it had also given the edge to Congress. According to that estimate, there was a neck-and-neck contest on the cards in Amethi and either candidate could win or lose by a margin of 3 per cent. However, Irani defeated Rahul Gandhi by a margin of nearly 6 per cent. This was a major political event in the history of independent India. I believe that the impact of this event and the shadow of Rahul Gandhi's defeat would haunt the Congress for a long time.

Rahul Gandhi had accepted defeat even before the result was officially declared. That was when I got fascinated to identify the factors that helped Irani in defeating Rahul Gandhi in the end. I spoke to several people. Nobody had a concrete answer. What happened in that place, which had been projected for years as the Nehru-Gandhi bastion, that Rahul Gandhi had to face defeat? The voters of an area, whose emotional attachment with the Nehru-Gandhi family continues to resonate in the political landscape, showed their displeasure with the family scion. It was from here that the plan to write a book on Irani's victory in Amethi started to take shape. However, my decision to not write on politics was coming in its way. Anyway, keeping my decision aside, when I started to uncover the electoral history of Amethi, a number of interesting facts began emerging. When I started reading about the previous elections in Amethi, intriguing incidents came to light. Many political manoeuvrings became visible. By this time, I had made up my mind about writing the book. Then it struck me that I should visit Amethi for fact-finding. I travelled throughout the constituency. I even went to those places about which I had read in a few newspapers and magazines. I also saw Irani's rented house in Gauriganj, which was at the centre of discussion during the election. It was described as being palatial. However, it turned out to be only an ordinary house. I also visited the Alok dhaba, where, according to a magazine, dozens of air conditioners were put up during the 2014 Lok Sabha election. However, I couldn't even find that many rooms there. The picture painted about Amethi had started to fade. After that, I met and talked to numerous people associated with the Indian National Congress (INC), Bharatiya Janata Party (BJP) and Rashtriya Swayamsevak Sangh (RSS). I also met the common people in different areas of the constituency and listened to their opinions. After speaking to all these people, only one thing came to my mind—Amethi was never a Congress bastion. In this book, I have discussed in detail why and how it was so. After visiting Amethi for the first time, I gradually came to know of several people who could give me insider accounts. I tried to meet all of them. A number of them spared their time, several others spoke over the phone. Some of them rudely turned me down, while some others retracted after promising to give their time. In the meantime, I visited Amethi thrice. After travelling across all the Assembly constituencies there, I realised that to make sense of Irani's historic win in 2019, one needs to analyse the entire period from the 2014 election to 2019. The activities in Amethi during this time have to be learnt. Speaking to people and perusing newspaper reports of that period seemed to be the only option. That was what I did. I caught up with people with links to the 2014 election and learnt about their experiences. After talking to the people in the Amethi Lok Sabha constituency, I felt that there was an urge for change among them. They were waiting for a party to contest the election wholeheartedly from there. The BJP fought the 2014 election enthusiastically. The party candidate reached every village. After that, I met those who had been active during the 2014 and 2019 Lok Sabha polls, among whom were people from both the BJP and the Congress. As part of this process, I went to Goa and met its chief minister Dr Pramod Sawant and listened to his experience. In Lucknow, I met people for several days and gathered information. The only purpose of sharing these stories is to tell you that most of the information in this book has been accumulated from primary and authentic sources. The book is now in your hands. I look forward to your opinions.

Anant Vijay

1 March 2021

Foreword

The Italian social scientist, Vilfredo Pareto, propounded the theory of circulation of elite to explain the process of transfer of political power from governing to the non-governing elites in undemocratic countries with the assumption that there are only two categories of people, i.e., elites and the masses. According to him, the governing elite enjoy power and authority on the basis of the so-called merit, popularity and moral authority. But subsequently, they become corrupt, authoritarian and irrelevant and gradually lose both social and legal legitimacy. But they adopt tricks to remain in power. For quite some time, such tricks and manipulative behaviour provide oxygen to them but ultimately, they are thrown out of power by the non-governing elites. Hence, the non-governing becomes governing elite and vice-versa. The role of common people is notional in transfer of power because the environment is undemocratic. To some extent, this model is also useful to understand the process of transfer of political authority in a democratic setting like India.

Indian National Congress in general and Rahul Gandhi in particular lost 2019 parliamentary election in the country and in

Amethi respectively because both of them lost ties with and support from citizens of this country. Both of them behaved like a rootless and non-responsive entity. Rahul Gandhi failed to connect with the people of Amethi, depended on power brokers, remained an absentee landlord and could not prove himself in spite of his victory in the 2014 election. There was near absence of development in an underdeveloped but VIP constituency like Amethi and an inability to understand pulse of the people. Rahul Gandhi and his party couldn't understand or counter the challenges created by BJP and Smriti Irani. Non-availability of dedicated workers for Rahul Gandhi played prime role in his defeat and in Smriti Irani's victory in the 2019 election.

Anant Vijay, the author of this book, rightly observed that constant contact with people of Amethi and honest concern for their miseries since the day of Irani's defeat in 2014 prepared a social background for her victory in 2019 election. She was able to establish and use vertical and horizontal linkages with voters of the constituency, opinion makers, dedicated RSS workers and well-wishers sitting in Delhi and elsewhere. Blessings of Prime Minister, who commands mass following, were more than sufficient in winning the battle. As the essential requirements to win the battle were absent in the Rahul Gandhi camp, neither Rahul Gandhi nor his supporters were able to understand pulse of the 21st century youth in Uttar Pradesh. They don't know development activities, if any, done by Indian National Congress and Rahul Gandhi in Amethi in the last two decades.

Anant Vijay is fair in saying that by contesting also from Wayanad, Rahul Gandhi proved that he was not sure about winning in Amethi. Of course he won Wayanad (Kerala) but it has long and short term political ramifications for Rahul Gandhi himself and the Indian National Congress, its followers and supporters, on both local and national level. There is a general thinking that in spite of various opportunities Rahul Gandhi could not prove himself. There are a number of reasons, both historical and contemporary, which I can't explain here due to the paucity of space. However, one of the consequences of such perception seems that in an era of coalition politics, strong political parties will think twice before creating electoral alliance with Indian National Congress in the years to come.

By enclosing a list of 134 developmental activities in Amethi since 2014, due to efforts made by Smriti Irani, despite her not being an elected representative during 2014–19, the author proves her concern for Amethi. It played crucial role in her victory in 2019. Needless to mention that these schemes are directly related to the welfare of farmers, students, wage earners, patients, travellers, women and children, persons with disabilities, senior citizens, the unemployed and so on. Many of these projects are directly related to the promotion of the agenda of 'Vocal for Local'. These are supposed to encourage the feeling of self-reliance and self-help among people of Amethi in particular. These efforts are both inclusive and sustainable. It is bound to bring attitudinal and behavioural change among people of Amethi in her favour. Such commitment and that too in a person who was not the elected representative during 2014–19, also put a question mark on the legitimacy of all those who were legally entitled to deliver but they were silent, absent and passive. It is an invitation to defeat in elections.

The book which is methodologically based on an integration of both 'field view' and 'book view' has a strong message for both the established and the emerging political elites who wish to retain and gain power and authority. In democracy, constant connect with voters and their concerns matters more in comparison to manipulation, false promises and tricks. The book provides a clear message that even if defeated, try to address the problems of the constituents, no matter whether you are successful or not. One has to increase the number of workers and retain their faith. Dependence on undemocratic tricks and manipulation is not fruitful today.

I congratulate Anant Vijay for publishing this book which is fit from academic and pragmatic viewpoint. Politicians and political workers are strongly advised to read this book.

Professor S. N. Chaudhary

ICSSR National Fellow

chaudharysn1954@gmail.com

1

A Victory Painstakingly Crafted

23 May 2019. The day when votes for the Lok Sabha election were to be counted. Smriti Irani was at her Gauriganj home in her Lok Sabha constituency of Amethi. She had got up at half past six in the morning. By eight, she had done her puja, had her breakfast and settled down in her room, a book in hand and earphones plugged on. She kept on listening to songs, kept on reading. All day long, people would call to ask what was happening, what the position was, what the news was from the counting centre, but she would say nothing more than 'counting is underway'. That was Irani's answer to everybody. Her colleagues and top leaders of the party were getting concerned because there was no concrete news from Amethi, and Irani was silent. Her colleague Pragya Tripathi kept urging, 'Didi, come outside and meet the party workers, come to the party office.' But it seemed that those words were not even reaching her. She was unflustered, and with a smile on her lips, continued with her music.

The Amethi constituency is unique for a number of reasons. The counting of votes for this most-talked-about parliamentary seat happens in three separate districts—Amethi, Sultanpur and

Raebareli. This makes it difficult to know and understand much without the coordination among its district magistrates. Therefore, Irani's office was in touch with all of them and efforts to gather information were on as well. When the EVM from the Jais area was opened, Irani fell behind her nearest rival, Congress's Rahul Gandhi, by 1,600 votes. This happened only once during entire counting of the votes. But as EVMs from other areas started to be opened, the road to Irani's victory became wider, her lead over Rahul Gandhi kept on getting bigger. Things came to such a pass that around half past five in the evening, Rahul Gandhi called a press conference in Delhi and conceded defeat. Furthermore, he publicly congratulated Irani for winning Amethi. Rahul Gandhi said at the press conference, 'Smriti Iraniji has won, and I want to congratulate her. The people of Amethi have given their decision and I respect that decision. This is a democracy and I hope Smriti Iraniji looks after Amethi with love. She must honour the faith shown in her by the people of Amethi.'

After this statement by Rahul Gandhi, Irani's phone began ringing frequently. She and her colleagues started getting one call after another on their mobiles and landline phones from leaders, journalists and colleagues from across the country. But Irani wasn't keen to answer those calls, and so she didn't receive them. She continued to be engrossed in music and maintained an innocent silence. About half an hour after Rahul Gandhi's statement, at eight minutes past six in the evening, she tweeted a line from the works of the noted Hindi poet Dushyant Kumar: 'Kaun kehta hai ki aasmaan me suraakh nahi ho sakta'. Soon after the tweet, on being goaded by the party workers and her supporters, Irani came out of her residence, sat in a car and reached the counting centre. There she was told that counting was still underway and the final result would take time to be officially declared. On hearing this, she went straight to Kalikan Dhaam. There she paid obeisance at the temple of the Mother Goddess. From there she went to offer her condolences to a party worker who had lost a family member. After that, Irani returned to her residence. All the while, her phone kept on ringing. Messages continued to pile up in her phone inbox. By and large, all the messages contained words like 'congratulations on the victory', but Irani's answer was the same: 'The counting is still underway, we should wait for the final result'.

People from the Prime Minister's Office were calling Irani. Calls were also coming from the Uttar Pradesh Chief Minister's Office, but Irani was calmly telling everybody, 'Before breaking into a celebration, we should wait for the Election Commission to officially declare the result.' She didn't want any celebration, any bursting of crackers before the Election Commission's announcement. However, the excited party workers were not ready to listen. They continued to gather in large numbers outside her residence. There were echoes of 'Didi Zindabad', 'BJP Zindabad' and more such slogans all around. But Irani was busy listening to music and replying to messages on her phone. Her answer was the same: 'Wait for the Election Commission's announcement'.

Irani this year was different from the Irani of 2014. She was now a mature politician, full of confidence. It seemed that Irani didn't want to leave any scope for criticism. Even after Congress president Rahul Gandhi had acknowledged defeat, she decided that she would issue a statement only after the Election Commission's official announcement. And finally, that moment arrived. At half past two in the night, the returning officer informed her that she had won the Lok Sabha election from Amethi. She sent her assistant Vijay Gupta to collect the certificate of election. While writing this book, when I asked her why she didn't go to collect the certificate herself, she said, 'Every party worker who had made even the smallest of efforts to ensure my victory had a right equal to mine over the certificate of victory'. It may be noted here that even when Irani had won the Indian Television Academy's best actress award for the first time, she didn't go to collect the prize herself. One gets the impression that it has become part of Irani's nature that whenever she reaches a landmark, her sense of fairness makes her indifferent towards jubilation.

After being notified of her victory by the returning officer, Irani went to the party office. There, after accepting greetings and congratulations, she asked the party workers if she should visit Delhi. Following chants of 'Didi Zindabad', the party workers raised their hands to greet her, as if all of them giving her their blessings. Then Irani spoke to the media for the first time before leaving for Delhi. She told the news agency ANI, 'Today, I express my gratitude to Narendrabhai Modi. He had allowed me to serve Amethi continuously for five years. In 2014, he had promised Amethi that he had come here with the objective of change. In the neck-and-neck battle that took place between the Bharatiya Janata Party and Congress, on the one hand you had a family, and on the other you had an organisation that works like a family. If I have to give credit today, I would just say that it should go to our organisation and our volunteers … and if I could dedicate today's victory to somebody, I would dedicate it to the party workers and their families who were killed in Kerala and Bengal.'

With this statement, Irani also responded to Rahul Gandhi's remark. Irani quipped, 'I am happy that Rahul Gandhi has so much faith in Narendra Modi's leadership and BJP's organisational abilities, and that he believes that I would be able to take care of Amethi. Today the people of Amethi have expressed the same confidence through their votes. I am grateful to the people of Amethi. I have stayed in Amethi for five years after a defeat, and now after victory, I will serve them for another five years. This I assure you, and people know that when I give my word, I honour it.'

Having embraced victory in this historic political battle in Amethi, Irani reached Lucknow airport at around 5 in the morning. People at the airport thronged her, and she was continuously being showered with applause. She received a warm welcome on the aircraft too, and all the passengers gave her a standing ovation. It seemed that the victory belonged to not only Irani or Amethi but also to all these people as well, and they wanted to celebrate it. They saw it as a triumph of the underprivileged over the privileged. As a result of this victory, faith in Irani increased across the country. As a leader, she started to be seen as an emblem of possibilities. Even people who were not acquainted with her now began to blindly follow her. Her appeal grew in several parts of the country, and continues till date.

But what led to Irani's historic win in Amethi? How did she establish an emotional bond with the people of Amethi between 2014 and 2019, from the time she entered Amethi as the BJP's Lok Sabha candidate to her transformation into 'Didi' for the people? How did she bring the organisation together and unite her party colleagues to raise a 'victory banner' in the Amethi Lok Sabha seat, hitherto considered nearly unconquerable? How was she able to convince the people that she would be rooted to Amethi and stand by them in weal and woe—people who had had to deal with promises being made and broken election after election? All these questions called for a thorough study.

Tryst with reality

'Amethi is like that traditional Hindu bride who would be called shameless if she lifted her veil, and who would be called backward and illiterate and stay suffocated otherwise. Didi, I 'm not sure you know that there are women who can't come out without their veils in daytime till their death …' These were the words of a woman who was standing among a handful of people gathered to welcome Irani in the Gauriganj area of the Amethi Lok Sabha constituency in 2014. Irani wasn't able to ask the woman her name at the time, but the pain in the woman's voice touched her to the core. She had come here as her party's candidate in the grand festival of democracy, that too in an area that has been regarded as a VVIP constituency by the national and international media for ages.

Irani was deeply saddened. Amethi and women: were the two really in such dire straits? Even after so many years of Independence, and despite being represented by the most powerful family of what is considered the nation's oldest political party, this was the state of affairs in this constituency! That its women had no knowledge of women elsewhere walking shoulder-to-shoulder with men in the nation's progress! That they were unaware of the world that existed beyond their veils and saw the plight of their constituency in conjunction with the condition of women burdened by the shackles of conservatism. Irani was surprised by what she saw and heard, and it strengthened her resolve to change the condition of women not only in Amethi but the entire country. She vowed that whatever happens, she would continue to work for the women of Amethi and the country as much as possible throughout her life. Although she was completely immersed in politics by then, Irani's vow was not a political one at all.

It was in 22 March 2014 that the BJP first broached the idea of making Smriti Irani a candidate from Amethi. Rajnath Singh was then the BJP president. Irani was in Delhi when Rajnath called her himself and informed her about the party's decision to nominate her as the candidate from Amethi and sought her consent. Irani remembers the day and the events that unfolded. 'Rajnath Singhji called at half past eleven in the night and told me, "I feel you should be the party's candidate for the Lok Sabha election from Amethi. You should contest against Rahul Gandhi." My quick response was that if the party orders me I would accept. However, I wanted to consult my husband Zubin Irani and the rest of my family once. Zubin was in Mumbai at the time. Rajnath Singh gave his permission. As soon as he hung up, I called my husband, Irani Sahab. As always, he said that he would support any decision that I took. After taking my family into confidence, I decided to fight the election from Amethi. I told Irani Sahab to let the children know when they got up in the morning. If you think that in the face of such a huge responsibility I was doubtful, frightened or even ecstatic, let me make it clear that having been a part of the organisation for so long and as a result of the discipline I inculcated there, I had enough self-control, and I was not touched by feelings of excitement or glee. The party had given me responsibilities earlier too and I had put in my best efforts to carry them out. So there was only one thought that came to my mind: I had to try and live up to the confidence shown in me by the party leadership.

'Here I must clarify one more thing: you won't find any redundancy among organised party workers because they are always in active mode. I got down to work that night itself … Before the election battle, I wanted to know more about the territory I was headed for. I had been to Amethi once before, with Rajnathji. For me, its culture, history, fame, ancestry and social dynamics held primacy over its political, caste and organisational structures.'

Irani recollected, 'Immediately after the party decided to send me to Amethi and upon understanding the region's geographical and mythological status, I started to consider what preparations I needed for Amethi, what the constituency was like, how the party was placed, how strong it was, where the cadres were, how many booths existed, how many villages, where we were strong or weak and by how much, and so on. Over the next couple of days, after consultations with my colleagues from across the country, I started to assign them their responsibilities. In between these political deliberations, I also took my children into confidence about my decision to fight the election from Amethi. I held discussions with my friends from the Yuva Morcha, Mahila Morcha and officials of the Rashtriya Swayamsevak Sangh, and only then did I enter Amethi and file my nomination. You would be surprised to know that after I filed my nomination, forget Congress leaders of Amethi, even the local BJP leaders started asking me when I was planning to return to Delhi. They were simply not ready to believe that a leader from the nation's capital would come here and contest an election with such seriousness. Leave aside the Opposition, even our people felt that since I had come from television and films, I was wealthy. As far as my political career was concerned, I was already in the Rajya Sabha. So what would I do in Amethi? Since I had filed my nomination, it was expected that I would move around a bit, create some hype and then go back … But things didn't turn out that way because they were not meant to. I had gone to Amethi to stay there, to do something meaningful, to work and serve. I understood that the soil, its people, my sisters badly needed my attachment and service.'

In the election of 2014, Irani accomplished something very significant: she adopted the locals, became one of them, convinced and assured them—to paraphrase—that she would remain one of them, their representative, no matter what the circumstances. 'Wherever I stay, in whatever condition I am in, I will still stay your own'.

Irani reinforced this idea in all her speeches and interviews. During every tour, rally and speech, she would come up with surprising revelations on Amethi—truths that not only the country but even the residents of Amethi were unaware of. Irani started to kindle hope in misery-stricken Amethi during that election itself. Although she had very little time on her hands, she was not lacking in hard work, ability, diligence and commitment. Anupam Kher once asked her during a conversation on the TV programme *People*, 'Amethi … 2014. You were fighting an election …' Irani retorted, 'I was fighting a family.' Kher asked further, 'What was your brief to yourself?' Irani replied, 'That this will not be a paper tiger fight. I think many people presumed even after I filed my nomination that I would obviously lose. People were not ready for me to battle it out.' That election, Irani was busy laying the foundation of Amethi's future; she was essaying a story that was to become history in the time to come. Indeed, having defeated the then Congress president Rahul Gandhi, Irani is today the Member of Parliament from Amethi. But let's return to the general election of 2014.

Why Irani from Amethi

On 5 May 2014, BJP's prime ministerial candidate Narendra Modi held a rally in Amethi, during which he explained the reasons for nominating Irani from there. There is an interesting story behind that rally that the then defence minister and former chief minister of Goa, Manohar Parrikar, revealed to me after the Lok Sabha election of 2014. He said that originally no rally in Amethi had been proposed in Modi's election campaign. But when Parrikar went on a tour of Amethi, he felt a change in the political atmosphere of the place. He had worked with Irani in the organisation earlier and he knew that Irani's understanding of politics was strong and she had a finger on the pulse of the people. While touring the constituency and speaking with his Goan colleagues who worked there, Parrikar suspected that Irani was fighting a lone battle. In Parrikar's words, 'I felt that if Smriti gets a strong support from the central leadership, she can cause an upset. I shared this with Narendra Bhai after returning from Amethi and suggested that he hold a rally there. Narendra Bhai asked the then Uttar Pradesh in-charge, Amit Shah to organise a rally for him in Amethi. That was when Modi's Amethi rally was fixed, that too on the last day of campaigning in Amethi, that is, on 5 May.'

Moments before Modi's speech at the Amethi rally, Irani spoke to journalist Barkha Dutt backstage. In between several other questions, Dutt told Irani, 'This is a Gandhi family bastion and some people say that even if Modi comes here nothing will change.' Irani replied, 'I think such people, who believe in these relationships that do not guarantee electricity, roads, water, educational facilities or employment, should be careful. If they treat their own people like this, how will they treat others?' Irani was not perturbed by who was in front of her. Instead, she was concerned—despite understanding the hold the Nehru-Gandhi family had over Amethi—about what Amethi could achieve. Unfazed by what the election result might be, Irani had nothing but Amethi on her mind.

But why only Irani from Amethi? The answer to this question was given by Modi himself in front of thousands in that rally on 5 May 2014. He said, 'When the party decided to send Smritiji to Amethi, people with old-fashioned and outdated thought processes felt that she is a celebrity, she is the "Tulsi" of the courtyard, and could achieve nothing in the courtyard of Amethi. At the most, Rahul bhaiyya would suffer a bit of discomfort. Today, I wish to disclose to the political pundits of the country the reasoning and strategy that led me to decide on sending Smritiji to Amethi after all. It was not about troubling Rahul bhaiyya, he is in a lot of trouble anyway, and we need not do anything. I did not send Smritiji to trouble Rahulji further, I sent her to alleviate the troubles of Amethi.'

Modi added, 'Smritiji works with me, she is a member of Rajya Sabha from my state, Gujarat. When she was elected to Rajya Sabha, I told Smritiji, do whatever you may in Rajya Sabha, but I am putting some of the backward districts of Gujarat under your tutelage. Show me some change there. Today I can proudly say that Smriti has made the districts that I had assigned her as a Member of Parliament exceptional and vibrant in a very short period. That is why I decided to send Smritiji to the district of Uttar Pradesh that was worst off. I did not have Amethi in mind at the time. I wanted to introduce a model of development, an alternative model. After a lot of brainstorming and discussions, it was found that if there was a district in Uttar Pradesh that was in a really poor state, it was Amethi.

I vowed that day itself that in the next sixty months I would change Amethi to such an extent that the world's universities would come visiting for case studies. Amethi would show the way for uplifting the backward districts of India. I chose Amethi for this. You have to now put your stamp on it by electing Smriti.'

Modi did not stop there. 'I have not come here to do politics of revenge. That is not my way. I have come to effect change and I trust my younger sister. Everybody has faith in their sisters, but I have special faith in this sister of mine. When she was sent to Amethi a month back, she would not have known which corner of the country Amethi was situated in. There is a family that has been talking about its ties with you for the past forty years. So if friends of the media can, let them do something. Put my younger sister in one corner and Rahul bhaiyya and the entire family in the other corner, and ask them the names of the villages within the Amethi Lok Sabha constituency. I am certain that if Smriti Irani can name a hundred villages, the family would not even be able to name ten villages together … A Congress leader had once asked who Smriti Irani is. I will tell you who Smriti Irani is—she is my younger sister. Over forty years, this place has been ruined. Smriti has come to revive it. We have sent her to improve lives here. She has come to wash away your [Congress's] sins, and breathe new life into the people of this place.

Emotional moment for family

From the very first day itself, Irani strived to kindle local pride in Amethi. She tried to instill this feeling among the people of Amethi to raise their self-esteem. So that the people would not be known simply for their loyalty to a dynasty and the lies peddled by the representatives of that dynasty. However, her challenges were not few. Her battle was on a completely different turf and against completely different kinds of people. On the outside, the Nehru-Gandhi family was the representative of this place, but the actual control lay with contractors whom Irani started to take on since the early days of her time in Amethi. In 2014, when Irani reached Amethi for the first time, a number of rallies were organised between her road trips and public outreach programmes.

She was on her way to one such election rally when her car stopped at a place in the evening. A man came and told her, 'You have come to contest the election from Amethi alright, but you do not even know what is going to happen to you. A bullet could come anytime from any direction and pierce your head.' Before Irani could register what had happened, the man fled from the scene. She was neither fazed nor frightened by this incident, but since it was related to her life, which her family had stakes in, Irani immediately narrated it to her husband. However, she did not disclose it to the local leaders and party workers because she had reached Amethi as a ray of hope for them. She did not inform the media because she feared it would be seen as a publicity stunt. Possibly, Irani was reminded of the incident on 14 March 1977 when Sanjay Gandhi's car was fired upon at the Munshiganj Crossing near Amethi, just two days before the Lok Sabha election that year. Questions were raised at that time, a minister from Uttar Pradesh termed the incident as fake. Vinod Mehta wrote in his book, *The Sanjay Story*, that he kept trying to access the CID report of this attack. But whenever he went to the CID office, he would be asked if he thought the incident was genuine. Mehta added that there was a lot of furore at the time over how Akashvani, in its 6 a.m. bulletin, relayed the reactions of twelve chief ministers of the country to an incident that had happened at around quarter past ten the night before. There were no mobile phones in 1977, and broadcasting techniques were not too developed either. At the time, the incident was considered Sanjay Gandhi's election stunt, Mehta wrote.

Having shared the death threat incident with her husband Zubin, Smriti moved on to other engagements. There is a mutual understanding between Smriti and Zubin that the latter would not interfere in politics at all. However, this was a case whose repercussions would have been far more on Zubin's and their children's lives than on Smriti's political life. For that reason, Zubin went the extra mile. He immediately contacted doctors in Mumbai to know what should be done if one was hit by a bullet, how to save a life during such an emergency, and which hospital was best at handling such injuries. His doctor friends informed him that in the event of a bullet injury, the patient should be rushed to the Medanta hospital in Gurugram. After this, Zubin, at his level, made all preparations to handle any kind of emergency. During that election, Zubin's car and the driver stayed with Smriti in Amethi even against Smriti's wishes. In the meantime, Zubin made it clear who would call him first in case of any emergency, how Smriti could be rushed to Lucknow in case of an emergency. There was no proper hospital in Amethi that could treat a critical bullet wound. That is why it would be necessary, in the event, to take Smriti first to Lucknow, and from there, an entire evacuation plan was prepared for taking her to Delhi and then to Medanta in Gurugram.

Perhaps it is not difficult to understand what Irani's family may have gone through in such a situation where she was going to stay put in Amethi for her election campaign. It was an emotional phase for Smriti, for Zubin and their children. Before embarking on the battle for Amethi, she had sat her kids down and talked to them for over an hour. She spoke to them about career and responsibilities and the need to handle every situation with passion. She told them that if something were to happen to her, their father would still be there to look after them. Irani talked longer with her elder daughter Shanelle, and readied her to be mentally strong in order to take care of her siblings if something unexpected happened to Irani during the Amethi election. With a heavy heart, Zubin also accepted the possibility that Smriti could meet with something untoward during the election. As far as Irani was concerned, in spite of being emotional, she remained calm. She was confident that her Bholenath was by her side. She was entering the electoral battleground of Amethi with Adidev's blessings.

Trust of her youth colleagues

Before reaching Amethi in 2014, Irani had been the BJP's Goa in-charge. She had a very cordial relationship with one of Goa's tallest leaders, Manohar Parrikar. Parrikar was also in constant touch with Irani during that election. He knew that Irani had a firm finger on the political pulse, so he took her words very seriously. One day, Irani called up Parikkar and requested him to send Satish Dhond, who was looking after the BJP's organisational matters in Goa, to Amethi. Apart from this, Irani also called Vikram of the Maharashtra Yuva Morcha to Amethi for assistance.

Dhond told all the BJP leaders who came from Goa to work in the Jagdishpur and Tiloi regions. BJP's leader from Haryana Subhash Barala was made the in-charge of Gauriganj. The Rashtriya Swayamsevak Sangh sent Balmukund Pandey, who was associated with the Akhil Bharatiya Itihas Sankalan Yojana, to Amethi. The Ranchi mayor at the time, Asha Lakda, was with Irani as well. Haryana BJP leaders Pratibha Suman and Amarendra also reached Amethi to aid Irani. Also joining ranks were Satish Gautam, BJP's second term MP from Aligarh, and RSS's Sah Sarkaryawah (Joint General Secretary) Dr Krishna Gopal.

At the time, neither the BJP leaders nor Congress realised that Irani had come to contest the Amethi election with such seriousness. After filing her nomination, when Irani dropped anchor there, the Congress started to work on ways to harass her. There is an interesting anecdote from this time. Dhond is known to undertake excellent surveys and is an expert in preparing strategic reports from an organisational standpoint. Ahead of the 2014 election, after many days of hard work, he came up with an organisational report on the Amethi Lok Sabha constituency, but a worker named Chandramouli disappeared with the report. Despite extensive searching, Chandramouli could not be traced.

In Irani's first electoral battle in Amethi, Irani's husband Zubin and her close associate Pragya Tripathi were with her. They had put up at Aalok Dhaba, close to Amethi. Six people, including Irani, had to adjust in a ten-by-ten room because no other accommodation could be arranged. They stayed in that small room for a week after which they were able to find a rented place to move into. The owner of Aalok Dhaba, Gyan Singh, told me that he had been witness to a number of elections, but in 2014, he felt for the first time that a BJP candidate was serious about the contest. 'Smritiji was aiming at not only her own victory, but she was also fighting for the people of Amethi,' he said.

After reaching Amethi and examining the state of affairs there, Irani requested her Yuva Morcha colleague, Shrikant Bhartiya from Maharashtra to set up an election war room in Amethi. All of Irani's Yuva Morcha colleagues were excited about her contesting the Lok Sabha election from Amethi. Shrikant Bhartiya did what he was requested to. A couple of days after the office was set up, BJP leader Govind Shukla alias Raja Babu, who is currently the general secretary of the BJP in Uttar Pradesh, refused to put up Narendra Modi's poster outside the party office. This led to a war of words with Bhartiya. Being a local, Shukla claimed one-upmanship and was unwilling to allow Modi's poster to be put up in the party office. When Bhartiya could not handle the situation himself, he called Irani. It was eleven at night. Irani immediately rushed to the party office and along with Bhartiya covered the entire wall outside the party office with Modi's posters. She did not stop there. She dialled Shukla from there itself and said, 'Modiji's posters have been pasted on the walls of the party office. Keep in mind that you belong to this place—please take care of the posters.' It becomes evident from this incident that in the 2014 election, even some BJP leaders were trying to be thorns in the side for Irani.

Victim of Apathy

Political wranglings had doomed the culturally and spiritually rich Amethi. Irani realised this soon after she had arrived. She was able to see and understand the deprivations that the area was facing every day. She learnt that during the revolt of 1857, Bhale Sultan of Umra village had posed a challenge to the British. Irani later became the first candidate from the Amethi Lok Sabha constituency in the history of independent India to visit Umra and commemorate Bhale Sultan.

Irani still vividly remembers many incidents from her early days in Amethi. Once while campaigning in the constituency, she saw an old woman picking up something from the road near the village of Nizamuddinpur. She stopped beside her and asked, 'What are you picking up?' The woman said that a few moments before, a vehicle carrying fodder had passed by that route and some of it had fallen on the road. Irani asked her if she was picking up the fodder for her livestock. The woman's reply left Irani shaken. She said that she was picking fodder for dinner. This was the same Amethi that was known as one of the most prestigious parliamentary constituencies of the country. It was represented by a dynasty that had been at the helm of affairs of the country for not one, not two, but more than five decades. In that same Amethi, a woman was scraping fodder, fit only for livestock, from the road so that she could make dinner for her children. In all these years, was that the model of development that the country's most prized parliamentary constituency could come up with? Irani found it difficult to understand. In the same way, the people of Amethi were once informed that an announcement had been made in Parliament to turn the Kasimpur-Jais town into a model station. But why did the project not materialise? Right to Information (RTI) queries revealed that such a recommendation had never been made to the government by the local administration; how then could the station have been built?

In 1983, Rajiv Gandhi had inaugurated a bus terminus in Tiloi. He was not only a Member of Parliament from Amethi but was also the Prime Minister from 1984 to 1989. However, till the time of the 2014 Lok Sabha elections nothing more was done there. The bus terminus was in a ramshackle state; its condition had not changed in all these years. There was no arrangement for water, no toilets and no sheds. Passengers' comfort was given a short shrift. It is not that the media did not show the real picture of Amethi. But there were always contradictory reports on Amethi in the local papers and those published from Delhi. While the national media regarded this as a VIP constituency and continued to give 'examples' of its progress, local newspapers always put primacy on problems at the ground level. In any case, media teams from Delhi would often accompany the Nehru-Gandhi family to cover their tours of Amethi-Raebareli, or they would move with the Nehru-Gandhi convoy during elections. Journalist Rajdeep Sardesai, in his book *2014: The Election That Changed India* has referred to many instances of scribes from Delhi waiting for hours to get a chance of interviewing the members of the Gandhi family or to be a part of their tours. However, for the local papers, the misery of the people was news too. The sorry state of affairs in Amethi started to find space in local papers more and more soon after Rahul Gandhi was re-elected from Amethi in 2009. The reason was more political than administrative. Amethi was a victim of the state government's apathy to such an extent that its people were getting crushed. It is difficult to understand if the state government was doing this intentionally or the Congress leadership was uninterested. Whatever the reason, the Congress was in power at the Centre and if its Member of Parliament could not lobby for his people, what was the point of him being there? Gradually, resentment started to take root among the people of Amethi against their powerful MP.

Rajesh Masala, an influential businessman of Amethi, says, 'To appease Rahul Gandhi, influential people and foreign companies and organisations, who needed the Congress government at the Centre to get their work done, used to linger in Amethi, catch hold of agents posing as his representatives, fix appointments with him, show him their faces, donate to the Rajiv Gandhi Foundation as much as possible and go away. The development of Amethi or its people was never on their agenda; and even if it was something that they cared about, they did not know the art of attracting attention to it. The less said about the grassroots understanding of prominent Congress leaders associated with Amethi, the better. They were unaware of the local requirements and hence, instead of leading to positive results, their efforts more often than not had the opposite effect.' He adds, 'Whatever undertakings, organisations and industries were set up in Amethi during the Congress's time were mostly done without considering if they would work here, or if the local people would benefit from them. For instance, the Institute of Information Technology, Amethi. It was opened in 2005 in Rajiv Gandhi's name in a thoughtless manner. In August 2016, the then human resource development minister Prakash Javadekar said in Parliament that the institute had been running illegally and was an extension centre of the Institute of Information Technology in Allahabad. Under the prevalent law, extension centres of such organisations cannot be opened. Every day, one teacher or another would visit this centre from Allahabad and take a few classes.' Javadekar said in his statement that in all these years, only one person from Amethi was able to study at this institute. According to Javadekar, the institute was of no use to the local students.

Even after losing the 2014 Lok Sabha elections, Irani not only maintained her relationship with the region but also continued to push for people-oriented development. During her tenure as the human resource development minister, she set up a satellite campus of the Ambedkar University, Lucknow in Amethi, so that the economically weaker local students could obtain higher education instead of students from outside belonging to the elite sections.

Rajesh Masala shared a tale about an underpass in Amethi that was interesting to hear but would otherwise put democracy to shame. 'The foundation stone of the underpass was laid in 2004. After the BJP government was formed at the Centre in 2014, there was an investigation into why the underpass could not be built. It was found that there never was a project of this sort. When no project existed, how could a budget be drawn up for it? When the government had no whiff of this project, how could its file be located? This was the state of development. That of the bypass was even worse. No tender could be prepared for 12-13 years. And when work eventually started, it could not be completed. Within two years, there were so many potholes that it could not be determined whether there were potholes in the road, or the road was in the potholes.'

Hard work, iron will

When Irani fought the Amethi election in 2014, hundreds of party workers and leaders volunteered to help her out and reached Amethi even without express instructions from the party. Asha Lakda says, 'When Smriti Irani didi got the ticket for the Lok Sabha elections in 2014, we could hardly wait to get to Amethi. We took a train to Allahabad and from there another train to Pratapgarh. We then travelled by road to Amethi. Soon after, we went to meet didi at her Gauriganj home. There were around twenty-five of us, women from Haryana, Madhya Pradesh and Jharkhand. And we started living there. Didi used to stay with us. All of us used to sleep on the floor. Didi used to sleep on the floor with us as well and used to eat whatever we ate. No matter how late she returned in the night from campaigning, she never forgot to ask if all of us had eaten and drank milk. Didi and the rest of us used to eat rice, dal, roti, vegetables and bread. Breakfast used to arrive early in the morning from Aalok Dhaba. We used to set off after breakfast and eat whatever could be found on the road for lunch.

'We were assigned different responsibilities. I was tasked with handling the Gauriganj Assembly segment. When I started to tour the area, I felt that it was quite backward. I come from a tribal-dominated place like Jharkhand, but the condition of Amethi was even worse. Firstly, there were hardly any roads and those that were there were so poor that you could not travel by car on them. You had to travel on foot. Apart from these indices of development, there was a strange atmosphere concerning women and Dalits. Whenever we went to meet the women, they would sit with their backs facing us. Initially, I simply could not fathom why these women sat that way even while talking to us. Gradually, when we started to interact more frequently with them, we realised that nobody had ever come to meet them, nobody had ever tried to talk to them, and so they were sitting in front of us in the same way that they used to sit in front of the men.'

Lakda remembers some of these incidents from the 2014 Lok Sabha elections like a film playing in front her eyes. 'We reached Pandey ka Purwa village for campaigning. While we were talking to the women there, suddenly some women sitting under a neem tree caught my eye. I asked why those women were sitting so far away. Some of the men present there replied that they were tribal women and so were made to sit at a distance. Even after sixty-seven years of Independence, that was the situation in the constituency that had been electing members of the Nehru-Gandhi family for decades. Then I told the villagers that I was a tribal myself, and asked the women to come closer. When the women came near us, they could hardly believe that a leader wanted to talk to them as well. Similarly, we went to a Dalit colony situated near a village of Thakurs. When I entered one of the homes, I said, "Behen (sister), please give me some water." One of the women said, "Are you joking? You will accept water from our hands?" I insisted, but she was incredulous. Still, she brought us water and all of us drank it. The women said that it was the first time that someone from outside their community had accepted water from them. They were also shocked to know that I was a political leader.'

There is a Durga temple called Mavai Dham in Amethi. This shrine is widely venerated. The ashram around it is spread over 15-20 acres. Asha Lakda told me, 'When I was campaigning for the BJP among the people there, some of them told me that I should meet "Mataji" at the shrine. I said that I would certainly meet her and sent her my message. I was immediately called inside. A woman sat there. She asked after me and wished that some development would happen in Amethi and it started to figure on the tourism map. She asked us if Smriti Irani would be able to usher in development in the region. When I assured her, she said, "You are a woman, and if you are assuring us on Smriti Irani's behalf, we believe you and we will vote for you." We paid her our respects and moved on.

'Likewise, one day we visited the villages of Jagdishpur. We came across a village where all the houses were thatched. There was not even a single pucca house. We went to every house and the people appreciated that at least someone had come to meet them and request votes. However, by the time we reached the last house in that village, the day had nearly ended. An elderly woman came out and said,

"People from the Congress had given us money, sarees. What will you give?" We were at a loss for words, but I said, "Mataji, we have not come to distribute sarees and money. We have come to share ideas." Then, slowly, people's faith in the BJP started to gain strength. I, along, with Aarti Singh, who is currently the president of the Jharkhand Mahila Morcha, and Ashwini Paranjpe worked together in Amethi in 2014. It was our duty to go to every village in our area and talk to the women and tell them about Modiji and Smritiji. That's what we would do. We visited several such villages where no political leader, let alone an election candidate, had ever gone.'

Lakda alluded to another important fact. She said, 'In 2014, people used to say in the national media that Smriti Irani would derive advantage from her on-screen image as "Tulsi". But in a place that had not been connected by roads, where voting is done merely for a saree, how would people have watched a serial on television? Smritiji got votes because of her simplicity. She embraced the people of Amethi as a daughter and a sister. She listened to the people, treated their sorrow as her own, and continues to do so; she tries to help them as much as possible and as quickly as she can. She continued her work even after losing the 2014 election from Amethi. Even today, when she goes to Amethi, she sits on the floor with the women there. Nobody in Amethi could believe that a central minister would do that. A leader sitting on the floor is not something that must be specifically underlined. Leaders have sat on the floor before as well, but it was a big deal for Amethi that a Lok Sabha candidate was sitting with them on the ground.'

Lakda continues, 'Let me tell you another story. We reached the biggest house in Yadav ka Purwa village to ask for votes on behalf of Smriti Irani. We were warmly welcomed and all the women of the village were asked to gather to meet us. Simply at the mention of her name, people were eager to join Smritiji. Her reputation of simplicity and ability to easily mingle with people preceded her in Amethi.'

On ground challenges

In 2014, Irani and her team were facing several challenges in Amethi. At the time, they were neither in power at the Centre nor the state. As a result, support from the administration and police was hard to come by. So Irani's aides found solutions to issues as they deemed fit. Asha Lakda remembers two such incidents even to this day. About the first incident, she says, 'When we reached Jagdishpur from Yadav ka Purwa, we tried to locate some old BJP hands. After meeting local leaders of the party and its affiliates, when we were on our way to hold a meeting, a few people came and threatened us saying they would not allow the meeting to happen. They said if we went ahead with the meeting, we could even be shot. I said, "Look, when the Naxals' bullets could not scare me, how can bullets in Amethi make me anxious? We are tribals, we love the people. But if someone threatens to shoot us, let me make it clear that if you fire, we will not sit quietly either. Fire a bullet and you will get two in return." Those people then said, "Let's see how you go from here." I said, "We will answer politely, hold the meeting with all sobriety and then leave." I remember we held the meeting there and returned peacefully. The days of threatening were over.'

The second incident took place in the Amethi bazaar. Lakda says, 'We had gathered people and were about to hold a meeting when suddenly a crowd of Congress supporters appeared. The henchmen of their local leaders were also in that crowd and started telling us that we could not stand at a particular place in the market nor hold a meeting. We could see that they had come intending to fight, and were meddling in our business unnecessarily. We handled the situation tactfully. The women who were with me and I mingled with the crowd and started to talk politely with those people. We knew that we could not win in a fight there. Hence we chose to reason with them. We made our point and listened to them too. In a short while, the people who had come to pick a fight were offering us lassi.'

Dr Pramod Sawant, who was then a Member of the Legislative Assembly from Goa and is now a chief minister, also stayed in Amethi for twenty-eight days during the 2014 election. His experience of Amethi was completely different. After voting for the Lok Sabha election concluded in Goa, the party directed him to go to Amethi. Let alone Amethi, he had never been to any place in Uttar Pradesh before that. After landing for the first time at Lucknow's Chaudhary Charan Singh Airport, he took a car to Amethi. On this trip, he stayed in Amethi for a week. The more he toured Amethi, the more surprised he was. It bewildered him that despite the Nehru-Gandhi family members' representing the area for so long, there was not a single proper hotel in the area. Vinod Mehta has written about a similar experience in his book *The Sanjay Story*. The book was published in 1978. Mehta mentions that there was no pucca house, no factory, no traffic of cyclists, no film poster, hardly any shops, no bank, no commercial activity, and not even the transistor—which was a symbol of prosperity in India at the time—to be seen in any household. Sawant adds that the place that he put up in Amethi had neither a reception nor laundry facilities. Even basic amenities like electricity, water, toilets were absent. So from 1978 to 2014, thirty-six years in other words, there was no discernible change in Amethi. For the first two–three days, Sawant kept touring Amethi alone, meeting people. Then Raja Khedekar of the Goa BJP office joined him and toured the constituency with Sawant, meeting women and children to know their opinion of the Congress.

Since the place had been represented by the Nehru-Gandhi family for so long, Sawant had expected its condition to be better than all constituencies in the country, but the reality was totally different. With development remaining a mere dream, the people here were utterly disappointed. There was despair all around. But quietly, they certainly hoped that someone would listen to their complaints and make better roads, medical treatment, electricity, water and employment available. People were disgusted that hooliganism, not democracy existed in Amethi. Contractors ruled the roost in Amethi. There was nobody who would listen to the people. Rahul Gandhi was out of reach for the common man. Sawant says that during his tour of Amethi when he would tell people that he was an MLA from Goa, they could scarcely believe that an MLA would even come to meet them. He adds, 'There was anger in people. They were living in fear, they talked in frightened tones, worried about their words reaching the Congress contractors. They had been voting, too, as a result of this fear. The state of education was poor, people wanted their children to study but there were no facilities. Surprisingly, apart from verbal assurances, the Congress leaders had no plan for the development of the people of this area. The state that Amethi was in could be experienced only after going there.'

After Amethi, Sawant visited the Tiloi Assembly area. There he put up in a guesthouse with eighty people. The objective was to reach every booth in the area and ensure victory. In order to do this, he started meeting people and trying to listen to their problems and understand them. He held ten–fifteen small meetings every day. Sawant says, 'It was for the first time that BJP representatives had reached every booth. The condition there was such that if somebody received even a hundred rupees, he thought he had made a fortune because it was far more than the daily wages. There was also a fear of booth-capturing among people. They were scared of the Congress leaders. They felt terrorised and believed if they did not vote for the Congress, they could even be shot. However, after touring the place, it became clear that if the fear could be banished from the minds of the party workers, the elections could be won.'

In the beginning, owing to this atmosphere of fear, even common activists were unwilling to work for the BJP. As a result, the party was facing considerable difficulties. It was getting tough to convince the activists. Sawant and his team met panchayat heads and gram pradhans. They met the literate people of the area. Forty groups, each comprising two people, were formed whose only task was to meet people every day, from eight to eleven in the morning, and convince them.

Sawant says, 'Among the local people of Amethi, there was a craze regarding the patka. We used to offer patkas to anyone we went to meet. It became a symbol of respect. Whoever I offered this respect was touched by the fact that I was doing so despite being an MLA.

'When I went to Amethi in 2014, it felt that no link had been established between the people and their representatives till then. Even the simplest tasks were difficult to accomplish. There were two types of people. One section was very rich and then there was a large section which was extremely poor. Between these two sections, besides the financial aspect, social disparity was quite wide too. Smriti Irani started to interact with activists from all walks of life, including the lower strata of the society. Their belief that a frontline leader could reach them reaped us rich dividends. People started believing that Amethi was going to change.'

Sawant worked for a long time in Amethi and had many interesting experiences. He explains, 'As a result of Smriti's tours and her habit of mingling easily with people, Rahul Gandhi came under pressure and he too sought to tour the constituency. Priyanka Gandhi and Sonia Gandhi had to hold rallies too.'

Having met the people, Sawant held a big rally in Tiloi for the BJP. He reveals, 'The plan of meeting people in small groups worked. People started to appreciate Smriti's simplicity and the party workers began to respond. This unnerved the Congress contractors, who began to terrorise people.' Sawant's team was confident of winning in two assembly segments. Activists from outside had to leave Amethi a day before the polling. Sawant says, 'The activists were summoned to the police station and threatened.' Sawant and the party workers accompanying him had to leave a day before the election. But they were in touch with the booth-level workers over phone.

A week or so before polling began, the then chief minister of Goa, Manohar Parrikar also reached Amethi. He held meetings at eight to ten places in the constituency and spent a night in Amethi. Party workers had also come from Madhya Pradesh to campaign for Irani. Sawant acknowledges, 'At the time, all of us thought Irani had a fighting chance in Amethi. There was a lot of enthusiasm among the party workers. I don't know about the common voters, but Irani's image was seen as positive by the activists and people of the town. The people of Amethi had no alternative. No candidate had contested with a 100 per cent seriousness before Irani. Had anyone done so, Rahul Gandhi would have lost even earlier. The people of Amethi were in search of another option, and Irani gave them that.'

Sawant had organised a meeting and a roadshow for Irani, and these events turned out to be pretty successful. Sawant adds, 'During that roadshow, Irani introduced me as her younger brother. After that, the party workers' love for me grew and they started to welcome me with garlands as well.'

Even after losing in 2014, Irani continued to visit Amethi for the next five years and working towards its development. She convinced the people of Amethi that even a top leader could come and live with them. People reposed complete faith in her. Irani's affable nature, her way of giving respect to everybody and taking everybody along with her were traits of a true leader. Even after the 2014 defeat, she was in touch with all her party workers. Those who had been with her in 2014 joined her again in 2019. It was no mean feat to have kept everybody together over five years.

BJP's Amethi district president Durgesh Tripathi says, 'When the BJP parliamentary board announced Smritiji as Amethi's Lok Sabha candidate in 2014, the party workers became very enthusiastic. The RSS and all other related organisations also joined hands.'

There is a process for organisational meetings before an election. Meetings are held with the RSS and its allied organisations. Ahead of an election, a strategy on the ways of coordinating with the RSS is set and only after that, does the election campaigning begin. In 2014, the aim was to touch every single booth. Tripathi says, 'Along with the plan of deep booth outreach, it was decided that didi would be taken to every booth. The Akhil Bhartiya Vidyarthi Parishad was working towards connecting with students.' Top office-bearers of the RSS, like the then prant (In its functioning, the RSS, divides the country into different Prant (states) as per their organisational need) pracharak of Kashi Abhayji, kshetra pracharak Shivnarayanji, vibhag pracharak Dhananjayji, zila pracharak Nitinji and sangathan mantri Chandrasekharji held a meeting. The Sah Sarkaryawah of the RSS, Dr Krishna Gopal also visited Jagdishpur for the meeting. That meeting was held in the house of a swayamsewak, Sanjay, in the industrial area of Jagdishpur.

Tripathi has come to admire Irani's simplicity. He tells me, 'People got a chance to know Smriti Irani when she came to Amethi.

Smritiji established close relationships with every activist she met. The affection in her behaviour impressed the party workers. It was in 2014 that for the first time she was addressed as "didi" (sister).' Pathak shares an interesting incident from the election campaigning in 2014. 'A day before polling, there was news of money being distributed at a village near Shukul Bazar. We went to didi at night carrying this news. At the time, didi was discussing the day's events with Balmukundji. It was close to midnight. We informed Balmukundji's assistant that we had to urgently meet didi. We were immediately called inside. I told didi about the money being distributed. Didi decided straightaway to go to that village and asked a volunteer Dharmendra to get the car ready. She got into the car and started for Shukul Bazar all by herself. Six party workers on three motorcycles followed her. The party workers riding pillion were carrying sticks. Balmukundji had asked didi not to go alone, but didi would not listen. She sat in the car and started off. An anxious Balmukundji called up didi's husband Zubin and urged him to call and dissuade her. She had gone alone. It was not safe for her to do so. Zubin replied, "When she did not listen to you, how is she going to listen to me? I am going to bed, you do the same. She will handle everything on her own."'

Voters shower love

Irani got very little time in the 2014 election. When the BJP made her the candidate from Amethi, there were only twenty-three days left before polling. She didn't get to prepare for the fight, the time was simply too short to reach every voter and every village. But even in this short period, with the help of the party workers, Irani gave the indication that if the party made her the candidate from this seat again in the next election, she could post a victory. The numbers were compelling. Despite a short, twenty-three day campaign, Irani had cut Rahul Gandhi's 2009 victory margin by 80 per cent. From 37,570 votes in 2009, the BJP polled 3,00,748 votes in 2014 riding Irani's hard work and enterprise. There is no official record of whether Irani got an indication from the party about its intention of making her the candidate once again, but after losing to Rahul Gandhi in 2014, she was in constant touch with the people of Amethi and stood by them in their weal and woe.

Fifteen days after the 2014 loss, Irani was back in Amethi because she had promised during her election campaign that whatever the result of the election, she would come back to the people of Amethi. Irani kept her promise. When she went to Amethi for the 2014 elections, people had told her that anyone who came to contest the election from there never looked at Amethi again after losing. But Irani told all the naysayers, 'Have faith in me, I will return.' And she did. 'I returned so that people understand that all leaders are not alike, nor does everybody run away after losing. So I continued to stay there,' said Smriti Irani, when asked why she didn't move on.'

She returned with a big vision and goal. She had made Amethi her own despite the loss. She had become a central minister. The new and youthful India under Narendra Modi was busy scripting fresh history and opening doors of new opportunities. Irani had set similar goals for Amethi as well. She started establishing personal relationships with the local leaders and workers of her party as well as the youth there. But whenever she was asked on a public platform if she would cross swords again with Rahul Gandhi in Amethi in 2019, she would say that the question could only be answered by her party president, Amit Shah, because in the party, the decision to nominate a candidate from a parliamentary constituency rests with the parliamentary board, not with the candidate. Defeated candidates do not usually have a positive outlook for the people of their constituency, but Irani was an exception. Despite her defeat, neither her ties with Amethi nor her resolve slackened. In an interview with journalist Tina Brown for the programme 'Women in the World', Irani said, 'No fight has ever left me wounded enough to not get back up again.' It would be wrong to say that Irani 'returned' to Amethi in 2019, for the truth was that when she reached Amethi in 2014, she became a part of the place. Irani made this even clearer in a November 2015 interview with journalist Barkha Dutt, who is perceived to be close to the Congress and Priyanka Gandhi Vadra. During that interview, between various other questions, Dutt asked her if she would return to Amethi for the Lok Sabha election in 2019 since she had given a tough fight to Rahul Gandhi and made the Congress nervous. Irani quickly answered, 'Why would you wait till 2019? I am in Amethi every two months. I think one needs to bifurcate and put into perspective two-three issues. When you contest, you contest because your party so desires, not because you pick a particular seat. That is not how karyakartas work. I don't know what assignment my party will give me in 2016, let alone 2019. I do not claim this false sense of victory that oh, the Congress is very nervous. I didn't go there to make anybody nervous or put down anybody individually. I think that fight was a fight between two kinds of ideas in our country. One where an individual is born in a very, very celebrated family, possibly with his every need being served to him on a platter, and on the other hand was this girl, who did not come from a very privileged background, but who had a whole nation rooting for her. So for me, that is what is memorable about Amethi.'

That is how Irani is. Very simple, yet very strong. A unique mixture of firmness and simplicity. There is a fascinating tale about her simplicity from 2014. Although Irani lost in Amethi, a BJP-led government was formed at the Centre under Narendra Modi. When Narendra Modi formed his cabinet, Irani was made the country's first woman Human Resource Development Minister. She was in Shimla when the results were being announced. At that time, she got a call from Modi about her inclusion in the cabinet. Following this news, she was on her way back to Delhi for the oath-taking ceremony, when she called her colleague Piyush Goyal to ask if she could get an extra pass for the ceremony. She wanted to take her daughter with her. Irani felt that she would be made a minister of state, and was wondering if she would be able get the extra pass. Goyal told her, 'I don't know if you're going to be made a minister of state or a cabinet minister, but any number of passes that you want can be arranged.'

In 2017, Anupam Kher asked Irani during an interview if she had met Rahul Gandhi after the Amethi contest. Irani replied, 'When I met him at my oath-taking ceremony, he did not say anything. I greeted Smt (Sonia) Gandhi. She said, "Smriti, when you were taking the oath, I was clapping for you." She was showing her magnanimity. Whenever Rahul Gandhi and I have walked past each other in the lobby of the Parliament … he hasn't said anything.' When asked what her advice to Rahul Gandhi would be, she replied after much persuasion, 'If your heart is not in a job, do not do it.'

On 10 October 2017, in a meeting that was attended by her party president at the time, Amit Shah, and the then chief minister of Uttar Pradesh, Yogi Adityanath, Irani assured her colleagues that regardless of who got the ticket from Amethi, the BJP would emerge as winner. Irani announced from the stage that day, 'The people of Amethi assure you today that no matter who you chose to lead them, the lotus will bloom there in the 2019 Lok Sabha polls.'

⌘

Rajesh Masala, who was Irani's election convener in Amethi, says, 'Although didi could not win in 2014, she became an elder sister to the youth of the entire area. This was not a premeditated strategy or a staged drama. Irani was whole-heartedly trying to carry out the socialisation that is expected in the relationship of a brother and sister during the Teej festival. She made everyone aware of the presence of an elder sister. Whenever she called someone bhaiyya (elder brother), he would automatically address her as didi in return. The trust in the bonds built by her over five years showed results in 2019. People voluntarily came forward during the election in 2019 and gave their all for Smriti Irani.'

Rajesh adds, 'Having witnessed and experienced the respect and honour that Irani gave to the people of the constituency, they went along with her. In this, Modi's vision worked its magic. One can understand that we are in a day and age in which your parents have the option of approaching the police if you misbehave with them. And here we are talking about the relationship between the public and a leader. If Rahul Gandhi had an emotional attachment to Amethi, he would not be flying to the US to have his cough and cold treated, while the people of Amethi ran from pillar to post for their treatment and fell into the clutches of middlemen. The truth is that if anyone from the Nehru-Gandhi family had ever established a meaningful relationship with Amethi, it was Rajiv Gandhi. He made an honest effort, and Rahul and Sonia Gandhi rode for twenty-one years on the back of that relationship. However, the faith in Rajeev Gandhi's descendants went on diminishing progressively.'

One of the main reasons for the Congress's loss in Amethi in 2019 was the leaders and workers of the party turning opportunistic and complacent. Even before the 2019 polls, Irani had taken a house on rent in Amethi. In contrast, Rahul and Priyanka Gandhi Vadra never stayed there. When Rahul Gandhi used to visit Amethi, he would often do a programme at the guesthouse of the Sanjay Gandhi Hospital and leave. Totally ignoring the interests of the patients in Amethi, he would use the hospital campus to carry out his political activities. This put the people in discomfort. Sometimes, he would stay at the guesthouse at Munshiganj and his cook accompanied him. A veteran journalist from Lucknow who has been witness to Amethi's politics from close quarters for a long time told me, 'The members of the Gandhi family don't even drink the water of Amethi and Raebareli. Their supplies of food, drinks, and even drinking water come from Satguru Kirana Store situated in Hazratganj in Lucknow.' On the contrary, when Irani went to Amethi, she went into the midst of the locals and ate with them. The fundamental difference between the two leaders was that the people had to approach one, while the other saw the people as the leader, and went to them herself.

While Irani was in charge of the ministry of human resource development, she wanted the life of every citizen of Amethi to be shaped by Prime Minister Modi's slogan of 'Sab ka Saath, Sab ka Vikas'. She put into effect a plan to build a central school in the area. There was no X-ray machine at the Amethi district hospital. She made it available. She arranged for CT scan, ultrasound and coloured X-ray machines. Two hundred-bed hospitals were started in Tiloi. These were all efforts at the grassroots that started to show immediate results. Rajesh Masala says, Smriti Irani was busy taking the projects to the micro level, while the Congress was happy with mere statistics. See it this way: the Congress had set up Samrat Bicycles, Malvika Steel Plant and a hundred other factories here, but those factories remained just in the record books. Boundaries were drawn, buildings came up, machines were put up, work started in those factories, and then it all came to a standstill. By 2019, things came to such a pass that even five factories could not be seen in operation in the industrial area here.'

Similarly, Pipri village of Amethi got relief from erosion in September 2018. When Irani had gone to Amethi for the first time in 2014, she reached Pipri that had been boycotting elections. Irani says, 'When I reached the village, the people there told me that they had never disrespected women in their village. However, the village elders got together and told me, "Don't mind, bitiya, but we will not vote for you. We will not be voting for Rahul either." I asked them why they have been boycotting elections. To this, the people said, "Our lands have been getting washed away by the erosive force of the local river, and we have been pleading with our MPs for nearly fifty years to save us and give our families a secure environment. We want our lands to be protected and our existence safeguarded. But nobody has done anything. In all these years, even Rahul Gandhi has never come to our rescue." I made a promise to them, then. I said, "Dada, it is completely your wish whether to cast your vote or not, but I will only say this much, that whether I win or lose, I will certainly come back to be with you." They laughed at the time and said no leader comes back. I said I would return and I did. When Yogiji became the chief minister, my first request to him was to build a dam in the village so that its faith in democracy, which it had lost over seventy years of Independence, could be restored. It was because of Modi and Yogi that faith in democracy has been restored in that village after seventy years.' For two years before Yogi's government was formed in Uttar Pradesh, Irani had been in talks with the then Akhilesh Yadav government to find a solution to this issue. Inspired by Irani's initiatives, Uma Bharti, who was the water resources minister at the time, also took an interest, but even so the project could not be completed. Finally, when Yogi Adityanath came to power in Uttar Pradesh, efforts were undertaken to address the problem of erosion in Pipri, and from September 2018, the people of the village started to get relief from the problem.

Sanjeev Balyan was the minister of state for agriculture when on 11 May 2015 he went to Amethi for the first time with Irani at her request. The first problem that was brought to his notice was that fertilizer shipments to Amethi did not reach in time, due to which there was no timely use of fertilizers. This badly affected the crops. Balyan was astonished to note the failure of the railways to transport urea rakes to a place like Amethi and the persisting woes of the farmers. In his own words, when he reached the meeting with Irani and this problem was presented to him, it felt like an electric shock. He was not being able to comprehend why such a small issue in a VVIP constituency was yet to be addressed. This may seem insignificant, but it was a big problem for the farmers. When the issue was raised at the meeting, Balyan talked to the then ministers of chemicals and fertilizers, food and railways from the meeting site itself. From the dais, Irani assured the people that the agriculture minister was speaking to Ram Vilas Paswan and a solution was being worked on.

Within a week of that meeting, fertilizer rakes reached Amethi. This sent a message to the farmers that there was someone who would listen to their difficulties. Assistant editor at the *Times of India*, Rohan Dua, who closely follows the politics of Amethi, concurs. He points out that bringing urea rakes to Amethi was a very sensitive issue for the people there, and Smriti Irani gained from her quick action.

Another issue that was brought to Balyan's notice was that there was no soil-testing laboratory in Amethi. Since this was directly related to the agriculture ministry, Balyan decided on it as soon as he returned to Delhi and a soil-testing laboratory was opened in Amethi. In this way, Balyan too grew close to the people of Amethi. Party workers from Amethi also began to visit his Delhi residence to meet him. Not only the party workers, common citizens of Amethi, farmers and the youth started to interact more and more with him. Whenever a delegation from Amethi came calling, Irani would made it a point to request Balyan to be present. Once some people from Amethi came to meet Irani, and she took them along to show them the Parliament House. There they were introduced to Balyan as well.

⌘

Right after the 2014 elections results, Irani began working towards winning over the women. The Amethi Lok Sabha constituency is dotted with neem trees. Neem is considered to be a goddess by the people of the area. There are a number of folk songs dedicated to the neem tree in the villages of eastern Uttar Pradesh. One such song is '*Nibia Ki Dariya Maiya Mori Dalailin Jhuluvva ki Jhuli Ho Jhuli Na, Maiya Mori Gavai Li Geet Ho Ki Jhuli Ho Jhuli Na*'. While campaigning for the 2014 election, Irani came across so many neem trees in the area that schemes around the neem fruit (nimboli) had started to form in her mind. Even after the 2014 defeat, Irani took steps to give a concrete structure to her idea. Irani's party colleague Pragya Tripathi says, 'Smritiji talked to an organisation from Ahmedabad called Utthan and convinced them to buy nimboli from Amethi. Women were to be persuaded to pick the fruit throughout the day, gather and dry it, after which people from Utthan would buy that fruit. In this way, a source of income was created for women of the low-income group without any investment.'

Utthan started to buy the nimboli at the rate of Rs 16 per kilogram. Irani kept the entire scheme under her watch, and this enabled her to connect with the women of the area in a big way. This scheme is in operation even today. Irani reaped direct benefit from this scheme in the 2019 Lok Sabha elections. Not only that, she also distributed sewing machines to hundreds of women in the area and arranged for potter's wheels for the potters. She also started training programmes to make pickles, papad and vadi, and arranged for the products made by the women to be purchased without having to go through middlemen. Tripathi says, 'These steps taken to make the women of the area self-reliant made their emotional bond with didi even deeper.'

Irani made an all-round effort to make Amethi her own. She made herself available for Amethi round the clock for five years. Earlier, most of the poor women in Amethi were not allowed to vote. Their voter cards and other identity documents used to be snatched away. Only male members of the households, or the head (pradhan) or former head of the panchayat would cast votes. Irani came to know of this for the first time during the 2014 election. Later when she started making regular trips to Amethi and engaged with the women in relation with the welfare schemes run by the Modi government and herself, she realised that something needed to be done to make these women direct participants in the democratic process. It was very important to stop the process of collecting women's voter IDs and only males casting votes in their place. For this, she began meeting women in groups. She started to educate them about the significance of their votes and encouraged them to take part in the festival of democracy in the same way as they took part in the Teej festival. Voting was not the right of only men but women as well. Irani tried to impress upon the women that they should go to the polling booths themselves and not part with their voter ID cards if somebody asked for them, even if that person was someone close.

As a result of these efforts by Irani, the poor people, especially the women got the message that this woman, despite being a central minister, and despite having lost the election, not only kept visiting them, mingling with them, and understood their sorrows, she also tried to dispel those sorrows. Along with their economic independence, she was also concerned about their democratic rights. She did not simply make empty promises, but had the will and courage to do something. As a result, all of them slowly began to pledge allegiance to Irani.

Muslims are not in small numbers in Amethi. Irani visited areas with Muslim populations regularly. There she never raised the topic of religion but talked with the Muslim sisters about their families and difficulties. She discussed their welfare. She enquired if they had toilets at their homes and gas stoves in their kitchens, whether their children went to school regularly, whether they were getting vaccinated, and what means of livelihood would suit them best. A large number of baskets were distributed for raising honey bees, all possible help was provided for fish farming. Everywhere, Irani would meet people, listen to their problems and solve them. She may not know the names of individual families, but she had created a bond with them, which she was shaping herself. Apart from Muslim, Dalit and backward-class women, she not only reached the poor households of the area but also tried to improve their economic conditions. She discussed with them ways to give a better future to their children.

Tripathi, who had worked with Irani during the 2014 and 2019 elections, says, 'When she was meeting the women in small groups, in many places, they complained about the village headman. They informed her about the lack of aadhaar cards, ration cards and toilets. Irani decided she would bring these items straight to the women. On the back of her efforts, block-level camps were set up for issuing aadhaar and ration cards. Similarly, she ensured help from the administration for building toilets in every household. She explained the importance of voting to the local Muslim and Dalit women. She told them that if they were concerned about the future of their children, they needed to go out and vote.'

In 2015, a fire broke out in a house in Amethi. The residents lost everything. When Irani came to know about this incident, she not only came forward and offered immediate financial help but also bore full cost of the weddings of the two girls of the family. She helped several girls in the Chhatoh block in their weddings. She sent gifts of mangalsutras, bindis, anklets, toe-rings, five sarees and clothes for the grooms' families. The family members told Irani after much hesitation that while most of the arrangements had been made, there wasn't any money for wedding jewellery. Irani arranged for ornaments for seven brides from her own pocket and sent them to their weddings bedecked with jewellery. Tripathi adds, 'When Irani heard about the plight of a boy of her constituency whose hand got severed, she played the role of a true didi, and not only paid for his treatment but also got him a prosthetic hand.' These efforts and assistance may seem small, but when news about such incidents spreads among the public, the image of a leader becomes increasingly stronger.

Tripathi explains, 'Didi did not become didi in a day. Such is her nature that she would establish a bond with people at the first meeting itself. She does not change her behaviour according to a person's status, rather behaves the same with everybody. She gives the affection of an elder sister to everyone, assures them of support in both good times and bad. Her brain works round the clock. She takes quick decisions. She listens to problems over the phone and provides solutions then and there. If she makes a promise, she keeps it.'

All-round benefits of Central schemes

While Irani's continued presence in the constituency, her behaviour and the tireless efforts of the party workers stood her in good stead in the 2019 elections, she also rode on Prime Minister Modi's goodwill and reaped the benefits of his work at the national level. As a result of Irani's efforts, the local people were being able to benefit continuously from the Prime Minister's schemes, which included provisions and insurance for the farmers, Pradhan Mantri Awas Yojana for the poor, and other welfare measures. The scheduled castes and other backward classes (OBCs) gained from the Pradhan Mantri Garib Kalyan Yojana, which freed the voters from the clutches of casteism.

It is believed that in the 2019 elections, a large portion of the votes of the Bahujan Samaj Party (BSP) went to the BJP based on the latter's work. According to political pundits, Dalits voted for Irani in large numbers. They were all influenced by Modi's vision and his style of functioning. The deprived masses gained directly from the Prime Minister's schemes and were able to raise their standard of living. Two of the BJP's MLAs from the Amethi Lok Sabha constituency, Dal Bahadur Kori and Suresh Pasi, are Dalits. The BJP was considered a party of forward and elite sections, but the enthusiasm of the Dalits and their support for the BJP in the 2019 elections demolished this belief too.

At the organisational level, lists were made of the beneficiaries of central and state schemes. The lists included households that received cooking gas under the Ujjwala scheme, assistance for building toilets, and financial help under the Pradhan Mantri Awas Yojana. Then these people were convinced to spread the word to their neighbours about the benefits that were available to them since the Modi government came to power and the extent to which their lives had been improved. The way Dalits and minorities gained from the schemes proved to be a morale booster for the BJP activists working to ensure Irani's victory. Irani had contacted all central ministries and gathered information on the work done in Amethi from 2014 to 2019. She had formulated a policy on how to use the Centre's efforts in her poll strategy. When the activists went for campaigning and outreach in the area, they carried with them lists of people in all of

Amethi who had benefited from the various central schemes; be it cooking gas cylinders, assistance for building toilets, homes under the Pradhan Mantri Awas Yojana or the opening of Jan Dhan accounts, all details were on the list.

There is a Dalit housing colony of 200 families in the Jagdishpur block of Amethi. Of these, sixteen families were the beneficiaries of the aforementioned schemes. It was explained to the rest of the families that if the BJP were to win from here in 2019, all of them would get the benefits of these schemes. The result was so positive that when the BSP leader went to Amethi, the Dalit community was not even ready to listen. They kept on asking the leader whom they should approach if there was a need. The leader had no answer and had to return dejectedly.

The BJP treated people from all communities equally in Amethi. It did not ask for votes on the basis of caste and community. Nothing was done separately for the Muslims. Benefits went to everybody without any discrimination. Both Hindus and Muslims derived benefit from the Pradhan Mantri Awas Yojana equally. Among the Muslims of the area, 70-80 per cent are poor. There is a big concentration of Muslims in Jais. Journalist Rohan Dua tells me that when he had gone to cover Jais, he saw boards hanging from numerous houses announcing that the homes had been built under the Pradhan Mantri Awas Yojana. According to him, around 1200 houses were built in Jais under the scheme. During the election campaign for the parliamentary election of 2019, a resident of Jais, Salman Hussain says, 'I think Prime Minister Narendra Modi will return to power. We are thankful to the BJP, whose leader ensured that we got pucca houses.'

According to a number of political experts, it is likely that some Muslim women voted for Irani over the triple talaq issue as well. They feel that wherever there were families with women who had borne the brunt of triple talaq, votes would have been cast in favour of Irani. After the BJP came to power at both the Centre and the state, work got underway in Amethi without any partiality. The role of brokers or middlemen was put to an end, and under direct benefit transfer, money was deposited straight to the bank accounts of the beneficiaries.

2

Relationship with Congress, an Illusion

If we go back to the counting day of the 2014 Lok Sabha elections, it became clear by afternoon that the then Congress vice-president Rahul Gandhi was on his way to victory. Irani fought tooth and nail, but Rahul Gandhi won by 1,07,000 votes. The situation after five years was completely the opposite. The counting of votes was going on very slowly and except for one round, Irani was always in the lead. Irani's victory was credited to a combination of her personality, Prime Minister Modi's popularity and the devotion of the Sangh workers.

When the 2019 general elections were announced and the BJP nominated Irani from Amethi, the entire party and Irani saw this opportunity from a unique angle. They considered the election to be related to national good and felt that to serve the nation, it was important to win in Amethi. Leave aside markets, hotels and stations, as we have seen, the state of education, roads, drinking water and healthcare was in a shambles in Amethi until 2014. No electoral contest should be taken for granted. And so, even after understanding and connecting with Amethi every day for five long years, Irani never took the election lightly despite the situation in 2019 being completely different from the one in 2014: BJP governments were in place at both the Centre and the state, and Irani was a union minister as well.

Amethi needed a candidate who could demolish the arrogance of the Congress. The people of Amethi saw such qualities in Irani. For one, she kept visiting the constituency even after her 2014 election defeat. If we analyse the tenures of the Congress MPs from Amethi, this act in itself was enough to show them the mirror on the amount of time they spent in the area and the interest they took in its development. Modi went to Amethi in May 2014, and that sent a positive message. After Modi's visit, the people of Amethi realised that their relationship with the Congress was but an illusion. Modi impressed a lot with his speech and fired the ambitions of a changing and youthful nation.

The Amethi Lok Sabha constituency was formed in 1967. Since then, the Congress had won most of the elections, but this area never progressed. Amethi was riddled with poverty, illiteracy and hunger, and nobody gave any attention to that. The simple truth was that the Congress was never really popular in Amethi. It is widely believed in political circles that Congress had always fought with its financial might. After Modi won from Varanasi in 2014, comparisons started to be made with the development taking place there and the lack of it in Amethi. The expectations of the people of Amethi were rising. They realised that Modi had opened the floodgates of progress in Varanasi, but Rahul Gandhi had done nothing for Amethi during his one-and-a-half decade tenure as an MP. The people started thinking that if Varanasi could progress, why couldn't Amethi? In any case, Irani had strained every nerve for the development of Amethi even without being an MP from the constituency, and so her candidacy not only raised the hopes of the people of the area, it filled the party workers with zeal. It would be worthwhile to note here that as a result of Irani's efforts, the railway ministry sanctioned Rs 358 crore for the doubling of the railway line between Raebareli and Amethi. In an interview with the *Times of India*'s Rohan Dua, the then minister of state for railways, Manoj Sinha, made the announcement. This was a decade-old demand of Amethi that Irani helped fulfil by dint of her efforts.

In the 2019 elections, the RSS and BJP stood firmly behind Irani. The Election Commission too was quite active. As a result, selfish elements in the administration were not able to do as they pleased. It was said that due to the Election Commission's strictness, the Congress could not distribute money this time around. Still, there were a few officers trying to sing the Congress tune, but then they feared for their careers as well because the BJP was in power at the state as well as the Centre. Consequently, most of them worked in silence, but justly in the end.

In the Lok Sabha elections, before 2019, Congress candidates used to visit Amethi for seven to ten days during which some outreach time was kept aside. Then they would go back to the special rooms arranged for them in the guesthouse, meet a few selected people and leave. After the Congress candidates filed their nominations and went back, the real game would begin. A week before voting, envelope politics would start at the block level. The BJP or any other prominent opposition party never took the Amethi Lok Sabha elections seriously, and this allowed for Congress walkovers. The media across the country tended to portray Amethi as the Gandhi family bastion. The RSS had readied its workers to counter this strategy of the Congress during the 2019 elections. Whenever the RSS workers came to know that a Congress car was on its way to dole out money, they would follow with cameras.

During the 2014 parliamentary election, many workers of other political parties joined BJP. But the experience with some of them was not good. They took money from the party leaders in the name of booth management and disappeared. The amounts lost were not too big, but the propensity for not working even after taking money and fleeing was seen as a big offence. So, ahead of the 2019 elections, the RSS prepared a list of all those people who had fled with money earlier. If a Congress representative went to any such pradhan, people from the RSS and BJP would tail them. They would enquire from the pradhan and would tell him directly or indirectly that even if he had accepted money, he should not distribute it. The BJP leaders claim they knew where the money was meant to be distributed to ensure Rahul Gandhi's victory. However, they did not want to conduct a raid and give the Congress a sensitive issue to exploit. Apart from the RSS, the people of the locality also helped the BJP to put an end to this envelope politics by tipping them off about money being distributed.

To stop electoral fraud, officers of the allied bodies of the RSS held a meeting with the district magistrate and all subdivisional officers posted in the district. In that meeting, all the administrative and police officers responsible for elections in the district were told in no uncertain terms that under no circumstances should money be allowed to be distributed this time around. A prominent Swayam Sevak of the RSS who was playing a key role in campaigning for Irani sent an indirect message that if the distribution of money did happen, the officers should be ready to face the consequences. With the BJP in power at all levels, the Congress was finding it tough to put its old tactics into practice.

Money did reach some big election managers, but they could not distribute it as they would have wanted as they were being kept under BJP surveillance. Whoever was suspected to have received money from the election managers, would have his opponents set after him so that if he tried to distribute the money, the BJP's poll managers would be instantly informed. Consequently, money, though distributed, could not reach the lower level election contractors. The outsiders, who wanted to come to Amethi to help the Congress with their financial might were finding it difficult in the Delhi and Fursatganj airports. A close watch was being kept on the outsiders leaving the airport and roaming around in the constituency.

The caravan grew, more and more people joined

According to the schedule of the 2019 Lok Sabha elections, polling was over on 18 April in the second phase in Sanjeev Balyan's constituency of Muzaffarnagar. Balyan took a train to Amethi on the night of 19 April. He says, 'I felt a lioness was fighting from Amethi. She was fighting alone. She was a Rajya Sabha member and a union minister. Why did she have to contest an election? But when a brave woman has been working passionately for the organisation day in and day out, having relinquished all luxuries and staying away from her family, why should a person like me not join hands to do whatever possible at my level? In any case, my attachment to Smriti Irani transcends politics. I consider her my younger sister, and when she is in the field of battle, how can a brother stay at home? He will go wherever needed and by whatever means possible.'

Balyan, currently a central minister, adds, 'Smriti Irani is a warrior who has no fear. When I came to know that she was fighting alone, I went to Amethi even without informing the party. One of the reasons was that Smriti Irani did not have a prior connection with Amethi. She was not aware of the local language and dialect. But the way she made Amethi her own, in a matter of just five years, impressed me a lot. Whenever I met Smriti Irani, I found her bubbling with positive energy.' When after a few days, the organisation called up

Balyan to send him to Haryana, he said that he was unable to do so. By that time he had already taken up election responsibilities in Amethi. He says, 'Witnessing the situation, I informed the party's Uttar Pradesh organisational general secretary, Sunil Bansal, and the national general secretary that the MP from Aligarh, Satish Gautam and I wanted to stay in Amethi and work there. I knew that it would be more challenging to work in Amethi than western Uttar Pradesh. Anyway, the political and social cultures of Muzaffarnagar and Amethi were totally different.'

Balyan had arrived in Amethi without informing Irani. He took a train to Lucknow and then went to Amethi by road. Till then, he did not even know where Irani stayed in Amethi. He did not call up Irani and reached her residence after asking people on the streets for directions. A policeman was posted at Irani's residence. When Balyan sent the message of his arrival, Irani's party colleague Pragya Tripathi called Balyan in the home. At that time, Irani was getting ready to go out for campaigning. Balyan had brought Satish Gautam and the chairman of the Baraut municipality, Amit Rana, with him. When he met Irani, he asked, 'Tell me what needs to be done. We have come for your election campaigning.' Irani was briefly taken aback, but she told Balyan to manage the party office and the functioning of the workers because she was finding it tough to manage them. After that, she left for campaigning.

Balyan tells me, 'Since there was no proper hotel in Amethi, we went to stay at Rajesh Masala's guesthouse. Then after cleaning up, I went out with my colleagues to inspect the party office.' Balyan remembers that day vividly: 'Though an election war room had come up by that time, there wasn't a proper system of coordination among the party workers. Even the provision of cars was not being streamlined. There needed to be a system regarding who was working where and doing what. Therefore, I started to hold review meetings of all offices. The party workers were travelling in the constituency in their own cars. I called the prominent functionaries from every office in the constituency, held meetings with them and told them to take party vehicle for campaigning.'

After Balyan's review, twelve new offices were opened for the party workers and a main office was designated to ensure coordination between all the offices. Balyan took all the party offices under him. His clear message to the workers was: 'Let Smriti Irani only focus on the elections, don't discuss management of public outreach with her. Nobody should call her regarding administrative matters; I am there for that.' The entire system was set up in three-four days. It is not that Balyan would meet Irani every day. They discuss election management system once in two-three days. Balyan had estimated that votes would be cast based on Modi's image with Irani being the face. Hence, he decided that he would only focus on administration and not hold or address a meeting anywhere. He chalked up a plan to reach the influential people in every village. He was astonished that whichever village any leader went to, the people there felt that God himself had arrived. Such was the state of affairs in Amethi.

Internal challenges

A significant part of the politics of the Nehru-Gandhi dynasty was centred around the Tiloi Assembly segment. Tiloi's royal house has been the cornerstone of politics in this segment. When Rajiv Gandhi came to Amethi, he put primacy on the royal family of Tiloi as well. Mohan Singh, who was linked to the Tiloi royalty, became an MLA on a Bharatiya Jana Sangh ticket in 1969. He later joined the Congress. He was twice an MLA from the Congress after that—in 1974 and 1977. In 1993, Mayankeshwar Sharan Singh of the Tiloi royal family became an MLA from the BJP. In 2007, he fought on a Samajwadi Party ticket and won. In 2017, he fought under the BJP banner again and won again. Before the Lok Sabha elections in 2019, the Congress had got in touch with Mayankeshwar Sharan Singh, the sitting BJP MLA from Tiloi constituency. A frontline Congress leader tells me that Priyanka Gandhi had spoken to Mayankeshwar Sharan Singh, and it was almost decided that the latter would support the Congress in the Lok Sabha elections. He had given his word to Priyanka Gandhi. When the BJP announced Irani's name, he started giving statements against her. He calculated that his words would reach Irani and she would react. Irani's reaction would have given Mayankeshwar Sharan Singh the chance to show his lack of interest in the BJP candidate and be supportive of the Congress. His words did reach Irani, but she did not respond at all. He then started to attack Irani even more, but it only dented his own image. This caused him to relent.

During the 2019 Lok Sabha elections, both Mayankeshwar Sharan Singh, and Gauriganj MLA Rakesh Singh were against the Jagdishpur MLA and state minister Suresh Pasi. One of the biggest challenges for the election managers of Irani was to resolve the conflict between Pasi and Mayankeshwar Sharan Singh. It was necessary to involve Mayankeshwar Sharan Singh in the election process fully. The task was cut out to dissociate him from the Congress. Some Thakur-dominated villages were unhappy with Pasi. They thought that Mayankeshwar Sharan Singh had helped Pasi and his family to prosper and now Pasi was going against his benefactor. It was under these circumstances that Balyan met Mayankeshwar Sharan Singh. Irani met him too. Mayankeshwar Sharan Singh was made an active part of the BJP's campaign. Balyan and Singh started to tour the villages. Singh began to take an interest in the election campaigning. Its effect could be seen in the constituency. A message went across to the Thakurs that there was no bad blood between Mayankeshwar Sharan Singh and Pasi. However, Irani's strategists were not satisfied merely with this. A parallel team was set up in Jagdishpur where support arrived from the Brahmins and Thakurs who held Pasi responsible for action against the forward castes of the area under the SC/ST Act. Since there was a considerable number of votes for Suresh Pasi in this area, he could not be ignored either.

The plan was also to render Rakesh Singh ineffective. This job was given to Sanjeev Balyan. Balyan decided to meet Rakesh Singh, who was the Samajwadi Party MLA of Gauriganj. Singh used to stay in his village. Balyan recollects, 'Rakesh would hold court every day in his village. I started to go every day to meet him. I became familiar with his men and a friendly relationship grew between us.' Balyan gradually won over Singh's team. Balyan says in Singh's praise, 'He is a very good human being and a dear friend as well. These days, whenever he comes to Delhi and I get to know about it, we meet without fail.'

It is said that Akhilesh Yadav had even called Rakesh Singh twice to discuss the latter's relationship with Balyan. He had indirectly advised Singh to distance himself from Balyan, but for Singh, personal relationships matter, not just party commitments. He continued to meet Balyan. The message that went across to the people of Amethi was that Irani had the latent support of Rakesh Singh as well. When ever the Congress leaders met Singh, or when ever they were planning to meet him, Balyan made it a point to do likewise. Once, Balyan came to know that Priyanka Gandhi was about to visit Singh, he pre-empted this by visiting Singh first. When Priyanka was made aware of this, she cancelled her plan. On the pretext of friendship and strategising, Balyan would often visit Singh, sometimes without prior notice, and chat a bit before returning. This resulted in an emotional bond between Balyan and Singh, which benefitted the BJP.

In the same way, Garima Singh, the first wife of Amethi royal family member Sanjay Singh, is a BJP MLA from Amethi. She was not active during the Lok Sabha elections either. As a result, there were difficulties in the Amethi Assembly segment. Garima Singh was indifferent towards the Lok Sabha elections because her son

Anant Vikram Singh had wanted to contest from Amethi. According to people close to Garima Singh, she felt that Irani's victory would not let Anant's career take off, but if Irani lost, Anant would prove to be a better alternative. When Garima Singh's son did not get the BJP ticket, she silently started working for the Congress. Garima, the doting mother, became inactive for the BJP. A local leader of the Congress even indicated that Garima Singh's son started to distribute money for the Congress. He even told me to ask Uttar Pradesh ministers Moti Singh and Mahendra Singh if I wanted to get more information. When Balyan came to know about this, he decided to woo Garima Singh over to Irani's side. Garima Singh's son-in-law, who lived in the US, was an old acquaintance of Balyan's. Balyan talked to Garima Singh's son-in-law and also to her son and requested them to work for the BJP. Garima Singh's office was run from her home. An election war room was set up there. But still, her involvement was not as expected. The BJP poll strategists were starting to get concerned about Amethi. There was a large proportion of Yadavs and Brahmins in the Amethi Assembly segment and efforts were revved up to win over the Yadavs. Rajesh Masala played a crucial role in this. Balyan took charge of three assembly segments, while Aligarh MP Satish Gautam took up Salon and Jagdishpur. Gautam undertook tours in the Brahmin-dominated areas too.

The BJP and RSS officials working in these areas began strategising at the grassroots levels on ways to deal with voters of the Bahujan Samaj Party and BS4. Six months before the election dates were announced, RSS officials had reached out to the BSP, or to put it more precisely, the prominent and educated people of all communities in the Amethi Lok Sabha constituency. People from the RSS would go to their places, dine with them and discuss who would be a better candidate for Amethi: Rahul Gandhi or Smriti Irani. The personalities and leadership abilities of both candidates were discussed. The RSS workers understood that the voters of Amethi were not necessarily emotionally attached to the members of the Nehru-Gandhi family. During this outreach drive, the RSS officials managed to convince most of the prominent people from all communities that Irani was better than Rahul Gandhi. Those who seemed to be bending towards the Irani camp were given the responsibility to spread the message among their communities as well. The pros and cons were explained to them.

Balyan reveals that he researched beforehand the backgrounds of these noted personalities, and then systematically visited their homes during his supervision tours to towns and villages. There is one such village in Amethi where a noted resident kept elephants. When Balyan came to know about him, he went to his home uninvited and said, 'Whatever happens, I would like to dine at your house today.' The host said that even Indira Gandhi and Rajiv Gandhi had come visiting once upon a time, but not Rahul Gandhi.

Balyan would prepare a list of such people and call them one by one in the morning and make appointments for them to meet Irani. The people of Amethi took to Irani because of her amiable nature and its effect began to show.

During this election, Balyan also went and met local activists of the Congress who were allegedly responsible for distributing money. Balyan devised a way to monitor every movement of these people. One or two persons were assigned to follow Congress leader and Gandhi family's confidante Captain Satish Sharma and Chhattisgarh chief minister Bhupesh Baghel round the clock and report to Balyan directly. The planning was such that Balyan would be informed even if a BJP worker quietly met any Congress leader.

Balyan says he understood that it was Irani whom people wanted to listen to. Tours of leaders were organised keeping in mind caste equations, but Balyan did not address any meeting and did most of his work in the background. Just before the counting of votes, a roadshow by BJP president Amit Shah was scheduled in the region. Through this roadshow, the party wanted to tell the voters that the entire party machinery was behind Irani. BJP general secretary Anil Jain and another frontline leader, Dr Mahendra Singh, arrived to make the roadshow a success.

The presence of Balyan provided another advantage. Most of the sector magistrates in Amethi were veterinary doctors. They were either Balyan's juniors or seniors. Balyan had a good rapport with them and the flow of information between them was smooth. Whenever a problem arose, a solution would be found immediately. The entire Lok Sabha constituency was split into units for ease of management. Three separate mechanisms were put in place for Irani in the constituency. The first was for cases that were handled by the party itself, the second by the RSS and the third was under Balyan's watch. Balyan's sphere was completely different from that of the party. It neither asked for anything from the party nor did it disappoint the party in any way. Balyan had called nearly 200 party workers to Amethi from western Uttar Pradesh to meet the on-ground requirements. Irani used to manage these three mechanisms herself, she would sit with all three groups and strategise.

An incident in 2019 proved to be the turning point in the Amethi elections, according to Balyan. When Irani arrived near the Purab Dwara village in Munshiganj during campaigning, she came to know that the fields there had caught fire, which was spreading continuously. There was a danger of the flames fanning out to some of the houses in the vicinity. Irani left her campaigning and went to the village. Fire engines were late to arrive, but in the meantime, Irani lent a hand in the efforts to put out the fire, at one point even pumping water from hand pump. The party workers who were with her also got down to assist the locals. She rebuked the officers of the district administration over the phone and reminded them of their responsibilities. The entire country watched those visuals on their TV screens. Balyan remembers that day because Irani had requested him to be present for the scheduled programme. While Irani was busy helping extinguish the fire, Balyan reached the place of the programme and told the people gathered there about the fire before apologising on her behalf. This humane side of Irani's personality deeply moved the people of Amethi. Everywhere people were discussing the incident. Needless to say, during an election, when a leader is seen in such positive light, it can only reap benefits.

Irani had a tough routine

6 May, or the date of voting in Amethi for the 2019 Lok Sabha polls, was nearing. The BJP, the RSS and Irani herself were ready with their gameplans. Irani had reached Amethi on 4 April and from the very next day, she began following a routine that she would stick to throughout the weeks leading up to election day. The RSS was involved very closely with Irani and her party in strategising, planning and executing her election gameplan. Irani's inputs were taken and a routine was chalked up. Her routine, including various meetings and programmes throughout the day, was fixed from eight in the morning to two at night. She would get up at seven in the morning; preparations and meetings would start from eight. In the first two hours, she would meet block-level workers and influential people from different parts of the constituency. In this session, the discussions would be focused on resources, election materials and problems. The meeting was attended by two workers from any block, four workers from any assembly constituency along with the assembly convenor and co-convenor. An RSS in-charge would also be present. Several such meetings were held at this time.

In the time given to the RSS, it was the organisation's responsibility to decide which block's swayamsewaks (volunteer) would meet Irani on which day. At this meeting, Irani sought all information on the area that was being discussed. If a problem was brought to her notice, she would suggest an instant solution. Irani has the ability to make quick decisions. Decisions on election materials like bags and badges and resources would be taken at this meeting. After this two-hour meeting, Irani would step out in to the constituency for campaigning and outreach. Her destination for the day was chosen considering travel time, so that she could reach by eleven. There were separate strategies for distant places. To put pressure on the Congress, poll planners of the RSS aimed to take Irani to every nyay panchayat.

After meetings and interactions throughout the day, she would return to her Gauriganj home by nine in the night, and after half an hour, leave to meet prominent residents of the area. These were people who could influence voters. These meetings could go on until midnight and sometimes longer. From midnight to the wee hours, she would prepare materials for the media and respond to the messages of journalists. After taking care of media work, she would retire around half past two or three in the night.

Irani stayed put in Amethi during the entire election campaign. She would get ready in the morning and do her puja. According to her party colleague Pragya Tripathi, 'Didi took care of everybody herself during the entire campaign. The election was happening in the summer, and she would prepare Rasna herself and serve it to the team members. After conferencing with the party workers in the morning, she would get into the car at half past ten. She would eat breakfast in the car itself. But she used to be mindful of whether those travelling with her had eaten or not.' Tripathi was with Irani throughout the election campaign. She adds, 'When she returned home at night, she would catch up with us and share her experiences of the day. Then dal-rice would be cooked, which is her favourite meal. She is very fond of ice-cream, but it was difficult to find it in Amethi. Often she would crave for ice cream like a child, but there wasn't even a proper restaurant here. There was however this eatery called "Kalptaru", and everybody seemed to be talking about it. One day Didi went there along with her party workers, and she was told that only five dosas were available; the restaurant only made that many every day!'

According to Tripathi, Irani has a wonderful ability to instantly connect with party workers. 'One day, she reached the party office after something like twenty-six meetings, and food was being prepared for the workers. Didi started to make pooris herself and treated the party workers. Often she would work with her party workers till four in the morning. But the discipline of the RSS was so strict that there had to be compulsory attendance at the meeting with block-level workers at eight in the morning.'

By repeatedly visiting the constituency since 2014, Smriti Irani had managed to develop an emotional attachment with the people. People who had earlier termed her as an outsider began to warm up to her. Ramrati Devi, a Dalit woman from Buddhi ka Purwa, says, 'Irani came but Rahul was never seen.'

Wherever she went, she made it a point to meet the swayamsevaks and pracharaks of the RSS of that area. She had a special interest in women's empowerment. In the early days of the 2019 election campaign, Irani held a meeting with 750 women in Jagdishpur. Her fiery speech there won the women over. There were no men at that meeting. Irani spoke openly to everybody present in that meeting and requested them to reach out to every women of their respective assembly constituency. Her spontaneity in interactions is her biggest asset. Even if an antagonist came to her with a grudge, she responded with an open mind and put them at ease.

Ramsuhag Singh, a resident of Salon, tells me, 'She was a union minister who had come from Delhi, she was a big star. Despite that, she would put her arm across the shoulder of any woman she met. This sense of affinity had a very positive impact. On the contrary, Priyanka Gandhi Vadra would come, wave her hand and leave.' At every meeting, Irani would goad the young women to claim their rights and do so with dignity. In fact, after a programme at the Indo Gulf company campus in Jagdishpur, young girls, having heard Irani, started saying that Didi Smriti Irani had to be made victorious at all costs. The impact of Irani's oration was huge on the youths.

Irani held a meeting in Jagdishpur a day before voting, but the former head of Sansarpur gram sabha and BJP worker Shivnayak Singh could not meet her. He was crestfallen that even after trying so hard, he was unable to meet Irani. He shared this with his colleagues. By the time it reached Irani's ears, it was already night. Irani wanted to leave right away for Singh's place in Sansarpur, but for some reason that did not happen. She went to meet him at five the next morning, which was the day of voting. Singh was so touched and enthused by this gesture that he devoted himself to work all day. In terms of the RSS's method of working, the zila pracharak of Jagdishpur, Satyendraji says, 'All the party workers got the message that Didi would look after them. She had given her heart and soul to the elections.'

When Manohar Parrikar told me that Irani had a sharp political acumen and ranked with the very best leaders when it came to understanding the pulse of the people, I thought he was praising a leader of his party for the sake of it. But Irani did certain experiments in Amethi that proved Parrikar right. During the 2019 Lok Sabha elections, Irani planned to divide the constituency into clusters for organising the Durduriya Vrat. During this vrat (fast), married women would worship Aushan mai (local goddess) on Thursday at over a hundred places, praying for Irani's victory. This created a positive atmosphere in favour of Smriti. The Durduriya Vrat had such a profound impact that the Congress camp became nervous. Its strategists thought about a counter and the next day, which was a Saturday, hurriedly conducted rival Durduriya pujas of Aosaan Mai at nearly twenty places. However, the Congress strategists forgot that this puja could only be held on a Thursday. Doing the puja on a Saturday had the opposite effect, and word spread among the women of Amethi that this action would annoy Aosaan Mai, and create more trouble for the women instead of putting an end to them. This blunder went a long way in queering the pitch for the Congress. The people of Amethi say that the women became so enraged that two meetings of Rahul Gandhi and three roadshows of Priyanka Gandhi had to be called off, as no one was ready to attend them.

Rise to the top through outreach

Irani was very particular about fulfilling the promises she made throughout her time in Amethi, to ensure which she undertook follow-up actions herself. She would publically confess if something could not be achieved, but her way of admitting to it was such that people would not feel short-changed in any way. Irani says, 'People are not unwilling to hear the truth, it is just that the manner of telling the truth should be polite. We are afraid of speaking the truth. But you need not be. Just present it properly.'

The list of her initiatives and personal care for the people of Amethi is long. For instance, when the son-in-law of the BJP mandal president of Bhadar block passed away, he was twenty-six. Irani recollects, 'That twenty-six-year-old youth was lying on the ground when his family called the hospital, only to be told that there was no one to drive the ambulance. There were sweepers but no doctors in the hospital. When I hugged his twenty-four-year-old wife, she said only one thing: "My husband died because there was no doctor in the hospital. Just tell Narendrabhai that when he becomes the Prime Minister, he must set up such a system that no other woman has to see the same fate.'"

Similarly in Haliyapur, the son of Rajendra Singh was martyred in Kargil's Batalik sector in 2006. Singh had himself served the country in uniform. People from the Congress in Amethi told him that if he wanted compensation for his son's martyrdom, he had to visit Rahul Gandhi in Delhi, and he would have to make the arrangements for their stay in the capital himself. The martyr's father did everything during that hour of grief and reached Delhi along with a local Congress leader to meet Rahul Gandhi. However, the meeting could not take place. Nothing came of the promise made to the martyr's family regading the gas agency and petrol pump allocation from special quota. Rajendra Singh received nothing from the government till 2014. When Irani came to know about his case, she not only visited the martyr's house but also extended help to his family. A resident of Haliyapur says, 'After Smriti Irani went to Haliyapur, Priyanka Gandhi came visiting too. But the martyr's father rebuked Priyanka Gandhi in public and she was forced to return.'

After winning the election, Irani arrived in Amethi as its MP for the first time on 26 May 2019 when her close associate and party worker Surendra Singh was murdered. She carried Singh's bier at his funeral. The images of Irani carrying her party worker on his last journey made national headlines. She went to Amethi next on 22 June for a two-day tour and then again on 6 July 2019.

Rahul Gandhi, on the other hand, came to Amethi only on 10 July 2019. He met party worker Mata Prasad Vaish and held a review session with activists at the Nirmala Devi Educational Institute. What he said there about Amethi was noteworthy. He said, 'I am not your MP now. But if you need me, I am here for you. I am not talking only about Congress activists, I am talking about every person of Amethi. I am talking about mothers, fathers and children. Whenever

Amethi needs Rahul, at night, in the morning, at four in the morning, Rahul will come and be present here … but you have to realise that somewhere you have made a mistake as well.'

Rahul Gandhi further said, 'The truth is, I am an MP from Wayanad, Kerala. However, I was your MP—Amethi's MP—for fifteen years and we have an old bond, a bond of affection. It is not a political relationship. Narendra Modi is the Prime Minister, Yogiji is the chief minister, and the MP here is from the BJP. I enjoy the role of opposition leader. You have to play the opposition in Amethi. You have to take care of the people's needs … there is no shortage of issues. I will keep coming here. But I will be required to spend time in Wayanad. I am an MP from that place and I have to devote my time there and develop the place. But I will lend my time here too. Do not think that I will not come here.' He accepted that Wayanad was his priority. The irony was, of course, that when he had been in power in Amethi and his party was in power at the Centre, Amethi continued to languish in misery.

3

An Equal Partner

As we've seen, in 2014, Irani did not have the opportunity to reach out to the people of Amethi fully, but by garnering over three lakh votes from a short campaign of twenty-three days, she proved that the road ahead would not be easy for her opponent. Sanjay Singh had won from Amethi twenty-one years ago. In 1998, Singh pipped Satish Sharma, who was trusted by the Nehru-Gandhi family. However, when the Atal Bihari Vajpayee government fell after thirteen months and Sonia Gandhi became the Congress candidate, the Amethi seat went into the Congress kitty again. Kalyan Singh was the chief minister of the state at the time and it was said that he did not put in a lot of effort in the Amethi elections. When Sonia Gandhi won the election, there were rumours in Amethi and across Uttar Pradesh that the Congress had distributed huge money and the BJP leaders had also got handsome shares. Whatever the truth may be, the fact was that when Sanjay Singh won from Amethi, KN Govindacharya, Sanjay Joshi, Vijay Malhotra and nine other pracharaks were active in the constituency, but no frontline leader of the BJP could be seen in Amethi in the election of 1999.

It needs to be discussed why all of them left the constituency and went elsewhere, or rather why the party pulled out these stalwarts from the constituency.

In 2014, when Smriti Irani reached Amethi, she was new to the region. The RSS karyakartas were all behind her and there was no shortage of enthusiasm to win the election, but there was no central figure who knew the pulse of Amethi and was familiar with the lay of the land. The search for such a person began, but by the time it could be completed, there were only seven days left for voting. The search ended with the emergence of Parmeshwarji, who was the zila pracharak of Amethi between 1996–2001. But due to organistional reasons, he could not be given the charge then. As per the RSS working style, when a pracharak leaves his station, he has to make arrangments for everything with regards to his existing work and responsibilities. It was not possible back then for Parmeshwarji to make the required arrangements in a short span of time.

Zila (district-level) pracharaks are very important in the organisational set up of the RSS, they have knowledge of every nook and corner of the district to which they belong. Full-time workers of the RSS are called pracharaks. They lead austere lives and are fully dedicated to the Sangh and the nation. They avoid becoming householders and remain unmarried throughout their lives. After a three-year training course (Tritya siksha warg), the swayamsevaks of the Sangh are recognised as pracharaks and entrusted with the responsibility of a particular place.

The main work of the Sangh pracharak involves opening new shakhas (RSS centres, where swayamsevaks do their daily exercise and prayers), improving the functioning of the existing shakhas, connecting newer people to the shakhas and vigorously spreading the Sangh's nationalist ideology to every section of society. The pracharaks are not paid a salary by the Sangh, and it is expected that they dine at the home of the karyakartas of the region that they are in charge of. They are given some travel allowance. A pracharak can be deployed anywhere in the country at any time. The organisation takes care of their basic facilities. They enjoy a very important position in the Sangh; in fact, two such Sangh pracharaks went on to become the Prime Ministers of our country: Atal Bihari Vajpayee and Narendra Modi.

When Irani was declared the BJP candidate from Amethi again for the 2019 Lok Sabha elections, the RSS gave the responsibility of managing the election to Parmeshwarji, who used to be a zila pracharak in Amethi. The RSS workers had become active long before the 2019 elections. The RSS had started to work in Amethi from November 2018. The entire constituency was divided into 116 nyay panchayats, and more than half of them were assigned to full-timer (poornkalik) and Mandal Karyawahs of the Sangh. Immediately after the dates were announced for the 2019 Lok Sabha elections, sixteen blocks of the Amethi constituency were placed under full-time pracharaks of the Sangh.

It is part of the Sangh's mode of working that when a major campaign is to be run in a particular area, full-time officials are appointed there. The way these officials function is unique too. They go all out to achieve their goal. They work according to the organisation's directive only, not according to the candidate's or local leaders' wishes. However, ensuring coordination is a priority for them. The coordination has to be such that there emerges no hindrance to their quest of fulfilling their objective. After full-time (poornkalik) officials were posted in all blocks of Amethi, the Sangh began work on booth composition. A plan was made to place twenty workers in each booth of the constituency. Special attention was given to the caste representation structure while posting these booth-level workers. Particular attention was paid to the fact that all castes and sections of society be represented in the appointment of booth-level workers. This process was set in motion in November 2018. At the outset, nyay panchayats were identified and set up all across the constituency. Each nyay panchayat covered seven to eight villages. By December 2018, the list of workers and trained workers of these villages had been made. Here too, the Sangh worked with such synchrony that it made the position of the BJP in Amethi even stronger. It began with the nyay panchayat heads identifying people who had been associated with the RSS in the past, in whatever capacity, in the villages under their jurisdiction: people who had been swayamsevaks or full-time officials of the Sangh but were no longer active. The nyay panchayat heads met them and got them involved again.

The list of trained workers and untrained workers was divided into various sections. Categories like females, males, teachers, businessmen, learned citizens, learned citizens among Dalits, farmers and so on were created, and duties were allocated accordingly. After such categorisation, the workers were split into smaller groups. Every day, the group head or pracharak of the RSS took meals at the home of some member of his nyay panchayat or the other. The group representatives were directed not to venture out of their designated nyay panchayats. All these people stayed put in their respective nyay panchayats from December 2018 till the day of the election, 6 May 2019. Apart from this, when the election was announced, duties were also allocated to the full-time householder workers at the block level.

Full-time pracharaks from the central and provincial levels were posted in 16 blocks of the Amethi parliamentary constituency. They used to keep a tab on the smallest details, and worked day in and day out for the success of the RSS's strategy. Full-time householder officials were involved in 116 nyay panchayats. After that, the blocks were placed under pracharaks and the responsibility of assembly segments was given to those full-time members who were either a part of the Sangh or were performing important roles in the Sangh's allied bodies.

The RSS felt this was imperative, having gauged the importance of a robust means of communication in the 2019 Lok Sabha elections. It developed a channel of communication across the constituency that ensured quick dissemination of information from the nyay panchayat level to the RSS's election-in-charge. This channel of communication was well tested too. Before the announcement of the election, the full-time members responsible for nyay panchayats, blocks and the Assembly constituencies of Amethi parliamentary seat would meet every second day. They used to share reports from their respective areas. If there was a piece of crucial information, it would be shared with the central leadership apart from the candidate (Irani), and the instructions that were sent back would be deliberated upon. One of the duties of these full-time officials was to keep an eye on the BJP workers. If any worker of the party was seen engaging in any wrongdoing, or if it was feared that they might do so, Irani would be immediately informed.

The RSS demarcates its own provinces and districts as part of its method of functioning. In the RSS's scheme of things, Jagdishpur in Amethi constituted a district. According to its zila pracharak Satyendraji, 'This entire process was set in motion before the 2019 Lok Sabha elections were announced.' The Sangh had also formed a separate group of lawyers who were assigned the task of staying connected with the Election Commission in order to ensure that there was nothing amiss. When the poll panel came out with the election dates, the BJP announced in its first list itself that Irani would be the party's candidate from Amethi. After this, Irani arrived in Amethi and took up the reins. As a result of the experience and lessons from the previous elections in 2014, Irani relied more on the local people this time around. The responsibility of managing her election campaign rested on the shoulders of the local leaders. There was no team from Delhi or Mumbai to assist her. It can be said that the people who came to Amethi with Irani in 2014 were outsiders, but after working there for five years, they became a part of the local populace. Irani had developed a distinct stature, having been a union minister for five years. Leaders, from Uttar Pradesh chief minister Yogi Adityanath to the then BJP president Amit Shah, had held rallies in Irani's constituency. There was a changed Irani in Amethi now, one who was self-confident and was present with a moral aura in the electoral battle of Amethi.

When she reached Amethi as a candidate in 2019, a system was put in place under which there used to be regular one-to-one meetings every morning with RSS functionaries. The RSS officials would share their plans with Irani and she would provide feedback. People who have attended these sessions say that Irani's feedback would be astute and precise. Some RSS officials also accept that Irani's political understanding is very nuanced. The RSS, which began preparing the ground for the election since December 2018, knew that most of the people of Amethi were attracted not to the Congress, but its envelopes. Therefore, they prepared to abolish these electoral envelopes.

Through its workers, the RSS formulated a plan to ensure that leaders of the Congress and its supporters coming from outside could not distribute envelopes, so that what happened to Sanjay Singh in 1999 did not happen to Irani. The Congress leaders were alert to these machinations and worried about how to fight the election. The Amethi Congress Committee, in fact, unanimously passed a proposal for Rahul Gandhi to contest the election from a seat in south India. The proposal of the Amethi Congress on 23 March 2019 went somewhat like this:

Honourable Shri Rahul Gandhiji, President, All India Congress Committee, New Delhi, represents Amethi and is also an MP from Amethi. There has been a proposal from the party workers from south India about contesting the election there. Shri Rahul Gandhiji is the national president of the party and the future Prime Minister of the country. Former Prime Minister Shrimati Indira Gandhi and Sonia Gandhi had contested elections from south India also, along with north India, and represented the entire country. This would be honouring the workers from north and south India. The district Congress Committee, Amethi unanimously proposed that Shri Rahul Gandhi should accept the proposal made by the workers from south India about contesting the election. This suggestion deserves to be welcomed.

There is a lot of enthusiasm and respect for him among the people of Amethi. Shri Rahul Gandhi would win handsomely from both Amethi and south India and become the Prime Minister of the country.

Kind regards,
Yogendra Mishra

Before this proposal could be made public by the Congress, it reached Irani. When TV journalist Pankaj Jha tweeted about this proposal of the Amethi Congress Committee, Irani sent a riposte at half past seven in the evening:

Amethi ne bhagaaya,
Jagah-jagah se bulaave ka swaang rachaaya,
Kyonki janta ne thukraaya.

#BhaagRahulBhaag

Singhaasan khaali karo Rahulji ki janta aati hai

This tweet gave rise to a political storm. A war of words started between the ruling party and the opposition. Be that as it may, the idea of Rahul Gandhi contesting from somewhere other than Amethi gave Irani a tactical, psychological and ethical edge.

Meanwhile, after boosting the administrative and strategic setup, the RSS turned its attention towards the 1,963 booths of Amethi. Along with promotions and campaigning, the RSS also identified the booths in which the BJP had got more votes than the Congress in 2014. Efforts were undertaken to beef up these booths so that even more votes could be garnered and the margin between the BJP and Congress reduced.

The RSS had made adequate arrangements at the booth level as well. A plan of sending election bags to every household was deliberated upon. The bags contained the candidate's publicity pamphlets, voting slip, flag, badge and patkas printed with the party's lotus symbol. One set of bags was distributed by the BJP, another by the RSS, and the third set was kept as an emergency reserve. A three-tier review of this process was also developed. At the first stage, the candidate, or Irani, reviewed it. Then there would be a review at the social level to see if the bags had reached every household, and if they had, what reactions they elicited. Did people use the flag and badge, for instance. If there was any report of suspicion or a lack of excitement, a whole mechanism would be set in motion and efforts made to ensure that the BJP flag was put up in every household.

As the Battle, so the Electoral strategy

While the Sangh was working in this precise manner that they can create an environment in favour of BJP candidate. They also tried to make impact of their efforts on the electors. Then they review the working of booth level volunteers. This three tier election mechanism had an positive impact. Congress leaders and their remaining workers were under the illusion that their old formula would bear fruit. A leader from Amethi associated with Congress says that the party felt assured the people would carry the day for Rahul Gandhi. One BJP sympathizer Ramnaresh Mishra told me that in Amethi the Congress cars carrying money would reach the booth level four days before the election and the prominent leader of that area would get one lakh rupees per booth. It was his responsibility to carry the money to the booth level, and then the booth in-charge was tasked with proper distribution of that money. And, as mentioned earlier, the headmen played a big role in this operation. However, this claim could not be verified.

Such 'revelations' were made by Congress workers also who received money and even those who did not. If this story is to be believed, then four days before the election, nearly Rs 20 crore would have been distributed in the 1,963 booths across Amethi, at the rate of Rs 1 lakh per booth. However, the preparedness of the RSS and presence of the BJP workers prevented this game of money from realising its objective this time around. The RSS had made another important preparation at the booth stage, and its benefit could be seen at two levels. First, the mechanism of information compilation; and the second was to avoid any kind of slip-up in strategic preparations. A study of the way that the Congress fights elections and experience from past elections suggested that the Congress leaders would try to divide the workers associated with the RSS and BJP. Such efforts were made this time around as well, but they were thwarted as a combat strategy was now in place at two levels. The kind of training that is imparted to the swayamsevaks and the culture that they are imbued with make it difficult to divide them. However, in politics, it is not easy to predict who might go astray—when, where, how or why.

Accordingly, preparations were made in case the Congress managed to lure away some BJP or RSS workers. A worker on a motorcycle was posted at every five kilometres so that in case of such deserters, he could quickly reach the area or booth and take up responsibility. These workers were trained to oversee the distribution of BJP election bags and keep vigil on the moves of the Congress.

Apart from firming up electoral preparedness at so many levels, the RSS also strived to connect directly with the voters. As discussed earlier, different groups of the RSS were assigned different tasks, including winning over voters from various communities. For this, some older members of the Vishwa Hindu Parishad were requested to join the election campaign. The RSS also roped in swayamsevak Colonel (Rtd) Dev, a resident of Rajasthan, who brought an entire team of maulvis along with him. Col Dev and his team worked for twenty days in Jagdishpur and Tiloi, areas with a large Muslim population. The RSS was also able to explain to the Dalit Muslims why voting for the BJP would be to their advantage. Those who called themselves Rajput maulvis also campaigned for Irani. This caused considerable damage to the Congress.

Moreover, the way the Modi-led government had taken a stand on the issue of triple talaq and the vigour with which Irani used to raise this issue in her rallies really struck a chord with women. It is believed that their fear of divorce decreased and women in most places made up their minds to vote for 'Smriti didi'. It was one of the reasons for Irani's win in Amethi. Most Muslim families were split down the middle on the question of voting for the BJP. The Muslim women threw their weight behind Modi and Irani gained from this. It would not be wrong to say that the decisions taken by Prime Minister Modi in the previous five years had ignited the flame of belief among the Muslim women of Amethi, the impact of which was felt by the Congress at the 2019 Lok Sabha polls.

Before the poll, the Sah Sarkaryawah (joint general secretary) of the RSS, Dr Krishna Gopal, visited Amethi twice. He met all the full-time workers in the area. Sangh activists held meetings in Prayagraj, Varanasi and Jaunpur as well, and there were deliberations on the preparations and strategy in Amethi. The RSS had given its all for Irani in 2014 as well, but as mentioned before, although there was no shortage of enthusiasm, there simply had not been enough time.

Sangh shakhas create a winning atmosphere

Dr Krishna Gopal had visited Amethi in 2014 too. The RSS activists became very active after that. It was a combination of the active role of RSS workers, the popularity of Modi, and Irani's hard work that earned the BJP over three lakh votes in 2014, despite a short campaign. The picture that emerges from the ground is that the RSS had started to increase the number of its shakhas in the Amethi constituency even before the 2014 Lok Sabha elections. By the time the 2014 Lok Sabha polls came around, there were 250 RSS shakhas across the villages of Amethi. By early 2019, over 300 shakhas had begun to function regularly in Amethi.

Both morning and evening shakhas were organised in Amethi. The morning shakhas were mainly for salaried people, businessmen and senior citizens, while the evening shakhas largely comprised students and the youth. Those who attended these shakhas regularly were called swayamsevaks. Becoming a sakha member is relatively easy and there is no official procedure involved. Anybody who wants to serve the nation and comes and salutes the flag can become a swayamsevak. Within the shakhas, members are organised into karyawahs (secretary), mukhya shikshak (chief instructor) and gana shikshaks. Apart from these three categories, the shakhas are divided into various sections that, in the Sangh terminology, are called Gat, the heads of which are called Gatnayaks. It is the duty of the Gatnayaks to look after the wellbeing of the swayamsevaks getting admitted to the shakhas. The entire structure and terminology of the Sangh has been borrowed from the Mahabharata. Given this mode of functioning of the RSS and its increased strength in Amethi, the dedication of the workers could be further channelled in favour of the BJP.

People's association with the RSS and the shakhas grows fast and deep because whenever a swayamsevak is absent, the Gatnayak asks after him and informs the sakha karyawah of the reason for his absence. After that, the sakha karyawah and Gatnayak visit the swayamsevak's house to enquire about his wellbeing and offer any help that may be required. This system leads to a sense of kinship.

Among ten swadeshi games that were played at the shakhas in Amethi were 'Main Shivaji' (I am Shivaji) and 'Mitra Raksha' (Protection of Friends). Apart from these, 'Dilli Hamari' (Delhi Will Be Ours) was played every day. Gradually, 'Dilli Hamari' started to gain prominence at the shakhas organised in the Amethi Lok Sabha constituency. This game involves one swayamsevak being made to stand in side a circle. Standing in the circle, he shouts, 'Who will win Delhi?' He repeats this question twice, and the other swayamsevaks present around him shout back, 'Dilli Hamari' (Delhi Will Be Ours). After that, all the swayamsevaks try to tightly fit into the circle. Whichever swayamsevak can fit tightly into the circle is declared the winner. The advantage of this game being organised regularly was that chants of 'Dilli Hamari' started to echo in Amethi. Cries of 'Dilli Hamari' began to be imprinted in the hearts and minds of the people.

Not only did this have a symbolic impact on the 2019 Lok Sabha elections, at a practical level it also helped a lot in creating the right atmosphere. This game played in the shakhas of the Sangh finds mention in the 'Sakha Surabhi' booklet. That this game could be used for election campaigning was proven for the first time in Amethi. A game played inside a circle checkmated the game of envelopes. Efforts were undertaken to strengthen morning and evening shakhas in Amethi and ensure the partnership of more and more people. Before the announcement of the election, a pamphlet was distributed in Amethi through these shakhas. The name of the Lok Sabha candidate was not written in that pamphlet, but it carried a description of the work done by Prime Minister Modi. There were examples of local people who had benefited from the decisions of the Modi government. This helped in turning the tide in the BJP's favour.

Seen from the perspective of the RSS's functioning, some parts of Amethi come under the Kashi province and others under the Awadh province. The Sangh has divided Amethi into two districts— Jagdishpur and Amethi. The Amethi district has forty-seven mandals of the Sangh while Jagdishpur district has fifty-one mandals. The system for administration has been strengthened by dividing these districts into seven khands. The geographical nomenclature made on the basis of the Sangh's organisational structure is different from official administrative systems. Before understanding this geographical nomenclature of the Sangh, it is important to know the organisational structure of the Sangh. At the grassroots level in the organisation are shakhas and above them are the khands. At least three and at the most twelve to fifteen shakhas together form a mandal. Keeping in view the system and geographical spread, ten mandals combine to form the town unit of the Sangh. In the same way, there are metropolitan units and district units. On average, in the Sangh's scheme of things, there can be several shakhas in a district. Above the district is the division and then comes the province.

According to the Sangh's organisational structure, at present, there are six provinces in Uttar Pradesh. These provinces are further divided into regions. Every year, the Sangh arranges Sangh Education

Class-First Year (Sangh Sikhsha Varg, Pratham Varsh) in Amethi, a training camp based on strict discipline. All kinds of activities are organised at the camp from four in the morning to ten in the night. For instance, there are physical exercise sessions in the morning and intellectual discussions in the afternoon and evening. The intellectual sessions comprise discussions on current affairs, conversations with subject experts and lectures. Usually, in the first year of these classes, entry is granted only to youths who are over sixteen. As a result of these classes being organised for years in Amethi, a whole assembly of trained men emerged. The third year of training takes place in Nagpur. Pracharaks are required to have completed three years of training, but all swayamsevaks who have undergone the third year of training do not necessarily become pracharaks.

Atmosphere of Belief

There was an atmosphere of belief in Amethi that a Modi-led government would be formed at the Centre again. It was explained to the people that if this came to pass and there was a non-BJP MP from Amethi, there could be hurdles in the process of development; whereas with the BJP in power both at the Centre and the state, developmental work would get a massive fillip.

Such an environment was created in 2019 that supporters in Amethi of the Samajwadi Party and Bahujan Samaj Party did not vote for their candidates or those whom their parties were supporting, even after being asked to do so by their leaders. Many youngsters from families that traditionally supported the Congress went against their parents. There were huge turnouts from the Hindu community. Regardless of the party they belonged to—Samajwadi Party or Bahujan Samaj Party—they considered themselves Hindus first. Intending to defeat the BJP, the Samajwadi Party and Bahujan Samaj Party went to their traditional supporters asking for votes in the name of caste and religion, but they could not succeed this time around. Mayawati followed the path taken by the Samajwadi Party and tried her best to shore up the Congress, but failed. The Sangh, energised by its success among the educated class, held separate meetings with the heads of the educational institutions running in Amethi, and made attempts to attract them towards the BJP. When this started to yield positive results, these meetings were made more regular. Apart from the swayamsevaks, the RSS also mobilised people associated with its allied organisations in outreach activities. Eight kinds of activities were apportioned between these organisations.

The Mahila Morcha was asked to focus on emotive issues connected to festivals that the women in Amethi celebrated. The Mahila Morcha contacted temples, maths and samitis, and organised Chhath Puja at the block level in which arrangements were made for those keeping chhath fasts. Mahila Morcha activists were given special bags to distribute, containing voter lists of particular areas, bindis carrying the BJP's election symbol, buttons, etc.

The Yuva Morcha was put to work among the youth. Representatives of the Kisan Morcha went to the farmers with the promise of solving their problems. Furthermore, separate teams of lawyers of the Adhivakta Parishad and other experts were formed that kept a tab on decisions made by central and state election officials.

The Election Commission too was keeping a close eye on Amethi, and strict arrangements were made. The questions posed by the Election Commission were answered, and information on the possibility of trouble in the constituency shared with the poll panel and steps according to the law were demanded. The team of legal experts was responsible for quickly replying to complaints if they were against the BJP candidate. This group objected to Rahul Gandhi's given name in his nomination papers. This objection indirectly questioned Rahul Gandhi's feelings towards the nation. A massive controversy erupted during the election campaign regarding his citizenship, name and educational qualifications.

A unique initiative of the Sangh was that everyone was given specific tasks, and the scope of their work was clearly outlined. The local activists were forbidden from getting involved in the platform of the central leadership and told to focus on their duties. The workers were instructed to not leave their respective blocks/areas even if a big leader was holding a rally in another block. There was also a ban on going to listen to their own leaders at public meetings because the focus was on small public meetings and the work assigned. All prominent and central leaders were intimated that their meetings would be small. Even the central ministers accepted this plan and started holding smaller meetings. The Congress leaders could not comprehend this strategy and they thought people were not gathering at the meetings called by frontline BJP leaders because they had lost interest in the party.

Even prominent journalists who had gone to Amethi from Delhi were puzzled by this strategy and started reporting on the small rallies of the frontline leaders as unsuccessful efforts. On 3 April 2019, ABP News ran a Nielsen survey story that predicted a big win for Rahul Gandhi from Amethi. The emphasis of the news story was on Irani's perceived loss than Rahul Gandhi's expected victory. However, voters had something totally different in mind. RSS fought the election battle of Amethi like the war of Mahabharat and worked on the basics of electoral battle.

Every booth a Hindu Rashtra

Voting in Amethi was scheduled on 6 May 2019. Booth-level preparations were done. The election-day challenge that was set for the swayamsevaks and BJP workers was to reach out to voters in every polling booth and tell them that they should vote keeping in mind the national interests. A district-level official of the Sangh, Satyendraji, tells me, 'People from all castes and communities were brought together and encouraged to vote as Indians. Based on the election list, responsibilities were assigned to conduct 100 per cent polling. The RSS representatives used to speak about the upliftment of the Hindu society. They did not take the name of any political party. Neither were sides taken nor was any party denigrated. National interest was stressed upon and the people were told that voting was their right. In the Dalit neighbourhoods too, the Sangh representatives used to talk about the nation and society.'

It has been mentioned earlier that the campaign had started from February 2019 itself in the form of small booth-level meetings. Although these meetings had had little impact on the Muslims, the Sangh activists continued to pay visits to their neighbourhoods. The frontline officials of the RSS had instructed for all allied organisations to be brought on a common platform and work towards a common goal. Gauging that the people were a bit disappointed with the Jagdishpur MLA Suresh Pasi, the RSS planned to send its swayamsevaks to the entire assembly area to work towards improving his impression, and each swayamsevak was allocated one or two villages. The booth in-charge was asked to treat the booth as a Hindu Rashtra and given the task of strengthening it. The booth in-charge was also directed to frame relevant strategies in order to ensure 100 per cent voting in his booth. The RSS had held two-day workshops in every assembly area to train the booth supervisors. It had formed a Lok Sabha Steering Committee and several Assembly Steering Committee under the leadership of its swayamsevaks. The Lok Sabha Steering Committee was working under Suresh Upadhyay. The Assembly Steering Committee was run by different people. For example, the Jagdishpur Assembly segment was under Vijay Shukla and the Tiloi Assembly segment was being looked after by Anil Bajpai.

These steering committees comprised different sub-committees which worked on their assigned jobs. All the sub committees had eight verticals. These verticals were called intellectual group, youth group, farmer group, religious group, national upliftment and political discussion group, women and Dalits group, business group and minority group. These groups had their respective duties based on which they went to their target classes and made appeals of voting for the national interest. The RSS also took upon itself a new task in this election—that of sending voter slips to every household. The worker who would go with voter slips would not engage in political discussions but simply talk about electing the deserving candidate. The booth-level team of swayamsevaks could also be regarded as chowkidars (guards). According to Parmeshwarji, 'Nobody slept on the night of 5 May 2019. The Sangh had made alternative arrangements for bags and booth agents. Over 350 swayamsevaks and over 500 workers had kept bags with them so that any emergency could be swiftly handled.'

Mrityunjay Tripathi, associated with the BJP in Jagdishpur, says, 'The people could see that households were getting toilets, and gas cylinders were being made available too. So they decided that they had to vote for Irani for the sake of Modi as well this time. People from the lower rung of the society made up their minds. There were long queues at polling booths on the day of the election. The central government assisted in this too. The RSS and BJP workers had the list of all those in the constituency who had benefited from the central government's schemes. Those handling assembly segments divided the list among themselves according to their respective regions. The veracity of this list was examined and was advertised in the constituency. The money distributed under the Kisan Samman Yojana had an effect too, as it gave the poor the confidence that the government was thinking about them. Public opinion was mobilised in the name of Prime Minister Narendra Modi, and the efforts bore fruit at the polling booths.'

Prominent Congress leaders from various states had also reached Amethi. Chief ministers and former ministers were in attendance. Vehicles carrying non-Uttar-Pradesh number plates had taken over the roads of Amethi. Irani had strategised very carefully here too. The BJP had kept local vehicles of Amethi for election campaigning, but those with number plates of places outside Amethi were used to keep a watch on the Congress vehicles. The reasoning behind this was that the drivers of local vehicles could easily become the informers of the Congress and pass on information on their movement to the Congress. Most of the vehicles carried Uttar Pradesh number plates and a few select vehicles that had arrived from Kanpur and Lucknow had Delhi number plates. These vehicles were there for keeping guard. They were spread across the entire constituency. Whenever it was known that a vehicle with a non-Uttar-Pradesh number plate was moving towards a village where the Congress had influence, a vehicle carrying BJP and RSS workers would be sent after it. When I asked the RSS's Parmeshwarji about this, he said, 'We wanted to foil any plan the Congress may have had to distribute money in the constituency, hence we laid such a siege. Often Congress vehicles laden with money would start off, but when they noticed another vehicle following it, they would turn back'. A Congress leader accepted that they were dented to a large extent by this strategy as their promises could not be fulfilled. Also, the RSS posted 10 workers at each booth, and they were tasked with keeping a round-the-clock vigil on the activities at the booths. Five of the 10 workers would be awake while the other five slept. Even the slightest possibility of any kind of disturbance or discrepancy in voting would be immediately conveyed to the booth in-charge.

Hit where it hurts most

During this time, the RSS understood that the voters of Amethi had a bond with Indira Gandhi, and to an extent, Rajiv Gandhi, but after their deaths, this relationship became progressively weaker and had almost ended. The people of Amethi say to this day that the voters were greatly valued till the time of Indira Gandhi, but after her death, they started to be forgotten. And after Rajiv Gandhi, as if Amethi evaporated from the minds of Congress leaders. Dinanath Shukla, whom I had met at the Amethi railway station, says, 'When Rahul Gandhi started to contest from here, the intervention of outsiders increased. Rahul Gandhi used to bring his foreign friends along for networking during campaigning. They aimed to earn some profits from the government. Neither were they concerned about the people of Amethi nor were they there for social service. They came only to fulfil their selfish objectives. Their prosperity could be seen from their big cars and attires. These people used to emerge seven days before and go back after a few days of voting tourism.'

Local Congress workers could not get anywhere close to their Rahul bhaiyya during election campaigns or visits, leave aside meeting him and speaking to him. This disconnect also played its part in making the ground fertile for the RSS and BJP's strategy to succeed. The Sangh sent its prominent leaders to dine at the houses of the local Congressmen. There was not a single Congress leader or important worker whose house the RSS officials and pracharaks missed. This had a psychological impact, and the local people of the Congress gradually softened towards Irani. While in the Congress, there was a culture of giving away jeeps and motorcycles to its workers, the RSS swayamsevaks were spending their own money to work.

The Congress had already sustained considerable damage for contesting an election on the back of local contractors and money power. Earlier, only those who did not get the money would be annoyed. In the election this time around, most of the people ended up empty-handed. This sent their anger soaring. The Congress' giving preference to contractors over the intelligentsia affected not only Rahul Gandhi's election campaign, but its adverse effect could also be seen on the ground on election day. The Congress workers themselves started to oppose leaders who had come from outside. During the 2019 Lok Sabha elections, former Haryana chief minister Bhupendra Singh Hooda and the Chhattisgarh chief minister Bhupesh Baghel met with protests at many places.

The RSS had put up a non-political platform in Amethi. There was a small group that talked about the interests of the nation and the Hindus. The members of this groups were trying to explain to the people that efforts were being made to fulfil the dream of an undivided India in the face of a society broken on the lines of caste and community. They were told that if the Hindus united, then victory could be achieved even on zero balance. Consequently, in many places on the day of voting, there were different opinions within one family. If the head of the family supported the Congress, the children were keen to vote for the BJP. Captain Satish Sharma's colleague Aditya Ojha says, 'I can pledge my allegiance to the Congress, but there is no guarantee of how my family members would vote.

Shambhu Shukla's family lives in Amethi. They have been with the Congress for generations, and they would vote for the Congress in every election. However, peeved by the behaviour of Rahul Gandhi and Priyanka Gandhi Vadra, this family started to campaign for the BJP candidate. Such incidents influenced the voters of the neighbouring areas as well. Even after so many years of Independence, Amethi was still backward. In the gram sabha areas of Gaon ka Purba and Budhi ka Purba, there are practically no pucca houses even today. Many residents of both the villages were in favour of the Congress. The people there were not ready to listen to any name other than the Congress'. On the initiative of Irani, the workers of the BJP and swayamsevaks of the RSS linked the names of these villagers with Aadhaar and also linked them with government schemes. Irani went to this village herself. She sat with the people there and had conversations. This raised the people's faith. The situation of the villages of Amethi was bad. This area had more poverty than the vananchal areas of Jharkhand and Chhattisgarh. A school is located five to seven kilometres away from the village. A person from Budhi ka Purba says, 'Only two girls have studied in the entire village. They had to travel eight kilometres from their village every day to study, though the village is only 18 km away from the tehsil.' Irani's conviction and behaviour ensured that an atmosphere was created in this village that was favourable for the BJP and in the 2019 election, 75 per cent of the votes went to Irani.

Looking at all the RSS swayamsevaks, pracharaks and full-time members who had campaigned in Amethi dedicate themselves back to routine work after Irani's victory, one is naturally reminded of the writing of former RSS sarsanghchalak K.S. Sudarshan in which he had quoted a poem as well:

Vrittapatra par naam chhapega, pehnoonga swagat samuhaar,

Chhor chalo yeh chhudra bhavana, hindu rashtra ke taaranhaar,

kankad-patthad ban-ban humko rashtra-neev ko bharna hai,

brahmatej ke kshetratej ke, amar pujaari ban-na hai.

(Names would be printed in documents, I'd wear garlands of recognition,

Leave behind petty thoughts, O saviour of Hindu Rashtra,

As stones and pebbles, we have to lay the nation's foundation,

Of the princely valour, of divine vitality, we have to be immortal worshippers.)

The thought expressed in the lines above properly identifies a swayamsevak. If people start clapping during any Sangh programme, the officials say, 'Why clap for doing a duty? If someone renders a service, does he beat the tom-tom, saying, see how well I have worked?' And so when a small booklet mentioning the aid provided by swayamsevaks at various fronts during the war with Pakistan in 1971 was presented to the then sarsanghchalak Guruji Golwalkar by a swayamsevak, he refused to accept it, saying, 'If someone else described it there would be no problem, but is it right for us to praise our own efforts?'

Smriti Irani's victory in Amethi was historic. And so, after carrying out their duties, the RSS strategists and workers moved on to their new assignments.

4

Rebellion

Rashtrakavi Ramdhari Singh Dinkar writes in his book *Sanskriti Ke Char Adhyaya*, 'Rebellion, revolution or revolt are not things that explode suddenly. A wound festers for a long time before erupting. Similarly, even after establishing itself against all odds, any ideology spreads in a half-baked state in the first few years.' Dinkar wrote these lines sixty-three years ago. When read in conjunction with the historic result of the 2019 Lok Sabha elections in Amethi, Smriti Irani's win was, without a doubt, nothing short of a revolution. It was an indication of the people of Amethi rebelling against the political dynasty. The wounds of poverty and lack of basic infrastructure had been festering for several decades before erupting. If the Amethi elections are assessed in terms of historic significance, there would be no better imagery than Dinkar's quoted in the beginning of this chapter.

In many parts of Amethi, people from various classes and communities were exasperated with the Nehru-Gandhi dynasty, but for the lack of a strong and serious alternative, they were compelled to vote for the Congress term after term. Previously elected leaders, who used the name of the Congress and the Gandhi family to come to power in Amethi, had never helped anybody, they had just fulfilled their own interests. Rahul Gandhi had created an image of a British-era lord who would undertake tours sometimes, show his face to the public and then retreat to his 'palace'. Often, he would exit through the back door without meeting anyone, while the people continued to wait for him outside. Rahul Gandhi fell prey to his own feudal ways. When the leader himself is out of reach of the people, how far can the party activists take the relationship under their own steam? Things came to such a pass that following in his footsteps, leave aside his local representatives, even small-time activists, bred on Congress money, lost touch with the people.

The Congress leaders did not reach out to the common man in Amethi. They could not connect with the society. They went to meet their contractors and then returned. The contractors were the only ones that got the benefit of government schemes. In spite of this lackadaisical attitude, people in the Congress believed that no matter what the people here would not abandon the Nehru-Gandhi family. But the distance between the public and the Congress party grew wider. Over three elections before 2019, the people of Amethi had seen the bubbles of promises made by Priyanka Gandhi Vadra burst. She had come to the constituency for the first time in 2003, accompanied by her husband Robert Vadra. The people here worshipped them. They were welcomed in every village. The entire area was draped in posters that said, 'Jijaji and Didi have come and brought with them fresh light'. After the elections, Jijaji and Didi were nowhere to be seen. And after that, the vicious cycle repeated itself: election, appearance, promises, and disappearance.

Rajesh Masala says, 'Priyanka had made numerous promises when she came for the fourth time as well, but when the promises were not fulfilled even after such a long time, the people of Amethi started to disapprove of her. Even rallies started to be called off. They cried wolf, people gathered again and again and kept on losing trust. What became of those Dalits at places they dined? They got no benefits. An event was arranged, they went to Dalit houses and ate while sitting on the floor, and then photos were taken. Photos were printed in newspapers, TV channels carried the news, but after that nobody asked after those Dalit families, nor did anyone come to meet them.'

There is another incident in this series of episodes. After becoming the Congress president, Rahul Gandhi was slated to visit Amethi on a two-day tour on 15 and 16 January 2018. A truckload of rose petals was arranged to be showered upon a statue of Rajiv Gandhi. At the same time, a controversial poster was put up in the name of Abhay Shukla alias Rijju at Amethi's Gauriganj station. This poster depicted Prime Minister Modi as the ten-headed Ravan, while Congress president Rahul Gandhi was shown carrying a bow and arrows as an incarnation of Lord Ram. This poster said, 'Rahul roop mein bhagwan Ram ka avatar. 2019 mein aayega Rahul Raj (Lord Ram has incarnated in the form of Rahul. 2019 would see the emergence of Rahul Raj [Ram Rajya]).' This poster had the opposite of its desired effect. The people got agitated and the rose petals dried up in the face of public rage. Such was the extent of people's ire against this poster that Rahul Gandhi could not even garland Rajiv Gandhi's statue during his Amethi trip. As a result of the public protests, he had to leave. This was a sign of the change that had taken root in Amethi. The story became national news, and local Congress leaders advised their president to change his constituency. Rahul Gandhi did not do this, but he did contest from two places.

However, Nadim Ashraf Jaisi, who was part of the Congress at that time and later broke away to join the Aam Aadmi Party, does not consider the BJP and Irani's victory as the triumph of the nation, nationalism, service and dedication. He argues, 'Amethi is not distinct from the nation, and so the effect of frenzied politics could be seen there too. There is an altogether different kind of attraction in the politics of frenzy. The BJP did frenzied politics in the entire country and its reverberations could be felt in Amethi as well. When Pulwama happened, Congress leader Chandrakant Dubey, who was managing Rahul's programmes in Amethi, warned the party workers that Amethi might be lost. There was a strong nationalistic tide. Rahul was looking weak and Modi's magic on the youth was doing wonders. The Congress could not measure the tide of nationalism and continued to compromise its ideals. It kept on giving importance to people like Imran Masood and Imran Pratapgarhi. If the BJP had Pragya Thakur and Sakshi Maharaj, the Congress put Masood and Pratapgarhi forward. The Congress failed to read the pulse of the people and painted itself into a corner as an anti-Hindu party.'

The Congress's strategic errors were in some way or the other responsible for Rahul Gandhi's defeat. The party could not do anything new. Its programmes were all stale. The leaders working in Amethi could not get new people associated with the Congress, and the older lot had lost contact with the public. The party could not sense this and its effect could be seen in the 2019 Lok Sabha polls. After Rahul Gandhi filed his nomination papers, there was next to no electoral management, the leaders simply assumed the people of Amethi would make Rahul Gandhi the winner because of their old relationship with the Gandhi family. Electoral management is important, but no centralised system for this could be formulated the Congress. Rahul Gandhi's representative Chandrakant Dubey made a separate plan; Priyanka Gandhi's associate Dheeraj Srivastava and Rahul Gandhi's close aide Kanishka Singh also made their own plan, and there was no coordination between them.

The second and biggest difference between Rahul Gandhi and Irani was that the latter established a bond with everybody. If there was a report of a disappointed party worker, the senior leaders on Smriti Irani's team would get in touch with him and address his grievances. Rahul Gandhi's nature, on the other hand, was completely different. A Congress party leader who is now in another party explained to me that if Rahul Gandhi was displeased with a party colleague, he became cold towards him, and eventually stopped talking to him. He would not even tell the party worker the reason for his displeasure. Dozens of such incidents happened within the Congress during the election and even before that. According to the local leaders of the Congress, a king is not supposed to be satisfied or disappointed. His duty, on the other hand, is to take everybody along.

A true leader takes everyone along, even the ones who disagree with him. Maintaining dialogue with the opposition at all levels is important. If a party worker has committed a mistake, point it out to them and coax them into changing their ways. If a leader has moved in the wrong direction, the top brass must make him realise his mistake and not castigate him or cast him aside. A failure of leadership in the Congress meant that new people could not be brought in, and instead, conflict with the older members kept mounting. A failure to identify good people was also one of the weaknesses of Rahul Gandhi's personality. He could not maintain his links with older supporters and could not establish emotional bonds with newer people either. He could not give respect to the older people nor could he expel those with whom he was dissatisfied. How could a party run like this? One example here is of Pramod Tiwari, who is apparently disliked by the Gandhi family; but the party is not able to show him the door, and he continues to be given responsibilities in every election. Under such circumstances, how can Rahul Gandhi steer anybody towards victory? Similarly, when a leader like Princess Ratna Singh the daughter of Denesh Singh, Raja of Kalakankar and the cabinet minister of Indira Gandhi's cabinet left the Congress, nobody in the party even talked to her or tried to learn the reason for her decision, let alone convince her to stay.

Nadim Ashraf Jaisi says, 'The Congress was in this condition in Amethi and the entire country because its leadership did not even know that the party workers craved for emotion. They were not salaried employees trying to save their jobs at all costs.' In Amethi too, people with new, bookish knowledge started getting primacy over the loyalty of the old associates. A game of statistics began to be played. Rahul Gandhi found himself in a mire because of his advisors. People with bookish knowledge of politics started gathering around him. They did not have an iota of understanding about Indian politics and the sensibilities of the people, leave alone practical and ground-level knowledge. People like Sandeep Singh, a product of the leftist students' organisation All India Students' Association (AISA) was Priyanka and Rahul's advisor. He is probably adept at theory and presentation, but he did not have the remotest links with grassroots politics. An Indian election is no computer game that can be won with a laptop.

Similarly, the broker culture in the Congress had been thriving for years, and had now assumed gigantic proportions. The party brass made no attempt to stop this. Rahul Gandhi or his lieutenants in Amethi could not replace the longtime party loyalists. The public of Amethi was enraged by the arrogance of these older functionaries, and if Rahul Gandhi could have substituted them before it was too late, the Congress might not have lost so badly despite the best efforts of the BJP. Whoever Rahul Gandhi pressed into action in these elections could not deliver victory to the Congress even in their own neighbourhoods, leave aside their panchayats and villages. Chunnu Singh is the general secretary of the Congress, but Rahul Gandhi lost heavily in his booth. Deepak Singh (Congress MLC) is ineffective and Sanjay Singh keeps changing his allegiances, and so the people do not take him seriously. In Ramnagar, the party lost in all four booths. The then Congress district president lost in his own booth. Some of the people that were made booth in-charges of the Congress were so intensely hated by the public that they did not even like to see their faces. How could such people deliver victory?

Another thing which harmed the party was that the local leaders did politics by making money even from the party workers to get their work done.

When the leaders themselves start looting the party workers, what good can possibly be achieved? The Congress workers were frightened of their own leaders, they did not carry money in their pockets because they feared the local leaders would snatch it away. Likewise, the local leaders of the Congress, or those who ran contracts in the name of Rahul Gandhi, accommodated their cronies in government schemes, contracts and leases, even brought them from outside so that they were not exposed and could carry on making money by looting. The local people did not get employment, there was nobody left to listen to the poor and weak. The local leaders used to take applications from the poor and weak but never forwarded them to Rahul Gandhi. In fact, nobody had direct access to Rahul Gandhi, which would have helped him to lobby and get genuine work done. All these factors had a very negative impact, and when the people got the first alternative, they ensured that Rahul Gandhi lost. A resident of Amethi, Ramchandra, says, 'Till the time the Congress workers were in the party office, they used to cheer for the party and Rahul Gandhi, but as soon as they came out of the party office and onto the road, they would abuse both Rahul Gandhi and the party. This meant that even if antagonised party workers were not openly joining the BJP ranks, they worked for the opposition secretly.'

The Congress's closed-door politics started to freely reach the BJP, and it helped them find answers to every challenge posed by the Congress. This was exemplified by the fact that the news of Rahul Gandhi deciding to fight the elections from Wayanad apart from Amethi was first broken by the BJP. This shook the confidence of the remaining party workers in the Congress. A leading government officer belonging to the scheduled tribe visited Amethi during the election and interacted with Chandrakant Dubey, Nadim Ashraf Jaisi and Congress MLC Deepak Singh. Suddenly, there was a police raid and that officer had to leave Amethi. This proves that the BJP leaders were keeping an eye on every move of the Congress.

Furthermore, the Brahmins of Amethi, who traditionally voted for the Congress, had become dissatisfied with the party. The fact that Deepak Singh, who was related to the princely state of Gauriganj, was made a member of the legislative council, and Sanjay Singh, who changed sides frequently, was made a Rajya Sabha member from Assam, upset the Brahmins. They felt that the Congress was giving more importance to the Thakurs. Sanjay Singh, a member of the Amethi royal family, was regarded as an opportunistic leader. In 1988, he left the Congress and joined Viswanath Pratap Singh's Janata Dal. When VP Singh became the Prime Minister, he promoted Sanjay Singh as the Union Communications Minister. When the Janata Dal broke up, he joined the BJP. In 1999, Sonia Gandhi came to contest from Amethi and Sanjay Singh was badly defeated. He was longing for a 'ghar wapsi' again and in 2003, came back into the Congress fold. In 2009, the Congress made him a candidate from Sultanpur—a seat neighbouring Amethi—and he reached the Lok Sabha from there. Then in April 2014, the Congress made him a candidate for the Rajya Sabha from Assam.

Before Sanjay Singh was sent to Rajya Sabha, there were reports of his displeasure with the Congress, and the Congress managers in Amethi felt that if he was not kept in good humour, he could hurt Rahul Gandhi in the 2014 Lok Sabha polls. As a result, he was made a Rajya Sabha member. In 2019, he contested the Lok Sabha elections from Sultanpur on a Congress ticket but lost to Maneka Gandhi. After this defeat, he started to search for a new address again, and is back with the BJP now.

Now, if we talk about the Muslims and Dalits, Rahul Gandhi built leads, although narrow ones, in 20 out of 23 booths of Jais. It was believed that this time around, the Muslims were united in not voting in favour or against any party. They could not be convinced that a particular party would be on their side. The Samajwadi Party also had a candidate contesting from Amethi. This resulted in the Muslim votes getting split. The Bahujan Samaj Party did not field its candidate from here this time, but it is doubtful if Rahul Gandhi could have derived any advantage. In 2014, the BSP did field a candidate, who got nearly 65,000 votes.

There is one more point that needs to be underlined: Rahul Gandhi's calling Modi a 'chor' (thief) again and again went against him. The more he chanted 'Chowkidar Chor Hai' (the gatekeeper is a thief), the more votes he lost in Amethi. It seems that those who came up with the 'Chowkidar Chor Hai' slogan had calculated that the 'Gully gully mein shor hai, Indira Gandhi chor hai' (the lanes are echoing with calls that Indira Gandhi is a thief) slogan had benefited the opposition. However, the Congress strategists could not sense the changing times. When this slogan was directed at Indira Gandhi, she had already become unpopular owing to the Emergency, whereas Modi was at the pinnacle of popularity as Prime Minister. Under this circumstance, much of the public strongly disapproved of the personal attack mounted on Modi. The Congress also had a precedent from the 2014 Lok Sabha elections, when Mani Shankar Aiyar had sunk the party with a derogatory remark on Modi's family background.

There is a leader very close to the Gandhis called Kishori Lal Sharma in Amethi and Raebareli. The Congress leaders, in their discussions, held him indirectly responsible for Rahul Gandhi's defeat. These leaders accused Sharma of telling them to work towards cutting Rahul Gandhi's victory margin. The reasoning was that if Rahul Gandhi's victory margin reduced, the importance of the local leaders would increase. Consequently, those associated with Sharma tried to decrease Rahul Gandhi's margin of victory. In this bargain,

Rahul Gandhi's votes plummeted so much that he ended up losing the election altogether.

It is said in hushed tones by local Congress leaders that ever since Rahul Gandhi brought Chandrakant Dubey to Amethi from Madhya Pradesh, Sharma had been feeling uncompertable. He was not being able to accept that Dubey remained in Amethi even after 2014. Sharma wanted to oust Dubey at all costs, and nothing could offer a better opportunity to do so than Rahul Gandhi's defeat in the Lok Sabha elections. It seems local leaders of the Congress were engaged in improving their status and power instead of those of their leader. It is said that Rahul Gandhi wanted to tour the villages of Amethi unaccompanied by any local leader. However, the local Congress politicians did not allow this to happen. Rahul Gandhi became enraged and he scrapped the plan of visiting the villages altogether. Irani, on the other hand, was going to every village of her constituency.

Rather than working on the ground, the local Congress politicians were only interested in creating a good impression on Rahul and Priyanka Gandhi Vadra. Congress leaders themselves admit that such politicians of their party used to take a lot of money but did not work. These people would surround Rahul and Priyanka Gandhi as soon as they came to Amethi, accompany them in their convoy wherever they went, but no sooner than they went away, these leaders would fall silent and turn their attention to their contractorships.

Hotelier Rakesh Pandey, the son of Jagdish Piyush, an associate of the Nehru-Gandhi family in Amethi, wrote a column in the 1–15 June 2015 edition of *Hindi Outlook*, in which he alluded to Rahul Gandhi's method of functioning; but nobody picked up on his signal. Pandey pointed out that Rahul Gandhi's activism had warmed up the Indian political atmosphere and he was suddenly being seen in the role of an opposition leader. He wrote that there was aggression in Rahul Gandhi's speeches, he was attacking the government. The Congress and Congressmen hoped that the party would get back on its feet again. But would the party be able to move away from the margins only on the back of Rahul Gandhi getting active? Pandey pointed out that Rahul Gandhi was on a three-day tour of Amethi from 18–20 May. Pandey wondered if the programme of meeting the farmers and other members of the public under the scorching sun would help bring unhappy voters back to the Congress party. He wrote that Rahul entered Amethi from Inhauna, Jagdishpur, and after the welcome, talked about 'false promises' of the Modi government, price rise and the land acquisition bill. People saw a Rahul Gandhi who was full of energy. Amethi was reminded of those times when Sanjay Gandhi and Rajiv Gandhi went to every lane and bylane of the Amethi constituency and bound the entire region in emotional ties, the benefit of which the Congress has been enjoying to this day. This could not be achieved overnight. Their assistants, whether it was Captain Satish Sharma, V George, JN Mishra, Kishor Upadhyay or KL Sharma, also played a role in accomplishing this. The situation has changed, and although Rahul Gandhi had people with him, he lacked the personality that was necessary to run a parliamentary constituency like Amethi. Rahul Gandhi had to pay for this in the previous elections in which his victory margin had shrunk from four lakh to one lakh. And buoyed by this, the defeated BJP candidate Smriti Irani had been preparing Amethi as her parliamentary constituency for contesting the Lok Sabha polls again.

Rahul Gandhi inherited the long political legacy of his ancestors in Amethi, and he was a three-time Lok Sabha MP as well. However, this became possible for Rahul Gandhi mostly because the people of Amethi had an emotional attachment with his father, Rajiv Gandhi. Many times, the representatives of different political parties contesting the parliamentary election supported Gandhi family candidates on different pretexts, Pandey wrote. It was only Smriti

Irani who was offering a challenge to Rahul Gandhi in Amethi. If a fire broke out in the villages, Smriti Irani would reach there first and start to distribute relief materials. Rahul Gandhi would come only afterwards. Similarly, over the issue of the scrapping of food parks, Smriti Irani reached Amethi before Rahul Gandhi. When a protest was organised at Delhi's Ram Lila grounds, 400 party workers reached Delhi from Raebareli whereas only 35 arrived from Amethi. Priyanka Gandhi had had an important role in Amethi as she looked after her brother's constituency. Sometimes demands were also raised for Priyanka to fight the election from Amethi. But this did not happen.

It is a known fact that politics and disputes can be handled through the leadership qualities of the person concerned. These can't be handled with the help of salaried employees or bouncers. Rahul Gandhi shouldn't have put his political career at stake by depending heavily on salaried employees instead of loyal party workers. He shouldn't have depended on the bouncer-like workers from Haryana, who didn't know the threads of the society of Awadh. Their language and way of speaking sometimes hurt the local people. Rahul Gandhi needed dedicated workers in Amethi, not salaried, so-called Congressmen, because of whom a disgruntled class of Amethi was regularly holding meetings in the constituency and expressing their opposition to Rahul Gandhi. It was this simmering fire in Amethi that Rahul Gandhi had to put out.

Rahul Gandhi's image was clean, but his salaried lieutenants, who had become his henchmen, were eroding his ground. They would present to Rahul Gandhi a scenario in Amethi that would safeguard their jobs. Rahul Gandhi had to find a solution to this. Where were the old and discouraged workers who had been disappearing from his meetings? Rahul Gandhi should learn from his mother Sonia Gandhi and find those dying faces. According to sources, if Sonia Gandhi did not see a veteran party worker during her tour of Raebareli, she would ask her associates why that worker was not present. This would have a positive impact on the party workers, Rakesh Pandey said in his Outlook piece. When a person like Pandey, who has been associated with the Nehru-Gandhi family for a long time, writes this, it speaks volumes.

Background of social rebellion

In 2009, there was a big agitation in Amethi over electricity. The pain and impact of that agitation on the residents of Amethi had not subsided till Irani reached Amethi in 2014. The issue of the miserable state of electricity in Amethi in those days was raised in the Uttar Pradesh Assembly as well, but mere questions and answers cannot dispel the darkness for the people. In those days, Amethi got only six to seven hours of power at the most. It reached the limit when the administration decided that leaving aside the big cities of the state, the rest of the places would get power in the night for one week and in the day for the next week. In this roster, Amethi figured at the top. This affected the local businesses which led the traders to rise in protest in 2009. In such a situation, instead of listening to the grievances of the traders, state repression was unleashed against them. Over a hundred traders were injured in the protests and police brutalities, and even then, Rahul Gandhi, who was the local MP at the time, enquired about Amethi only after many weeks. By then, the damage in terms of how the public perceived him was done.

The scary situation that prevailed here becomes clearer if you read the newspapers of that time. In July 2009, the people of Amethi were so distressed over electric supply that news of their plight featured almost every day in dailies like *Dainik Jagran*, *Hindustan*, *Swatantra Bharat* and *Janmorcha*; but the MP from the area Rahul Gandhi and the local Congress MLAs were not bothered. Amethi resident Subodh Misra, a witness to those times, says, 'It seemed that the darkness of Amethi had covered the eyes of the MP too.'

Among the newspaper headlines of the time were, 'Agitation over power intensifies', 'Demonstration planned over power problem', 'Harassment of traders won't be tolerated', 'Amethi residents crying for power', 'People take to the streets', 'Anger over power cuts', 'People upset with daily changes in power roster', 'Memorandum calls for two-phase power supply in city', and so on. But when nothing could be achieved, the people took recourse to torch processions, memoranda and demonstrations. Then they got tired and decided to hold strikes, which ultimately turned into a complete shutdown of the city. Still, the administration was unmoved. Neither Lucknow nor Delhi was concerned about Amethi, even though in the media coverage of these protests, the name of Rahul Gandhi was figuring everywhere. The citizens of Amethi, stricken by power cuts, gathered in thousands at Gandhi Chowk and made the administration feel the power of democracy. Not a single shop in Amethi opened in the bandh called against the irregular supply of electricity. The agitators jammed Gandhi Chowk from the morning of the bandh. The Pratapgarh-Jagdishpur road was blocked till late evening. Local officials looked on helplessly at the sea of people out to protest. Thousands of women, under the leadership of the then nagar panchayat president Chandrama Agrahari, took part in the agitation. When the agitation started intensifying, superintendent engineer of the electricity department Mukul Sonkar held several rounds of talks with the agitating leaders at the main police station in the afternoon. These talks were, however, inconclusive.

The next day, more than five thousand people took out a procession in the town under the leadership of Rajesh Agrahari, president of the vyapar mandal, Chandrama Agrahari and other leaders, demanding a change in the power roster. More than two thousand women participated in the procession. It made its way through Sagara Tiraha, Station Road bus terminus, and turned into a public meeting after reaching Gandhi Chowk. Soon more than twenty thousand people gathered at Gandhi Chowk. The agitators put up tents in the middle of the road and blocked the Jagdishpur-Pratapgarh and Jagdishpur-Durgapur highways.

All small and big schools and colleges in the town, including Shiv Pratap Inter College, Rajkiya Balika Inter College, Saryu Devi Saraswati Vidyamandir Inter College, RR PG College, remained closed. Technical training institutes like SIIT, ICT, NET and others were shut too. When Mukul Sonkar came for talks following this massive show of protest in Amethi, he told the trade leaders that no more than eight hours of power could be provided. The enraged protestors then entered the main police station with chants of 'Murdabad'. They encircled the gate of the police station and held the superintendent engineer hostage. Deputy Collector Abhimanyu Kumar Tiwary and CO (Circle Officer) Rajmani Mishra posted personnel from half-a-dozen police stations in addition to the PAC force for security in Amethi.

In fact, before this protest, a torch procession was organised in the town to spread awareness among people and ensure that the bandh was a success. During the march, people shouted slogans against the electricity department. The torch taken out from the Devipatan temple travelled through various parts of the town before reaching Gandhi Chowk. Despite all this, neither Rahul Gandhi nor any of his representatives came to meet the agitators.

Hurt by indifference, not lathis

No representative of the then Congress MLA Amita Singh could be seen at this massive demonstration organised by the people of Amethi. The people expressed disappointment at the indifference of their representatives. It was a VVIP area in name, but its misery was not going to go away through the statements of its leaders. The police responded to the people that had come out into the streets by going on the offensive. The next day, the newspaper headlines were even more condemning: 'Rahul's parliamentary constituency turns into Kurukshetra for power', 'Barbaric police lathicharge raises temperature', 'Amethi scared as police go berserk', 'Women mistreated in their homes at midnight', 'Children's face brunt'. The sorry state of power supply in Amethi and news related to it made headlines in the local editions of all newspapers. The detailed news in all the newspapers were: 'Amethi remained closed in protest against the lathicharge on the people demanding electricity in Amethi, the parliamentary constituency of Congress general secretary Rahul Gandhi. After the incident of lathicharge and stone-pelting on the traders of Amethi, who were sitting on dharna demanding electricity, several traders of Amethi town were arrested by the police. In protest, shops in the town remained closed. Amid the dharna by the residents of Amethi against the unprecedented power shortage, the administration argued that there was a meeting going on at the Amethi police station when the irate mob started stone-pelting. Around six police personnel, including a police inspector, were injured in the stone-pelting. A fire brigade official was also injured. Following this, the police resorted to lathicharge and fired rubber bullets. As a result, about twelve people were injured. Several vehicles were damaged in the incident. In this connection, twenty-four people were identified and five people were arrested at night. Meanwhile, the Congress claimed that Rahul Gandhi would be visiting Amethi himself on 17 July. He might meet the people injured in the lathicharge. His approach towards the state government could turn aggressive. The state spokesperson of the Congress, Akhilesh Pratap Singh called the lathicharge a barbaric action and said that it had brought back memories of the British Raj. The people were demanding for power and they were getting lathis.

The Congress alleged that the police had lathicharged the people demanding for power in Amethi on the orders of chief minister

Mayawati. It was portrayed as revenge politics. On 15 July 2009, newspapers reported that the superintendent of police and kotwal had to pay the price for the lathicharge on the protestors; both Superintendent of Police at that times RK Chaturvedi and Kotwal SN Singh were transferred. A magisterial probe was ordered into the incident by the Uttar Pradesh government two days before Rahul Gandhi's visit. It was believed that this action was taken so that other political parties would not use this episode to their advantage in Amethi.

Apathy of the representatives

The same day, the Lucknow editions of many newspapers such as Dainik Jagran and Amar Ujala carried reports about the step-motherly treatment of Amethi. The reports, based on interviews with the local people and surveys, revealed that the people of Amethi were also miffed at the indifference of the public representatives responsible for the power problem. Dr Surendra Pratap Yadav, a lecturer at a local college, was quoted as saying, 'Electricity should be supplied properly. Whatever electricity you get should be given systematically all through the day and night. It should not be the case that electricity is supplied one week in the daytime and the next week at night.' Businessman Nikhil Bhalothia blamed the apathy of public representatives for the problem, saying, 'Amethi elects the Gandhi family as its representative. But MP Rahul Gandhi's indifference towards the problems of the constituency is shocking. The MP should talk to the state's chief minister regarding the power problem. A public representative should be an equal partner in the problems of the people. He should solve public problems or fight for them.'

Local councillor of that time, Mohammad Ishtiaq said, 'The electricity department collects commercial rates for power from the people of the town, but supplies are given to rural areas. Why is that so? The neighbouring areas are supplied power according to an equal day and night roster, while for Amethi a one-week-day and one-week-night roster was fixed, which was beyond comprehension.' Another resident of Amethi, Avdhesh Mishra, said, 'Amethi is bearing the brunt of its allegiance to the Gandhi family.' Sameer, a trader, complained, 'Our businesses are collapsing as a result of the power crisis.' Harishankar Jaiswal added, 'The electricity department officials in Amethi have gone out of control and become irresponsible. The electricity department is behaving like an enemy of Amethi.'

The names of the protesters were published in the newspapers and included people from all walks of life. President of Yuva Udyog Vyapar Mandal Harishankar Jaiswal, Prem Maheshwari, Ravindra Kumar Singh, Councillor Mohammad Ishtiaq, Pawan Kasaundan, Pramod Shukla, Advocate Ashok Saroj, Nikhil Bhalothia, Balakishan Agarwal, Surendra Jaiswal, Usman Gani, Mohammad Kalim, Chironji Lal and others were involved. Amethi was at the mercy of Rahul Gandhi's corrupt contractors who had turned deaf to the people's complaints.

Rahul Gandhi was elected as an MP from Amethi for the first time in the general elections of 2004, after which his representatives took up the responsibility of developing the area. There were many Lok Sabha constituencies that had seen the light of development because of their representatives. Rajdeep Sardesai, in his book, *2019: How Modi Won India* compared the Amethi Lok Sabha constituency with Maharashtra's Baramati—the place from which Nationalist Congress Party leader Sharad Pawar had been a long-time MP. Pawar had done a lot of development in his constituency as an MP, Sardesai writes. However, it has been a part of the tradition of the Nehru-Gandhi family members to be less available for the people of their constituencies. This family has always behaved like kings, and its representatives have looked after the real work. These representatives, in turn, have tended to act as landlords. In 2014, Aam Aadmi Party candidate Kumar Vishwas had tried to create a triangular contest in Amethi by also going from one village to another. He said during his campaigning that Rahul Gandhi was a prince and the people of Amethi craved to meet him, but if *he* was elected, he would be available to the people at all times. Vishwas bid goodbye to Amethi the moment he lost the elections.

Rahul Gandhi's associates claimed that it was because of his representation that this parliamentary constituency was accorded a special status. Due to his efforts, many development schemes had been implemented in Amethi and many others proposed. However, these claims were less real and more fake. Far from the facilities available to VIP parliamentary seats of the state, Amethi had no education, health, roads, or transport to speak of. Despite their backwardness and misery, the people of Amethi, for a long time, felt proud that they were being represented by a national-level leader. An advocate from Gauriganj, Shivnath Shukla, typified this line of thinking when he told a newspaper, 'Recognition is more important for us, not development. Wherever in the country we used to go and say that we were from Amethi, we would be honoured and Congress members would come forward to help. This had more value for the local people.'

Then why did Amethi not vote for Rahul Gandhi in 2019? The younger voters played a central role in the election of Irani. The Congress may well believe that frenzied politics was behind this but the people of Amethi had become tired of false promises. The exasperation of the public was on display when black flags were waved at Rahul Gandhi during his election campaign in the Gauriganj Assembly segment. Ram Sevak, a Congress worker from Musafirkhana, puts it very clearly, 'Irani reached them and helped them get scholarships, jobs and so on. The youth could see new hope for their future. The local BJP leaders acted as a bridge between Irani and the people of Amethi. This was the reason Amethi voted in 2019 for its own good.'

Sonia Gandhi and Priyanka Vadra reached Raebareli on a two-day tour to analyse the Congress's debacle in Uttar Pradesh in 2019. While Rahul Gandhi was absent from Amethi after the result, it was the first time that Sonia Gandhi had reached Raebareli so soon after the results were declared. After 2014, Sonia Gandhi's visits to Raebareli had to be reduced. She was not in the best of health. Nearly all work related to Raebareli was being looked after by Priyanka Vadra, even before she was made the Congress general secretary or the in-charge of eastern Uttar Pradesh. Sonia Gandhi and Priyanka Vadra had officially reached Raebareli for reviewing the reason for the party's defeat in Uttar Pradesh, but the real reason was Amethi. Sonia Gandhi's representative Kishori Lal Sharma, and Zubair Khan, who used to look after Priyanka Gandhi's work, had stayed in Amethi for three days to review the reasons for the loss. After that, Rahul Gandhi's representative Chandrakant Dubey and Congress district president Yogendra Mishra resigned. The party has still not declared what came out of the review. But according to media reports, before the session, anger could be seen among the district and town presidents of the Congress. These functionaries were extremely unhappy with Rahul Gandhi's approach. The Congress officials complained that Rahul Gandhi did not share his opinion about the candidates and was not part of the electoral strategising. District presidents of eastern and western Uttar Pradesh were also called for the review. The Congress leadership was everybody's target. The truth is neither Rahul Gandhi nor Sonia Gandhi or Priyanka Gandhi Vadra could have imagined a loss in Amethi. It could also be that the Congress leadership underestimated Irani in the Gandhi family bastion the same way Uttar Pradesh chief minister Yogi Adityanath took the Bahujan Samaj Party-supported Samajwadi Party candidate in the 2018 Gorakhpur by-election lightly. Yogi Adityanath has accepted that was the case, but the Congress leadership is still not able to publicly acknowledge they took Amethi for granted.

In the initial stages, it seemed that the entire Gandhi family had started to distance itself from the 'once Gandhi family bastion' Amethi after just one defeat. After her win, Sonia Gandhi had written a letter thanking the people of the Raebareli parliamentary constituency. Through the letter, Sonia Gandhi expressed her gratitude towards the workers of the Samajwadi Party, BSP and Swabhiman Dal for their efforts. She wrote, 'My life has been like an open book before you. You are my family. The energy that I get from you is my real asset.' Addressing the residents of Raebareli, she also said, 'I know that the coming days are going to be even harder, but I am totally confident that on the strength of your support and faith, Congress will be able to overcome all challenges. No matter how long the battle might be, I assure you that I will never back down from sacrificing my all to safeguard the fundamental values of the country.'

As for Rahul Gandhi, despite being associated with Amethi for years, he did not write a letter even to his party workers regarding his loss. Instead, he went straight to Wayanad. However, there too, he did not take the name of Amethi and instead said he felt he had belonged to Wayanad since birth. To reinforce his message, he tweeted a photo of nurse Rajamma hugging him at the time of his birth in Delhi. Contrary to Rahul Gandhi, Irani did not cut off ties with Amethi even after her defeat in 2014, and after her victory, she has been touring the constituency regularly, and news of her house being built there also made headlines in the media.

5

The Making of a Winner

Irani's family situation during childhood and adolescence taught her several valuable lessons. There were shortages in life, there were struggles, but at least there was no suffocation and none of the compulsions of a girl child because she was brought up in a modern environment. Her personality was shaped by her childhood and that gave her the gumption to reach the stage where the biggest party in the country sends her as its representative against the political scion of a family at his so-called bastion. While writing this book, I spoke to Smriti Irani on several occasions. She shared many memories from her childhood, especially those full of dreams, confidence and the will to be someone. Her thoughts about the girls of this country revolves around her own struggle If she can be successful, why can't the other women do the same? Although Irani did not dream about politics in her childhood, she was confident that one day she would become famous and everybody would know her. Her friends and family members laughed at this but didn't discourage her when

Irani shared these thoughts. Irani knows the value of labour and she feels no work is small or big. As a teenager, she had sold beauty products and fashion accessories on the streets of Delhi, been a Miss India contestant. She also worked as a cleaner at McDonald's. Even in tough times, Irani would tell herself, 'If I ever get a chance to serve the nation, I will definitely do something. Something that can change society, contribute to the nation's progress, something for posterity.' Over time, these childhood dreams came true. Since the time she entered politics, her resolve to serve her country and the people has became stronger. The reason for this is the deep imprint that her mother and maternal grandfather have left on her personality. Irani's maternal grandfather, Nirmal Chandra Bagchi, was a big influence in her life. He was a dedicated worker of the RSS; in Sangh terminology, a swayamsevak. Irani used to stay near her grandfather's house in Delhi's Rama Krishna Puram. She was dear to her grandfather and so spent a lot of time with him. She would listen to the discussions between swayamsevaks and pracharaks of RSS who used to visit her grandfather's place from other parts of the country. When these people used to talk about nationalism, duty, the atrocities in Kashmir, Partition Vedas, Puranas, religion, culture, India's glorious past and justice, she would be deeply influenced. Often she would accompany her grandfather to the Sangh shakhas organised at Rama Krishna Puram. The culture of service, righteousness and commitment that developed in her after visiting the Sangh shakhas can still be seen in her character. Irani's grandfather Nirmal Chandra Bagchi had a lot of faith in her. He would always say that she would go a long way in life and do something big.

Before entering politics, she had become a TV superstar. She gained considerable fame by playing the role of Tulsi in the iconic Ekta Kapoor-led Balaji Telefilms' serial *Kyunki Saas Bhi Kabhi Bahu*

Thi. She was interested in acting, but her interest in literature, culture and social service was stronger. Even during shoots, she would often have a book in hand.

Irani is the eldest of the three daughters of Bengali mother Shibani Bagchi and Punjabi Brahmin father Ajay Kumar Malhotra, who lived in Maharashtra. Being the eldest child, she developed a sense of responsibility and duty towards everyone in the family. Her mother was a member of the Jana Sangh. So when the Maharashtra BJP leader Gopinath Munde inspired her to join active politics, she did not hesitate for even one moment. He had understood that what people called saffron politics and Hindutva ideology was already clear to her through the poems of former Prime Minister Bharat Ratna Atal Bihari Vajpayee. Several poems of Atalji are imprinted in her mind in such a way that she can recall them at any occasion. Among them are 'Haar nahi manoonga/raar nahi thanoonga/Kaal ke kapaal par/likhta hoon, mitaata hoon' (I will not give up, I will not give up, I write and erase on the forehead of time, I sing a new song); 'Bharat zameen ka tukda nahi/jeeta jaagta rashtrapurush hai' (India is not a piece of land, it's a living entity); 'Aur baadhaayein aati hain aayein/ghire pralay ki ghor ghataayein/paanvon ke neeche angaare, sir par barse yadi jwaalaayein/nij haathon mein hanste-hanste, aag lagaakar jalna hoga/Kadam milaakar chalna hoga' (Let more hurdles come our way/Let the dark clouds of apocalypse gather around us/Even if embers burn under our feet and fire rains down on our heads/Gladly we'll carry a flame on our bare hands/We will march together.) These are lines from some poems by Atalji that Irani never fails to mention.

She has been listening to two poems since her childhood, and wants every Indian to read them at least once. The first poem is 'Mai akhil vishwa ka guru mahaan' (I am the great leader of the entire world), in which Atalji composed matchless verses of national pride.

'Main akhil vishwa ka guru mahaan
Deta vidya ka amar daan
Maine dikhlaya mukti marg
Maine sikhlaya brahma gyaan

Mere vedon ka gyaan amar
Mere vedon ki jyoti prakhar
Manav ke mann ka andhkar
Kya kabhi samne saka thahar?

Mera swar nabh me ghahar-ghahar
Sagar ke jal me chahar-chahar
Iss kone se uss kone tak
Kar sakta jagti saurabh may.'

(I am the great leader of the entire world,
I offer the immortal donation of learning,
I have shown the liberation route
I have taught divine knowledge.

My knowledge of Vedas is immortal,
My light of Vedas is bright
Has the darkness of human mind
Ever been able to offer resistance?

My voice reverberates in the sky,
It travels in the waters of the ocean
From this corner to that
I can fill the earth with fragrance.)

She is also very fond of the second poem, Hindu Tann Mann, Hindu Jeevan (Hindu body, Hindu life). Although this poem is quite lengthy, Irani believes that for one's pride, even if it cannot be memorised, its essence can be internalised through repeated reading. This is because Atal Bihari Vajpayee had openly accepted that he himself, and like him, every BJP member, every party worker and every person who loves the nation does not feel guilty for being a Hindu, rather acknowledges it with pride. Irani remembers a number of stanzas from this poem:

> 'Hindu tann-mann, Hindu jeevan, rag-rag Hindu mera parichay
> Mai Shankar ka wah krodhanal kar sakta jagti kschar kschar
> Damru ki wah parlay dhwani hoon, jisme nachta bheeshan sanhar
> Ranchandi ki atript pyas, mai Durga ka unmatt has
> Main Yam ki pralayankar pukar, jalte marghat ka dhuandhar
> Fir antartam ki jwala se jagti me aag laga doon mai
> Yadi dhadhak uthe jal, thal, ambar, jad chetan toh kaisa vishmay
> Hindu tann-mann, Hindu jeevan, rag-rag Hindu mera parichay

* * *

> Main ek bindu, paripurna Sindhu hai ye mera Hindu samaaj
> Mera iska sambandh amar, mai vyakti aur yeh hai samaaj
> Isme maine paya tann-mann, isme maine paya jeevan

Mera toh bas kartavya yahi, kar dun sabkuch iske arpan
Main toh samaj ki thi hoon, main toh samaj ka hoon sewak
Main toh samshti ke liye vyshti ka kar sakta balidan abhay
Hindu tann-mann, Hindu Jeevan, rag-rag Hindu mera
    parichay.'

(Hindu body, Hindu life, my every vein has Hindu
    identity!
I am that anger of Lord Shankar that can destroy the earth.
I am the sound of apocalypse emanating from the damroo,
    in which dances great destruction.
I am Ranachandi's unsatiated thirst, I am Durga's
    hysterical laughter.
I am Yama's call of death, I am the smoke from
    crematorium flames.
I set the world ablaze with the fire inside me.
If water, land, sky and consciousness tremble, then why
    be amazed?
Hindu body, Hindu life, my every vein has Hindu identity!

* * *

I am a drop, full-to-the-brim Indus is my Hindu society.
My ties with it are immortal, I am an individual and it is
    the society.
It has given me my body, it has given me my life.
My only duty is to sacrifice everything for it.
I am a trustee of the society, I am a servant of society.
I can sacrifice the person for the collective without fear.
Hindu body, Hindu life, my every vein has Hindu
    identity!)

Irani is also very fond of English writer Rudyard Kipling's historic poem 'If'. Kipling had written this poem in 1895 as a tribute to Leander Starr Jameson. This poem first appeared in the 'Brother Square-Toes' chapter of *Rewards and Fairies* in 1910 and is an important piece of world literature. Reading 'If' gives you a sense of Irani's literary understanding and sensitive mind. The poem goes like this:

If you can keep your head when all about you
Are losing theirs and blaming it on you,
If you can trust yourself when all men doubt you,
But make allowance for their doubting too;
If you can wait and not be tired by waiting,
Or being lied about, don't deal in lies,
Or being hated, don't give way to hating,
And yet don't look too good, nor talk too wise:

If you can dream-and not make dreams your master;
If you can think-and not make thoughts your aim;
If you can meet with Triumph and Disaster
And treat those two impostors just the same;
If you can bear to hear the truth you've spoken
Twisted by knaves to make a trap for fools,
Or watch the things you gave your life to, broken,
And stoop and build 'em up with worn-out tools:

If you can make one heap of all your winnings
And risk it on one turn of pitch-and-toss,
And lose, and start again at your beginnings
And never breathe a word about your loss;

If you can force your heart and nerve and sinew
To serve your turn long after they are gone,
And so hold on when there is nothing in you
Except the Will which says to them: 'Hold on!'

If you can talk with crowds and keep your virtue,
Or walk with Kings-nor lose the common touch,
If neither foes nor loving friends can hurt you,
If all men count with you, but none too much;
If you can fill the unforgiving minute
With sixty seconds' worth of distance run,
Yours is the Earth and everything that's in it,
And-which is more-you'll be a Man, my son!

Feelings over politics

As mentioned above, Irani had become a big TV star before coming to politics. How bright her career was could be gauged from the fact that even today Tulsi, the character she portrayed, is known in every household even though the show has long finished. Furthermore, she not only won the Indian Television Academy's best actress award for seven consecutive years, but she also became the first Indian to represent the country at the Monte Carlo Television Festival and be a part of its prestigious jury. But in the midst of all these achievements, her desire for social service did not diminish. Even when she was following her career in film and television, she was associated with non-government organisations like Cancer Patients Aid Association and the Vatsalya Street Kids Foundation. In 2007, she set up an NGO called People for Change, whose goal was to provide scholarships for higher education to children from economically weaker sections. In Nashik, this organisation provided sports scholarships to many children, and considering the need, through its own initiative, provided tube wells in more than thirty-five villages of Maharashtra. During the floods, with the help of the radio station FM 92.7, People for Change gathered and distributed over 10 tonnes of relief material. Irani's charitable work not only continues but has also become more widespread since she became a minister. Despite this, Irani harbours no hubris. Even after reaching such a position, she does not consider herself to be different from the common woman and man. An example of this is that notwithstanding her current status, whenever she gets a chance, she appears on social media, sharing things from her personal life and family, giving us glimpses into her life as an elder sister, wife, mother and aunt. It is another matter that with the presence of Instagram, Twitter and so on, photos and news related to her continue to make the headlines in the media. Over one crore people follow her on Twitter. Her Facebook page is followed by 5,357,397 people. The same level of popularity is reflected in the likes on her Instagram posts. But these platforms were not there at the beginning of her career.

Irani does not hide her attachment with her family, society and friends. Truth and naturalness form her identity. Her easygoing nature is evident in her old interviews as well. When her children were younger, she said in a TV interview about her dreams and desires, 'I get peace of mind walking barefoot in the wet grass at India Gate at night, having kulfi for a few rupees from the kulfi seller there, and spending time with my family at a calm and secluded place. What else can one want?' She added, 'I have heard that these days some people do boating at India Gate. I just enjoy walking on the lawns in front of the India Gate. Sitting there for some time. What more is there in life than being with your near and dear ones?' This Smriti Irani is completely different from the Smriti Irani who has been portrayed in some sections of the media as an aggressive political leader by her detractors and opponents. She is indeed bold and determined and believes that every girl must be like that. Even at this stage, some of her childhood dreams are intact. She says without hesitation that if she had the opportunity to meet any historical characters, she would want to meet Chhatrapati Shivaji Maharaj, Vishnugupta or Acharya Chanakya, the Knights Templar and Field Marshal Sam Manekshaw. She does not stop here, but says without flinching, 'It may sound silly, but if possible, I would definitely want to meet and spend time with my Lord Bholenath. After all, what is life without Augharnath?'

Irani's self-education never stopped. Greatly influenced since her childhood by the stories of Laxmibai's struggles, she always wanted to do something exceptional in life and be someone of note. But she did not know that the future would be presenting to her a fortress in the political battle of modern India by the name of 'Amethi', whose tale of victory would go down in history books. Irani has been influenced by Subhadra Kumari Chauhan's poem 'Jhansi ki Rani' on the courage and valour of the queen of Jhansi Laxmibai. There is hardly any Indian who knows Hindi that has not read this poem:

> 'Simhasan hil uthe rajbanshon ne bhrikuti tani thi
> Budhe Bharat me aayi fir se nayi jawaani thi
> Ghumi hui Azadi ki keemat sabne pahchani thi
> Door firangi ko karne ki sabne mann me thani thi
> Chamak uthi san sattavan me, wah talwar purani thi
> Bundele harbolon ke muh hamne suni kahani thi
> Khoob ladi mardani wah toh Jhansi wali rani thi.'

> (When thrones quaked, dynasties were anxious,
> In senile Bharat had come youthfulness again,

The price of lost freedom everyone understood,
To drive away the British everyone vowed.
Glittered in the year fifty-seven an old sword,
Religious singers of Bundelkhand have told the tale,
She fought valiantly like a man, she was the queen of
Jhansi.)

In the same way, Irani has always admired the life of the brave Joan of Arc, who was born in a peasant family in eastern France on 6 January 1412. She has read Joan of Arc's story in English innumerable times, but Munshi Premchand's biography of Joan of Arc by the same name is imprinted in Irani's mind, and she has absorbed the message hidden in it. Perhaps it is this understanding that has been inspiring her to work for women's rights. This story by Munshi Premchand was published in the April 1909 edition of *Zamana* under the title 'Joan of Arc'. Although the index of the magazine mentioned the author's name as 'Dal-re aj Ambala' and 'Dal-re' was printed at the end of the biography, it was written by Munshi Premchand. Upanyas Samrat (King of novels) Premchand used to write under pseudonyms in those days, what with the ban on his collection of Urdu stories, *Sozé Vatan*. With the life story of Joan of Arc, Premchand, while making observations on the situation of women in the Indian society and across the world during that era, wrote a lot about their courage and valour. Those words have played an important role in making Smriti Irani who she is today. Munshi Premchand wrote, 'Those who consider women as unsuccessful and worthless are completely mistaken. There has been no era in which they have not established their prestige and glory among people. History bears witness to the fact that even in a battlefield, they have produced such astonishing scenes of courage and valour that have amazed people when they have read and heard about them. When women, who are synonymous with virtuous behaviour, move towards knowledge and art and kindness and integrity, then unsolved riddles come into sight. And if they take to the battlefield and face the enemy armed with bow and arrows, they wipe out rows after rows and even beyond. They are no less than men in any aspect whatsoever. Their true enthusiasm, patriotism, self-respect, purity, sympathy and other qualities are worthy of worship. Such incidents come to light from across India and especially Rajputana that prove that Indian women have sacrificed their lives for their country, purity and loyalty, but have not let any danger touch their religion and motherland till their last breath. Ahilyabai, Rani Padmini, Razia Begum, Chand Bibi, Nur Jahan and others sacrificed their lives at the altar of their country, and their names shine like the sun and moon. These women made India glorious. The main reasons for our national decline today is that we have patronised them, not treated them equally, and have deprived them of the treasures of knowledge and art. We have shut the doors of education for them. The result has been what we are seeing today.'

Munshi Premchand wrote further, 'The progress and prosperity of any nation depends upon those young children, who are raised by the mothers, not the men. By keeping them behind the veil and ignoring them, we have kept them away from the glimpses of freedom and progress in the new age. They went on getting weaker physically and mentally, and that weakness, infirmity, ignorance and illiteracy is what we inherited. It is our mothers that make us brave and talented; the foundation of prosperity and progress is laid in their laps. The courage and determination of mothers provide the strength to the makers of national edifices. Mothers instill these qualities in the children, who then give their all to the cause of humanity in generations to come. To be proud of the splendour of the past is like standing on a high mound. You never know when it will get demolished by adverse winds. Russia, Japan, Britain, France, Italy—take any empire … at the source of the success, prosperity, independence and the system and stability of that country are its highly courageous women.

'Joan's personality had immense power and purity. She was healthy and strong, both physically and mentally. The glow in her face was matched by her flamboyance. A painter had once drawn such an image of Joan that epitomised her spirituality, piety, beauty, simplicity and all other qualities that were the strongest elements of her life.

'Joan's valour and saintliness were clear as daylight from her childhood. She had an infinite ability to perform great deeds. She was ever ready to face difficulties. She had a surprising capability to breathe life into people. An eyewitness to all her victories and acts of bravery and sacrifice has written, "In all the incidents that I have seen, or heard about, I have found her to be affectionate, pious and unassuming."'

These lines are ingrained in Irani's mind. She has set such ideals for herself. Perhaps, for this reason, the dignity of women is bigger than any win or loss or anything else for her. She does not make any compromises when it comes to the dignity of women.

An incident that happened prior to the 2019 Lok Sabha elections is worth mentioning here. Irani was informed that there was one Shukla family in Amethi who were close to the Gandhis, and controlled around 20,000 votes in the area. The BJP's district and provincial level leaders had been trying for a long time to woo this family over to their side. Even the local unit of the RSS, and its workers attached to Amethi, were in favour of this. The head of the Shukla family, sensing the winds of change, was ready to side with the BJP on the condition that they do so respectably before Irani. After both sides agreed, a meeting between Shuklaji and Irani was fixed.

At this meeting, all the prominent local leaders of the BJP and RSS were present. Shuklaji started to speak. He pompously claimed to know several Gandhi family secrets, and even went so far as to make very distasteful comments about Priyanka Gandhi Vadra. He said that he could tell her how many moles there are on Priyanka's body. After hearing this, Irani lost her cool and told Shukla in no uncertain terms that he could not be made a part of the BJP. After that, she left the meeting without thinking about what effect that incident might have on her election campaign.

The local leaders of the BJP and those associated with the RSS tried to explain to Irani the benefits of an alliance with the Shukla family and how making him an enemy could cost them dear, but Irani was not ready to budge. She argued that there was no question of being associated with a person who did not respect women. Despite repeated persuasion, Irani was not ready to compromise on the 'honour' of a woman, even if that woman happened to be her main opponent in such a crucial election. Priyanka Gandhi, on the other hand, at that time had been opposing Irani tirelessly. During the 2014 Lok Sabha elections, Priyanka Gandhi had replied, 'Smriti who?' to a question on the challenge posed to Rahul Gandhi.

Frank and fearless

Irani believes, 'Say what you think, do what you want, as long as you do not break the law, and nobody is inconvenienced or their dignity violated. How can you cross your limits, how can you not respect women, or not provide justice to the oppressed, or not help the needy and not secure the rights of the poor?' She did not become the Smriti Irani that she is today all of a sudden.

While shooting for *Kyunki Saas Bhi Kabhi Bahu Thi*, once Smriti Irani left the sets during a three-four-hour break, to go on a dharna at the call of local party workers. There she was picked up by police. Back at the set, people started to search for her. When she was called, the crew realised she had gone for a dharna and been detained. Thankfully, she was released after a little while and returned to work.

The mayor of Ranchi, Asha Lakda, remembers some incidents from a few years ago: 'When Smriti Irani became the national president of the Mahila Morcha in 2010, I did a lot of work with her as a national secretary in the Mahila Morcha and as the in-charge of Delhi, West Bengal and Jharkhand from 2010 to 2013. When Smriti didi was in the Mahila Morcha, seeing her dedication, we, leaders and workers, would discuss that she be made a Lok Sabha candidate in 2014. It was not known at that time that she would get the ticket to such a challenging seat like Amethi. Didi is not just our leader, she is like that guardian of our family, whose shelter not only gives you peace and saves you from adverse situations but also strengthens you for the coming times.

'If I talk about myself, at one point of time, I was faced with such misfortunes in my personal life that had Smriti Irani not been there, it would be difficult to say where I would have been. In 2012, Naxals shot and killed my husband. When I heard the news, I was in a market in Ranchi, and fainted on the spot. My whole world came collapsing around me. My health deteriorated. My family members were upset.

'No sooner had Smriti Irani heard about the incident than she reached Ranchi. She had no other political engagement there. She visited my house, saw my condition and suddenly proposed to my family members that they let her take me to Mumbai to stay at her house. She said that though she could not expunge my grief and trauma, she believed that a change of environment would be a balm on my sorrows. When Smritiji proposed this, my relatives found it difficult to believe. In any case, she was neither my kin nor was I her responsibility … there were a lot of quiet discussions among my relatives. People raised a number of doubts and questions, but when Smritiji decides to do something, she does it. She convinced my family members and brought me on a flight to her Mumbai home. She started my treatment without caring about the cost involved. But more than the doctor, the biggest medical treatment was done by didi herself, by preparing me mentally.

'More than a leader and star, she is someone full of compassion and sympathy, which sets her apart from her contemporaries. When I reached Mumbai with her, I was not even able to stand properly, but didi gave me support. The kind of support that can never be forgotten. Even amid her busy schedule, she would find time to comfort me. She would counsel me and take me along on her tours. She took complete care of me during those tours. When I reached Delhi on the first tour with her, I was almost tottering at the airport, but she held my hand, and ushered me out of the airport. When there was a demonstration at Srinagar's Lal Chowk, she took me along there too. I stayed with her for forty-five days at her Mumbai residence, and during this time, she took me on all the tours that she had scheduled. I would like to mention something special that I noticed during that time.

'In those forty-five days, I never saw Smritiji sleep for more than three hours. There were times when I stayed in the house for the entire day. During that time, her two children—they were young at the time—would take great care of me. I used to like dalia a lot during those days and would eat it often, and the children would come to me and say, "Eat good food and you will get well soon." Smritiji has stressed on making her children humane and has given them very good values. No matter how busy she is, her children get her complete affection. These children were quite young in 2012. When she would be away from home during the day, they naturally used to miss her. Perhaps that is why whenever she used to return home, she would meet her children first. When she is in Mumbai, she prepares and sends them to school. I can say with conviction that her near and dear ones feel her love.'

Amethi in Irani's political journey

Irani joined the BJP in 2003 and became the vice president of the Maharashtra BJP Yuva Morcha the following year. In 2004, the party gave her the responsibility of fighting the election against Congress's Kapil Sibal from Delhi's Chandni Chowk parliamentary seat. Irani was living in Mumbai at the time and had no experience of fighting election. But she fought with gusto. She went from lane to lane and campaigned. She polled only 47,981 votes as opposed to Sibal's tally of 1,27,396 votes.

After the election result, Pramod Mahajan, a prominent BJP leader at the time, admitted in an interview to senior journalist Rajat Sharma that the party had given Irani a tough seat. Even though she could not win from Chandni Chowk, she maintained her association with the party. It is worth mentioning that after joining the BJP, she became a much loved younger member of the wider BJP family because of her behaviour, values and humility. On 7 February 2005, a documentary on patriotism in Indian films was screened at the home of senior BJP leader LK Advani. It was directed by Advani's daughter Pratibha. After the screening, Modi called Irani the 'daughter of Gujarat' in front of TV cameras of the national media.

Irani became the national secretary of the BJP in 2010, and in June that year, she was appointed the national president of the

BJP Mahila Morcha. By then, the BJP leadership had decided to use Irani's political combativeness and oratory skills to the party's benefit. That is why the party leadership decided to send her to the Rajya Sabha. In 2011, she became the party's youngest member of the Rajya Sabha from Gujarat. Her name was proposed by the then Gujarat chief minister Narendra Modi. It was Modi who signed first on Irani's nomination paper as proposer. In the Rajya Sabha, Irani made life difficult for the then ruling government with questions on women's interests, Gujarat and other matters of national importance. She would go fully prepared and raise questions and participate in the debates.

Society & politics

> 'Siyasat ki shiraon me hai madhoshi
> Priyadarshan Itihaas kanth mein
> Aaj dhwanit ho kavya bane
> Vartman ki chitrapati par
> Bhootkal sambhavya bane.'

> (Intoxication in the veins of politics
> Pleasant history in the voice
> Echoes today in poetry,
> On the canvas of the present
> The past is possibly made.)

The above lines are by Hindi poet Ramdhari Singh 'Dinkar'. The form of politics seen in Amethi is not new. Indian society, which is thousands of years old and whose civilisational progress has been accustomed to seeing the image of God in every particle and seeing divinity even in natural symbols like the river, mountain, tree, fire, cloud and wind, would traditionally be attracted towards able people. In any case, this is the way that political systems have developed across the world. Whether in the East or the West, in the development of human civilisation, early governance was established as a symbol of power on the back of the valour of the warriors. That is how the biggest monarchies were established. Over time, it transformed into a system of dynasties, and often descendants of the early rulers took over the reins of the princely states, until another strong dynasty, mighty individual or invader attacked and established his rule, or a new descendant or mighty warlord overthrew the king by force and set up his own empire. The biggest gift of the tribes of the ancient era and the system of governance in the medieval age was that the entire centre of power, prosperity and strength was divided between the king and those who had stakes in his rule. Not only the king and his family, his relatives of any level and even his subordinates and their families were so special that their kins' clans went on prospering and became established as the elite.

We would find it difficult to swallow this bitter truth of human history, but the reality is that when India was hounded by foreign invaders and Europe boasted of an improved governance system and claimed to be close to God, and wanted to give that struggle the moral clothing of a clash between religion and the State, even then the fight was one over the supremacy of the personal arrogance of the 'concerned person' more than that of these institutions. This becomes clear if we dig into history. In the West, the main reason for the power struggle between religion, at the head of which was the Church, and the State that the emperor ruled, was personal. This was not a battle of ideas, as has been taught to us or recorded in texts. At that time, two people in positions of power in the Church and the State clashed with each other over the use of power, its sphere of influence and their supremacy. Over time it resulted in the eventual victory of the State. According to the 'Doctrine of Two Swords' concept that was behind the system of governance in the West, God created two types of power to govern the world, the temporal and the other-worldly. The emperor was designed to hold temporal power, while the master of otherworldly power was considered to be the head of the Christian Church, the Pope. The Bishop of Rome, being a successor of Saint Peter, was considered the head of the entire Church and the representative of Jesus Christ on earth. While the emperor had his courtiers, ministers, landlords and the army, the Pope exercised his power through bishops and devotees. In this way, every citizen was equally loyal to both. But there was an anomaly in this system. The bishop who followed the Pope's orders was appointed by the emperor.

At that time it was an ideal, ethical governance system. The two did not interfere in each other's work, and the whole of Europe used to follow it. But Gregory VII stopped the practice of bishops being appointed by emperors as soon as he became the Pope in 1076. His order was a challenge to the then emperor Henry IV. This is where serious differences and conflicts between the Church and the State started. The two attempted to remove each other from their posts, and in the end, the emperor had to give up. He apologised to the Pope, but this clash affected European politics. No sooner had Pope Innocent III ascended the throne than he claimed supremacy over all the states of Europe. He made the Church so powerful and supreme that no ruler of Europe could refuse to obey his order.

In 1296, a war was going on between France and Britain. At that time, Pope Boniface VIII was at the helm of the Church. Emperor Philip IV of France, also known as Philip the Fair, who was fighting the war with Britain, coveted the vast land assets of the Church that had hitherto remained 'tax-free', to fill up his emptying treasury. He taxed the property of the Church, and under pressure from the French, who were devoted to the State, and from temporal power, the Church for the first time had to give way and Pope Boniface had conceded defeat. He accepted to pay the tax. But Philip IV did not stop here. He captured a representative of the Pope and prosecuted him in his court. The Pope considered this a gross insult and tried to establish that it was a violation of the authority of the Church by the State, but Philip IV did not accept this argument, and instead, took Pope Boniface prisoner, accusing him of being corrupt and tyrannical. With his death in 1303, the State's domination over religion was established, even though unofficially.

After the death of Pope Boniface, Benedict XI became the Pope. But before he could do anything, he was poisoned to death. After this, Philip IV succeeded in getting the chief bishop of his choice to be the Pope. Before he could celebrate his success, Louis IV of Bavaria was elected as the Roman emperor in 1314. In contrast to this, some feudal lords and kings elected Frederick of Austria too for this post. This way, with two contenders for the same post at the same time, the State got entangled in a power war within itself. The point to note here is that just as the Pope was the head of the Bishops, the emperor used to be chosen from among the kings. The Church once again took advantage of this conflict between the European kings, and in 1316, when John XXII became the Pope, he declared that only that king could hold the post of the emperor who had the support of the Pope. Using this authority, he excommunicated Louis IV from the Church, but this situation could not be sustained for long and eventually, the Pope was defeated in this struggle, and the supremacy of the State was established.

In this war, when seen from the outside, the supremacy of the State may well have been established, but it proved extremely bad for the public. It further reinforced the old evils of 'subjectivity' and 'centralisation' of power. An autocratic monarchy was established in France, based on the divine doctrine of kingship, in which the king had unlimited powers. During the reign of Louis IV, between 1643 and 1715, autocracy reached its height, and he declared, 'I am the State.' By making laws according to his will, he led to an excessive centralisation of power in the hands of the monarch. Louis XV and Louis XVI took cover under this system despite being unworthy. In spite of being an indolent and inept ruler, Louis IV snobbishly declared, 'This is legal because I wish it to be.' The entire system in France at that time became dependent on hereditary bureaucracy, on which there was no system of control. The entire French society had disintegrated.

On one hand there existed the privileged clergy and oligarchs and on the other, the deprived masses. By this time, France's financial system had sunk in debt. Elsewhere, the American freedom struggle put a stamp on the bankruptcy of France. This gave birth to the glorious French Revolution. It is to be noted here that when the European civilisation was entangled in a battle between religion and state and was waiting for its golden age, India had lost the battle to save its illustrious past. The vast India of Chandragupta Maurya and Harshavardhana was divided into so many small states that it had become easy pasture for the Greek, Arab and Turkish invaders. Whether Mahmud Ghazni, Muhammad Ghori, Aibak, Genghis Khan, Khilji, Tughlaq and Timur Lang can be called attackers, invaders or rulers, all were arrogant and had their own selfish motives. Then again, the arrogance of the Islamic invaders vis-a-vis India's ideal of Vasudhaiva Kutumbakam was due to their monotheistic beliefs. This line of thinking continued from the establishment of the Mughal empire after Babur and through the rule of the East India Company to the setting up of the British regime. This not only snatched the Indian kings' thrones and their respect, but it also took away their pride. Nobody cared for the masses. They were like sheep in front of the king.

The rest is history, in which mass movements helped establish democracy. But could democracy ever free itself from the influence of 'person', 'specific person', or 'person's uniqueness'? The widespread recognition that was accorded to early democracy by the monarchy even if it was under compulsion, was, in fact, a way in which kings, landlords and other influential sections tried to change form and maintain their hold on power. Even in that period, when the share of the individual in the State started increasing under the effect of democracy, the 'subjective' supremacy could not be prohibited. It became stronger under the influence of capitalism and the storm of modernisation. Even the theory of classless society envisaged by Marxism and communism could never move away from its influence at any point in time. Modern political theory and individualism, which developed with the ideals of individual freedom and self-reliance, and which believed that the individual should not subject his conscience to an elected or any other kind of leader, could not find an answer to the 'charismatic personality'.

It is no less surprising that individualism that strongly supported concepts like restricting the rights of the State, free market, freedom of expression and personal property, proved to be a total failure in this regard. Such a doctrine, which held that a government is formed with the consent of individuals in the form of citizens, and its role ought to be limited to the protection of the rights of those very citizens, could not save democracy from the evils of 'individual worship'. After India gained independence in 1947, it seemed that our parliamentary system and federal state structure, in their special democratic form, would be spared given the guidelines of the Constitution, but time is witness to the fact that every year, in elections at every level, this element has only become stronger. Even in a society based on a deeply entrenched caste system, that influences voting behaviour, everybody fails against the 'charismatic personality'. Even communist, socialist, liberal, conservative, capitalist, nationalist or any other idea or ideology could not find a solution to it. Not even social, regional, party, linguistic and ideological attachments have been able to break it completely.

～

Mahatma Gandhi had once maintained that the highest power in parliamentary democracy was vested in the masses, but what he did not realise was that the semi-literate masses, who were immature towards their rights cannot be aware of even their fundamental rights, leave alone supremacy, in front of the 'parliament' and 'powerful lords'. That is why he explained in the book 'Constructive Programme', 'We have long been accustomed to think that power comes only through legislative assemblies, I have regarded this belief as a grave error brought about by inertia or hypnotism. A superficial study of British history has made us think that all power percolates to the people from parliaments. The truth is that power resides in the people and it is entrusted for the time being to those whom they may choose as their representatives.' But in reality, could the masses remain supreme after Independence? On the contrary, even the parliament went into the grip of some influential groups, individuals, parties and sections. The masses fell under the influence of 'individuals' rather than debates and ideologies. Even Mahatma Gandhi, who was venerated as the 'Father of the Nation', being turned into a superhuman or a godlike personality, was a reflection of this Indian mentality. There would be hesitation to accept that 'Indian politics' is a game of ideologies and the foundation of these ideologies is subjective. The individual is the hero, he is the villain, he is the superhero, and is even venerated and worshipped. Even to the extent of other ideals and democratic values looking its subordinate. In many respects, unlike the rule of the people, by the people and for the people, it is the rule of a particular person, particular family, influential people and groups, even if it looks different from the old monarchy and the system of dynastic rule. But it is certainly neither fully individualistic nor completely democratic. That is why because of being 'individual-centred', the leader's personal charisma has always remained paramount.

The Nehru-Gandhi family had, from the beginning of their political journey, not only gauged this emotional frailty of the Indian masses, but also learnt to use it to their advantage, and this has continued over generations. Under this circumstance, if a party has successfully countered this influence, it is the BJP. At the level of the country and also at the level of Amethi. If we look at the history behind this, we find that owing to a disagreement with the policies of Jawaharlal Nehru, Syama Prasad Mukherjee laid the foundation of the Bharatiya Jana Sangh. The Bharatiya Jana Sangh, which was formed on 21 October 1951, took part in the first general elections and could get only three seats. However, alternative politics had begun. American author and historian Craig Baxter has underlined this alternative politics in his writings. After this, the second challenge to individualistic politics came in 1967 when Samyukta Vidhayak Dal governments were formed in many states across the country. These were known as SVD governments. At the time, leaders like Syama Prasad Mukherjee, Deen Dayal Upadhyay and Ram Manohar Lohia challenged Nehru. In the Indira Gandhi era, this challenge had started to become a bit lax, but Atal Bihari Vajpayee and Lal Krishna Advani kept the flame burning. After the Atal-Advani era, Narendra Modi emerged on the political horizon of the BJP. In the 2014 Lok Sabha elections, Amit Shah emerged as a key ally of Modi on the national scene. An important name in this series is that of Smriti Irani who breached what was considered to be an impregnable political fortress of the Gandhi family.

6

The Politics of a Dynasty

In Indian democracy, the constituency has a significance of its own. The constituencies of prominent leaders are discussed and the eyes of the entire country are turned towards the political activities and development projects taking place there. Members of the Gandhi family have for ages represented the Amethi Lok Sabha constituency in Uttar Pradesh. Consequently, this has been termed as a VIP constituency, and often journalists, in their enthusiasm, have called this the Gandhi family bastion, but it was a fortress that had never faced a serious challenge. And when it did, it fell in just five years.

How did the Gandhi family come to select Amethi? How did their bond grow stronger election by election? To know this, we have to understand the political thinking of this family, beginning with Pandit Jawaharlal Nehru selecting the Phulpur parliamentary constituency during the first ever Lok Sabha elections in 1951-52 all the way up till Rahul Gandhi's choice of Amethi and Wayanad seats during the 17th Lok Sabha elections in 2019. Raebareli, Chikmagalur and Medak would fall on the way too. It begs the question that after Independence, in the first parliamentary election, why did Pandit Nehru select Phulpur instead of Allahabad as his constituency given both are located in the same district? Pandit Nehru not only strolled to his victory in the election of 1952, but he won the 1957 and 1962 elections as well.

In the second Lok Sabha election in 1957, Pandit Nehru polled 2,27,448 votes, while his opponent Chet Ram could get only 61,322 votes. In 1962, Nehru was challenged by the famous socialist leader Ram Manohar Lohia, but still, he got 1,18,931 as opposed to Lohia's 54,360 votes. Therefore, it is not difficult to see why Phulpur attracted Pandit Nehru more than the city where he was born, where he was initiated into the freedom struggle, and where his father set up buildings like Swaraj Bhawan and Anand Bhawan and influenced not only his city but his party, the Congress, and the country with his eloquence and prosperity. Were Phulpur's rustic surroundings, backwardness, caste configuration and geographical position more important to Pandit Nehru than those of Allahabad?

Phulpur is a town situated 30 kilometres from Allahabad. Despite being the parliamentary constituency of India's first Prime Minister, the pace of development in Phulpur has been painfully slow. The backwardness of this place was a stairway for the Nehru-Gandhi family that reinforced their charismatic personality and helped them to win elections. Older people of the town tell a story from the Nehru era. When the Lok Sabha elections were held for the first time in the newly independent country, Pandit Nehru arrived in his constituency to campaign. In those days, stages were not built for political meetings. No matter how big the leader was, a white sheet would be spread on benches and the meeting would start. It is said that at the time, the ruler of the princely state reached the venue of the meeting riding on an elephant, but was stopped by the District Magistrate. An argument broke out between the two. The king was not ready to accept the new system of someone else getting more special treatment than himself, that too in his own kingdom. On the other hand, the district magistrate was committed to protect the honour of the Prime Minister, who was the head of the executive under the new democratic system. Pandit Nehru saw this and ran to the king. He said, 'Maharaj ki Jai' (Hail the King), and following him, the public also started shouting slogans of 'Maharaj ki Jai Ho'. And then the king came down from his elephant, took Pandit Nehru's hand and not only seated himself on Nehru's election campaign bench, but also appealed for votes on Nehru's behalf. Older people recollect that while returning to Delhi, Nehru told the young collector that the king wanted to be saluted and he wanted votes. Nehru advised, 'I gave the king what he wished for and he gave me what I wished for. Democracy does not have any problem with this, nor do I. So you should not be uncomfortable with this, young man!'

Possibly the above incident did not happen exactly like that, but it reveals Pandit Nehru's vision as a politician. It is not for nothing that Pandit Nehru became an architect of democracy of his own kind in new India. He knew very well the weaknesses of the people and the importance of their opinion. That is why even when his fame was at its peak, he selected for himself a comparatively backward parliamentary constituency. Such a constituency on which he not only had an emotional and linguistic hold but on which his personality has had a considerable bearing. It has been the misfortune of Indian democracy that Pandit Nehru's descendants adopted this tactic in a rather permanent, and often, detrimental way.

Like Pandit Nehru, his family members also chose those parliamentary constituencies that laid the foundation of the family's triumph on the back of its backwardness. Barring a few exceptions like Raj Narain's victory in Raebareli and Smriti Irani's win in Amethi, this dynasty has always considered particular constituencies as their fifedom. Over the years, able people from these places richly benefited by being agents of the family, but the rest of the population only got empty promises. It is worth remembering that Indira Gandhi, who had entered active politics while Pandit Nehru was alive, did not think Phulpur to be a place fit to contest elections from. She went to Raebareli, though she too was born in Allahabad and had started her marital life there. After Pandit Nehru's death, his sister Vijaylakshmi Pandit went to Phulpur to fight the parliamentary election. In 1964, she polled 1,10,549 votes to defeat Socialist Party's Janeshwar Mishra in the Lok Sabha bypoll. Mishra got a mere 52,529 votes in this election.

In the fourth Lok Sabha elelctions in 1967, Vijaylakshmi Pandit's rival was once again Janeshwar Mishra. Pandit's votes decreased this time around. She polled only 95,306 votes, but it was still more than the 59,123 votes that Mishra got. She won the election but was unable to establish a relationship with Phulpur. After only two years, she resigned from the membership of the Lok Sabha and went to work at the United Nations. Phulpur had to face a bypoll again in 1969. This time around, the people sided with Mishra—a leader who had worked among the people. In this way, the people put an end to the so-called relationship of the Nehru-Gandhi family with Phulpur.

Indira's chessboard in parliamentary polls

Lal Bahadur Shastri occupied the post of the Prime Minister after Nehru's death, but Indira Gandhi was his real political heir. Indira Gandhi, who was a Rajya Sabha member from August 1964 to February 1967, decided to fight the elections by going directly to the people during the fourth Lok Sabha polls in 1967. She started scouting for a constituency that would be influenced by her personality even without being told to do so. She deemed the Raebareli parliamentary seat ideal for this. Her husband Feroze Gandhi had represented this seat in 1952 and 1957. In the 1957 Lok Sabha poll, Feroze Gandhi got 1,62,595 votes over the 1,33,342 votes cast for his rival, Nand Kishore. It is said that Indira Gandhi had campaigned for him in this election as well. It is another matter that the relationship between Feroze and Indira Gandhi was better then. Feroze Gandhi was not only criticising Nehru's capitalist policies in

Parliament but was also exposing the corruption that had begun to take over Indian politics and politicians. Very meticulously, he exposed the nexus of corrupt people, as a result of which, many people had to go to jail, the insurance industry was nationalised and the then finance minister had to resign.

When Feroze Gandhi started a campaign against the corruption in the Congress in 1955, that same year Indira Gandhi became a member of the party's working committee and the Central Election Committee. Similarly, in 1959, when Indira Gandhi became the president of the Congress, she tried to dismiss the first elected communist government in Kerala and impose President's rule in the state. It is said that one day there was a heated argument between Feroze and Indira Gandhi at the breakfast table in Anand Bhawan. Things came to such a pass that Feroze Gandhi called Indira Gandhi a fascist in Nehru's presence. This incident is mentioned by Bertile Falk in his book *Feroze: The Forgotten Gandhi*. Feroze Gandhi was perhaps the only member of the Nehru-Gandhi family who, after much thought, chose a backward area in the form of Raebareli as his karmabhoomi. Feroze Gandhi was the kind of MP who would corner the government of his own party in Parliament with his questions based on matters concerning his constituency and related to public interest. He was a staunch supporter of India's federal structure and was against the centralisation of power. He was connected to the common man and was popular.

When Feroze Gandhi died all of a sudden, Indira Gandhi jettisoned his legacy altogether. Had she any special bond with Raebareli, after Feroze Gandhi's death, Indira Gandhi would have himself contested the bypoll from Raebareli. But, necessitated by the death of Feroze Gandhi, RP Singh and Baijnath Kureel were made the Congress candidates from this parliamentary seat in the bypoll of 1960 and in the third general elections in 1962, respectively. Despite attaining the pinnacle of popularity, Indira Gandhi took a long time to enter the electoral politics. In fact, till the 1967 election, Indira Gandhi was busy making herself stronger in the organisation.

Seeing her father's popularity in parliamentary elections, Indira Gandhi had understood that the masses felt strongly connected to symbols and had the tendency to deify larger than life personalities. So it was important to maintain an image that symbolised greatness and commanded attention. Moreover, Purvanchal was known to her since childhood. They were not royals, but the heft of her family was like that of any princely state. History bears testimony to the fact that from arriving in Raebareli in 1967 to losing to Raj Narain in 1977, Indira Gandhi was not only invincible in this constituency, but was the pride of the people here. The residents of Raebareli would boast about being represented by the heir of the Nehru-Gandhi dynasty, the most powerful leader of the country.

When Indira Gandhi fought from Raebareli for the first time in 1967, she polled 1,43,602 votes as compared to 51,899 votes for her nearest rival BC Seth. In 1971, Raj Narain gave a tough fight, but in the end, he too lost to Indira Gandhi's charisma. As opposed to the 1,83,309 votes polled by Indira Gandhi, Raj Narain got 71,499 votes. However, he did not give up even after electoral defeat and challenged Indira Gandhi's election legally by accusing her of misusing the Prime Minister's Office, using her influence and engaging in electoral irregularities. Amidst a lot of legal wrangling, on 12 June 1975, the Allahabad High Court quashed Indira Gandhi's election from the Raebareli parliamentary seat on grounds of electoral irregularity. This verdict by the court and the intensifying opposition attack enraged Indira Gandhi.

Indira Gandhi, who used to put the position of the Prime Minister above the parliamentary process, was overcome with anger, and instead of resigning, ordered the arrest of the opposition members. As the Prime Minister, she declared Emergency in the country, though it was not the country's period of crisis but rather a personal moment of crisis for Indira Gandhi. This step by Indira Gandhi is considered the biggest blunder of her political career, and she would come to realise that later. Her image among the Indian masses suffered in a way she could not have imagined.

On 5 February 1977, reporting from a rally called by Indira Gandhi at Delhi's Ramlila Maidan, a BBC correspondent wrote that the organisers had tried their best to gather people for the rally. School teachers, employees and labourers of the Delhi Municipal Corporation were brought to the Ramlila Maidan in packed buses. Indira Gandhi was in a bad mood. She was shocked. In her hard-hitting speech, she ridiculed the Janata Party as a 'khichdi'. But in the middle of Indira Gandhi's speech, some women sitting at the front started to get up and leave. The workers of Seva Dal tried hard to persuade them to join the meeting again but failed. The people made so much noise by talking among themselves that Indira Gandhi had to suddenly stop her speech midway. This trouble in Delhi stayed with Indira Gandhi in Raebareli as well. She was fighting a losing battle in the 1977 Lok Sabha polls. Here, in comparison to Raj Narain, who got 1,77,719 votes, Indira Gandhi could muster only 1,22,517 votes.

A long time has passed since then, yet it is difficult to imagine what India's political history would have been had Indira Gandhi not imposed Emergency. How would have the Congress been viewed if the Emergency had not been imposed? If Indira Gandhi had respected the verdict of the court and resigned from her post, what would have happened to her? What if she had not misused her prime ministerial post? If the general elections had taken place on time in the country, what would the result have been? Who knows, Indira Gandhi might have won by an even bigger margin. But this leader, who had the most charismatic image in a given period of Indian democracy, was perhaps destined to be remembered as one who presided over a dark age, and so she could not call upon the courage that her Italy-born daughter-in-law Sonia Gandhi showed in a similar situation by resigning from her Raebareli seat. Perhaps Sonia Gandhi did this learning from the experiences of Indira Gandhi. It is another matter that even after the Raebareli defeat and ouster from power, Indira Gandhi did not quit politics. She planned her political comeback by deciding to contest a bypoll from Chikmagalur, a nondescript Lok Sabha constituency in Karnataka, in 1978. Chikmagalur means 'little daughter's city'. According to a predetermined strategy, the MP from the constituency, DB Chandra Gowda, vacated his seat for Indira Gandhi, and she made a grand re-entry into Lok Sabha.

According to senior journalist Sagarika Ghosh, who has written a book on Indira Gandhi, there was a famous slogan in Chikmagalur, 'Ek sherni sau langur, Chikmagalur, Chikmagalur' (One lioness and a hundred langurs, Chikmagalur, Chikmagalur). The Janata Party exerted full force to defeat Indira Gandhi. In this entire bypoll, Indira Gandhi campaigned for eighteen hours every day and subsisted on peanuts and fruit. Whenever she went somewhere at night, she would put a torch between her feet and turn it towards herself so that people could see her face. She had so much stamina that she could walk faster than any Indian politician living at the time, writes Ghose. The situation of voters in Chikmagalur was favourable and the chief minister of Karnataka at the time, Devaraj Urs, was popular. As a result, Indira Gandhi registered a historic victory in this election, wining by 70,000 votes. At a time when she was besieged by political opposition and the Janata Party government was bent upon initiating legal proceedings against her, this win proved useful in her political journey. However, within a fortnight of Indira Gandhi's election from Chikmagalur, she was expelled from the Lok Sabha. Members associated with the ruling Janata Party found Indira Gandhi guilty of breach of privilege and contempt of the House for obstructing a parliamentary inquiry into the functioning of the automobile company owned by her son Sanjay Gandhi. After a few days, she lost membership of the Lok Sabha. She was also sent to jail for a short period.

The truth is that if 1977 is a big milestone in Indian politics because of the defeat of the Congress and the first non-Congress government of the country coming to power, the year 1978 is remembered for the fighting spirit of Indira Gandhi on the back of which she wrote the script of her return. In many respects, Smriti Irani's win in the 2019 Lok Sabha is identical. Even after losing the Lok Sabha elections in 2014, she maintained a connection with Amethi, and through public relations, affection and developmental work, wrote a script of victory that was unprecedented.

Indira Gandhi used the slogan 'Ek sherni sau langur' to demolish the idea of coalition. At that time, the idea of coalition was new to the Indian parliamentary and legislative system. Although, after 1967, Samyukta Vidhayak Dal governments were formed in several states, their lifespans were not long. The leaders who had joined hands in 1977 to defeat Indira Gandhi, soon started pointing swords at each other for their own selfish interests. This created political anarchy for some time and the Janata Party government collapsed before its term. It is said that Indira Gandhi had started working on a plan to return to power with the advice of Jai Prakash Narayan. The same Jai Prakash Narayan, who had played a major role in toppling Indira Gandhi from power with the slogan, 'Singhasan khali karo ki janata aati hai' (Vacate the throne, the masses are coming). A few months after the loss in March 1977, the killing of eleven people, including eight Dalits, in the nondescript village of Belchi near Nalanda in Bihar, provided her with the ammunition she needed.

Indira Gandhi had internalised Jai Prakash Narayan's advice of staying attached to the public. She reached Belchi under very adverse circumstances and in even that pre-electronic-media and pre-social-media era, ensured that her trip made headlines. As per a BBC report, former Bihar chief minister Dr Jagannath Mishra, who accompanied her on this trip, said, 'Saroj Khaparde, Pratibha Singh and Kedar Pandey were also there with Indira Gandhi. People told her that cars cannot go there. Indira Gandhi said they would walk to that place even if it took the entire night. At first, she took a jeep but it got stuck in the mud. She then took the help of a tractor, but after a while, that too failed. That place was full of floodwater. Then an elephant was brought for her. It was already dark by the time Indira Gandhi reached Belchi. She talked to the victims and gave them solace. From that moment, Indira Gandhi had started her political comeback.'

Journalist Janardhan Thakur gave an interesting account of this trip in his book *All the Prime Minister's Men*. He wrote: "No lunch, let us leave," said Smt Gandhi firmly. Not to be deterred, when aides mumbled that the route was bad and no car could reach, she said: "We shall go on walking. We shall go on walking even if it takes us all night." Outside the town of Bihar Sharif, the road petered into a muddy track. When the jeep got stuck, a tractor was pressed into service but even that got stuck ... Smt Gandhi was walking through the mud ... Some Congressmen refused to go saying there was waist-deep water ahead but Smt Gandhi was still marching on, her sari raised above her ankle. "Of course I can wade through water," she snapped at her frightened companions. A thoughtful local suggested an elephant. "But how will you climb an elephant?" aides asked. "Of course I will," she said impatiently. "This is not the first time I have ridden an elephant. Bahut dino baad haathi pe chadh rahi hun" (It's been some time since I climbed an elephant).' Images of this incident held India in thrall for a long time. The people present there were shouting slogans like 'Aadhi roti khayenge, Indira ko bulayenge' (We will eat half a meal, but we will call Indira), and 'Indira tere abhav mein harijan maare jate hai' (Indira, in your absence harijans get killed). Statistics say that in the fast-changing political atmosphere, in the mid-term elections to the Lok Sabha, Indira Gandhi made a comeback in every sense as the head of the 'Indira government' amid slogans of 'Chuniye unhe jo sarkar chala sake' (Elect those who can run the government). An officer posted in the Intelligence Bureau of Biharsharif at the time, who was later posted to Delhi to look after the Prime Minister's security, shared with me the entire incident. The officer stuck with Indira Gandhi all through and in the dispatch that he sent to the Centre after returning, this trip was interpreted as the harbinger of Indira Gandhi's comeback.

This nationwide political change had had its effect on the Raebareli constituency too, and representation by the Nehru-Gandhi family had stymied local development. In the Lok Sabha polls of 1980, Indira Gandhi was re-elected from Raebareli. But it is said that despite regaining her reputation in national politics in a matter of just three years, she could not recover from the shock of the electoral defeat in the 1977 Lok Sabha elections throughout her life. Indira Gandhi had lost interest in Raebareli. In this election of 1980, she also fought from Medak, which was then located in Andhra Pradesh. The argument was that this would strengthen the Congress in both the north and the south. Not only did Indira Gandhi come back to power, but she also won from both the seats. In Raebareli, as compared to 50,249 votes polled by Rajmata Vijaya Raje Scindia, Indira Gandhi got an impressive 2,23,903 votes. In Medak, Indira Gandhi recorded 3,01,577 votes, while her nearest rival, S Jaipal Reddy, could get only 82,453 votes.

Whatever the reason, Raebareli, known for its attachment to the Nehru-Gandhi family and as Indira Gandhi's parliamentary constituency, was cast aside by Indira Gandhi. This is not surprising if the political or electoral history of the Nehru-Gandhi family is studied. Letting go and grasping, grasping and letting go was its favourite pastime as far as slecting and leaving the constituencies was concerned. Raebareli has always been completely committed to this family. Even Gandhi family's distant relatives were given the same respect by Raebareli electorate without expecting anything in return, making them victorious. Leave aside Raj Narain in 1977 and the BJP's Ashok Singh in the elections of 1996 and 1998, either the Nehru-Gandhi family itself or its near or distant relatives have occupied the Raebareli parliamentary seat. Among them are Arun Nehru, in the bypoll of 1980 and general elections of 1984; Sheila Kaul in the parliamentary elections of 1989 and 1991; and the family's loyalist Satish Sharma in 1999. In the 1984 by-election, Arun Nehru received 1,76,456 votes, while in 1984, the wave of sympathy following the assassination of Indira Gandhi ensured that he won by a record margin. In the Lok Sabha election of 1984, Arun Nehru polled 3,14,028 votes. It is not surprising that this tally recorded by Arun Nehru could not be matched by anybody until Sonia Gandhi took the field in Raebareli in the 2004 Lok Sabha polls. Sheila Kaul got 1,97,658 votes and 1,02,331 votes in the 1989 and 1991 Lok Sabha elections respectively. Similarly, while Ashok Singh of the BJP got 1,63,390 votes in the 1996 Lok Sabha elections, in the 1998 poll, he managed to secure 2,37,204 votes. When Captain Satish Sharma came to contest the elections with the support of the Nehru-Gandhi family, he received 2,24,202 votes.

Sonia Gandhi came to Raebareli for the first time during the 2004 parliamentary elections. She got 3,78,107 votes as opposed to 1,28,342 votes for the Samajwadi Party's Ashok Kumar Singh. Although she had to resign within two years due to the controversy created over office of profit (she held the chair of the National Advisory Council), in the bypoll that took place in 2006, she won by a bigger margin. As opposed to her nearest rival Raj Kumar's tally of 57,003 votes, she raked in 4,74,891 votes. In the Lok Sabha elections of 2009 and 2014, Sonia Gandhi got 4,81,490 and 5,26,434 votes respectively. In the 2019 polls, she won by securing 55.8 per cent or 5,34,918 votes. Looking at these figures and viewed from a historical perspective, the Nehru-Gandhi family has always been connected to Uttar Pradesh. And in that too, the affection of the people of

Raebareli and Amethi, leaving aside a few exceptions, has always kept this family in the Parliament. But instead of cherishing the people's affection and considering these places as their home, the members of the Nehru-Gandhi family perhaps used them as their property. Whenever they felt like, they would take eight to ten cars and go on a two to four-day trip. They would meet a few select people, try to know the problems of the two constituencies only from them and then return, leaving a trail of dust in their wake. In the eyes of the world and the media, a completely different impression would be produced from the photos of the tour that was far removed from reality. But a social resentment was brewing behind this rosy picture. It is difficult to say if Rahul Gandhi had any idea of this or not, but Irani had felt it back in 2014 itself.

The Nehru-Gandhi family's relation with Amethi has never been as egalitarian as it appears or has been made out to be. In a way, it has always been a party of satraps, landlords, heads of maths (Hindu monasteries) and middlemen. Mahatma Gandhi had understood this in the initial days itself of his association with the Congress, and for that reason, had advocated the disbandment of the party after Independence. Amethi was not beyond this. This party, governed by a high command culture, maintained its relationship with the powerful sections, and the pains and sorrows of the masses were just tools for it to grab media headlines.

The Nehru-Gandhi family's relationship with Amethi started from the threshold of the Amethi royal house. Older people of Amethi say that the foundation of this relationship was laid a long time before Independence. This bond goes all the way back to the king of Amethi, Raja Madhav Bakhsh Singh, and the noted lawyer Motilal Nehru. Although Pandit Motilal Nehru was known for his advocacy and role in the freedom struggle, he was also known for his luxurious lifestyle.

According to historical records, owing to the looting and massacre in Delhi, Pandit Motilal Nehru's father Pandit Gangadhar Nehru migrated to Agra. But before he could properly settle down there, he passed away in 1861, aged thirty-four.

Pandit Gangadhar Nehru had three sons. The eldest among them was Bansidhar Nehru, who, after Victorian rule was established in India, went to serve in the justice department. Younger to him was Pandit Nandlal Nehru, who was the diwan of a small princely state called Khetri in Rajasthan for almost ten years. Later he returned to Agra. At Agra, he studied law and began legal practice. Pandit Gangadhar Nehru's third son was Pandit Motilal Nehru. Three months after the death of Pandit Gangadhar Nehru, on 6 May 1861, Pandit Motilal Nehru was born. Pandit Nandlal Nehru brought up his younger brother Motilal and arranged for his education.

Pandit Nandlal Nehru was counted among the successful lawyers of Agra. With a high court set up in Allahabad, he had to spend most of his time there in connection with cases. So he built a house in Allahabad and started permanently residing there along with his family. Pandit Motilal Nehru pursued his education there. He was educated at Allahabad's Muir Central College, but could not appear for the BA final year examination. However, he did Bar at Law later from Cambridge University, and become one of the most expensive and sought after advocates of the country. It is a fact that Pandit Motilal Nehru was one of the few first-generation Indians to receive a western education.

In that era, when the average income of an ordinary Indian was not even a hundred rupees, his monthly income was in thousands. He had travelled to Europe several times in relation to cases or on tours, and so, as compared to other Indians, he was an expert in understanding the people of the West. He had easy access to British officers and jurists. This was when he bought a sprawling house in Allahabad's Civil Lines. He reached the pinnacle of his career as a lawyer when in 1909, he secured an approval to be an advocate in Britain's Privy

Council. In 1909, when under the Indian Councils Act, also known as the Morley-Minto Reforms, Indians got representation for the first time in the Governor General's executive council, and in 1910, when elections were held to the central and provincial legislative councils, Pandit Motilal Nehru contested the legislative assembly election from the United Provinces and won.

It is said that Raja Madhav Bakhsh Singh of Amethi openly supported Motilal Nehru owing to their old relationship. Noted journalist Vinod Mehta alludes to this in his book *The Sanjay Story*, while referring to a person from the Amethi royal house. Mehta writes, quoting that person, that the king's (Rananjaya Singh) father gave Motilal Nehru a break and offered him many important cases. One could say that the Anand Bhawan in Allahabad was built with money from Amethi. It was, in fact, Raja Madhav Bakhsh Singh, who once advised Pandit Motilal Nehru to build a mansion matching his status. After that, on 7 August 1899, Pandit Motilal Nehru purchased a bungalow spread over 19 bighas from Raja Jaikisan Das for Rs 20,000. A huge one-storey building was already in place. Before this bungalow was purchased, the Nehru family used to stay in a bungalow at 9, Elgin Road, and before that, they lived in an old neighbourhood of Allahabad called Mirganj. It was at this Mirganj house that Pandit Jawaharlal Nehru was born on 14 November 1899. The house in Mirganj no longer exists because under a clean-up drive in 1931, the civic body pulled it down.

Anand Bhawan was purchased when Jawaharlal Nehru was ten years old, and the whole family moved there. Jawaharlal Nehru writes in *Meri Kahani*, 'The result of practising law with hard work and dedication was that there was a flow of cases, and a lot of money was earned.' After purchasing Anand Bhawan, Motilal Nehru had further construction done on it. However, electoral politics connected him to the masses and the Congress. He started to use his massive house and enormous wealth for the cause of the country as well. It was at Anand Bhawan in 1928 that Jawaharlal Nehru first wrote his 'Poorna Swaraj' speech. The contours of the Quit India movement were shaped here. Furthermore, the outlines of all historical decisions were formulated here. For that reason perhaps, on 21 June 1954, Jawaharlal Nehru wrote in his will about Anand Bhawan, 'For us and many other people, this house has become the symbol of all those things that we value in life. It is much more valuable than a brick-and-concrete building and a private property. It is connected very intimately with our freedom struggle and great incidents have taken place within its walls. And very important decisions have been taken.'

The intention behind describing the lives of Pandit Motilal Nehru and Pandit Jawaharlal Nehru here in such great detail is to find out why this family did not choose Allahabad in their parliamentary journey despite being so closely connected to the city. Why did the Nehru-Gandhi family deem Phulpur, Raebareli and Amethi to be closer to it in its electoral journey and for fulfilling its political ambitions? Was it just so that it could derive its interests from these areas? It is worth noting also that this family has been successful in doing so.

Like Motilal Nehru, in 1926, when Jawaharlal Nehru contested from the Faizabad-Machhlishahr joint seat, he also made the Amethi princely state his political centre. It was from here that he conducted the election. In return, when after Independence there was a campaign for the merger of the princely states in the country, and the Amethi royal house was merged with the Republic of India, Pandit Nehru offered Rananjaya Singh, the then king of Amethi and the father of Sanjay Singh, the post of a minister. He, however, refused. Though Rananjaya Singh did not enter parliamentary politics directly at that time, he had a considerable hold over politics in the entire Amethi region and his ties with the Nehru family remained strong.

After Pandit Jawaharlal Nehru and Feroze Gandhi, when Indira Gandhi chose the neighbouring seat Raebareli for herself, Amethi was selected for her son Sanjay Gandhi. There is another interesting story behind elections in Amethi. Sanjay Gandhi had emerged on the political horizon before the Emergency. The Congress leaders felt that Sanjay Gandhi would be the one to take the Congress legacy forward. An army of sycophants started gathering around him. Giani Zail Singh wanted Sanjay Gandhi to contest from a Lok Sabha constituency in Punjab, Shyama Charan Shukla kept on sending messages to Sanjay Gandhi to make Madhya Pradesh his place of work, and Jagannath Mishra wanted the Congress crown prince to oblige Bihar. Vinod Mehta writes in his book that in April 1976, the Raja of Amethi arrived in Delhi with the local MP and five MLAs of the district. All of them met Sanjay Gandhi and suggested that he contest the election from Amethi. At this, Sanjay Gandhi said, 'Which election, which seat? I do not know when elections would take place, it is too early to say now. I have not made up my mind.' Apart from family ties, the additional reason for Sanjay Gandhi's election from this place was, by and large, the same as that for choosing Raebareli. The high political ambitions of the Amethi royal heir Sanjay Singh were no secret. The Amethi royals already had a relationship with the Nehru-Gandhi family. In this situation, a friendship between two young men with high political ambitions, Sanjay Gandhi and Sanjay Singh, was but natural. Both of them had stepped into politics at almost the same time. Remember in the 1980s, Sanjay Singh was twice elected as an MLA in Uttar Pradesh and had also served as a minister. On the other hand, Sanjay Gandhi played his cards tactically and made the backwardness of Amethi a pivot, and this strengthened the friendship between Sanjay Gandhi and Sanjay Singh.

Sanjay Singh's father Rananjay Singh and Congress MLAs of that time from the district, were putting pressure on Sanjay Gandhi to contest from Amethi. On 18 May 1976, the local MP Vidyadhar Bajpai openly proposed to Sanjay Gandhi that he should contest from Amethi. According to a BBC report, in 1976, when the 'dark age' of Emergency imposed on India was being discussed not just in the country, but all over the world, in November, Khairahana village near the town of Amethi in Uttar Pradesh's Sultanpur district suddenly captured the headlines for a different reason. What happened was that Sanjay Gandhi arrived in this village with some of his associates and wielded a shovel to inaugurate the construction of a road. Youth Congress workers in large numbers from across the country joined him. Hundreds of shovels, spades, crates and other necessary items had already been sent. This shramdaan (offering of labour) continued for not one or two days, but over a month. The people who had come for shramdaan stayed. Food was cooked for them, villagers made arrangements for their stay at their own homes, and there were daily cultural programmes for entertainment. All in all, the atmosphere remained festive for around one and a half months.

The head of Khairahana village at the time was Ramnaresh Shukla. His elder son Rajendra Prasad Shukla, recollecting that episode, says, 'Sanjay Gandhi's politics started from shramdaan. The shramdaan happened on three roads. Later, all three roads were covered by asphalt. People were coming from various states to participate in the shramdaan. The DM, SP and all senior officials were camping here.'

The reason for this was clear. Sanjay Gandhi had already arrived on the political scene before the Emergency, but he had not yet entered parliamentary politics. Indira Gandhi was an MP from Raebareli and she could not have found a safer seat than this for her son. Therefore, road construction was just an excuse; the truth is that Amethi had been chosen to prepare the political ground for Sanjay Gandhi. Credit has to be given to the Nehru-Gandhi family for turning an ordinary parliamentary constituency into a VIP constituency, even if a ceremonial one, by adopting it at a political level. It is another matter that it did not lead to any progress in the lives of the residents of this place. Veteran Congress leader from Amethi, Umakant Dwivedi, who played an active role during the shramdaan, says, 'Till 1971, Vidyadhar Dwivedi was the local MP. He hailed from Unnao but used to contest elections from Amethi. He was very close to the Gandhi family, and when it was learnt that Sanjay Gandhi was looking to enter politics, he, in a way, adopted Sanjay Gandhi and publicly announced that he would be vacating his seat for him.'

Sanjay Singh reminisced about those days speaking to the BBC in 2017, 'Nearly a thousand Youth Congress workers had arrived. There were gatherings all through the day and night. I was a player at that time and not interested in poitics, but when Sanjay Gandhi arrived in Amethi and said we would have to stay here, I along with my freinds shunned our love for sports and got down to construct the roads.' There have been other roads, schools and markets built in the village, but the people say nothing has matched the festive atmosphere of those two months. Extraordinarily, not even a stone or a mark related to that event exists in Khairahana village today. Some of the younger children of the village do not even know who Sanjay Gandhi is. But there are others who remember everything. According to Ramsagar, 'People used to come from various places. Many educated girls had come too and they engaged in shramdaan. We used to toil all through the day because we did not just get to eat well, we could also listen to songs.' Amaravati Devi, a woman from the village told the BBC, 'Those days, women did not leave their houses too often, but when women from outside came here and started building roads for us, seeing them, the women of the village also ventured out. Everyone was working following the lead of one another.'

Sanjay Gandhi, however, got no advantage from this political arrangement because by then Emergency was declared in the country. The next year, in 1977, when he took the field of election for the first time in the Lok Sabha polls, he faced defeat in Amethi. Vinod Mehta has written in his book that Sanjay Gandhi campaigned for an urban election in a rural area, which was one of the reasons for his defeat. People were enraged over Sanjay Gandhi's infamous sterilisation drive during the Emergency, and that contributed to his loss.

7

You Scratch My Back and I Will Scratch Yours

The Samajwadi Party and Bahujan Samaj Party have always quietly supported the Congress in Amethi. Often they would not field candidates in the parliamentary elections, and even when they did, they would strategically choose people who would benefit the Congress. It was rumoured in Amethi that the Samajwadi Party and Bahujan Samaj Party decided their candidates in Amethi only after conferring with Sonia Gandhi. The people could discern which candidate was there to fulfil his interest and which candidate was there to serve the people. The state had seen the reign of the Samajwadi Party, which was marked by casteism, muscle power and money power. The BSP would always talk about the Dalits but work for the rich. Be it Dalits or the backward classes, they were nothing more than vote banks for these parties. Besides the local people of Amethi, many people in Lucknow said that during the BSP's reign, the objective of governance was only to earn money, and hooliganism and communalism were rampant. There was talk about the power of the people, but work was done by money power. There have repeatedly been discussions over note-counting machines in Uttar Pradesh. During parliamentary elections, the Bahujan Samaj Party (BSP) used to be with the Congress on the pretext of national issues and during Assembly elections, the issues would become local so that the party could field their own candidates. An Amethi resident, Rakshit Shukla, spoke of Mayawati's love for flattery and wealth. The Samajwadi Party and BSP governments in the state supported the Congress in Amethi so that the central government represented by the Congress would turn a blind eye towards all their misdeeds. In this way, there was an unwritten understanding between all of them regarding Amethi. Educated people associated with the Samajwadi Party and BSP in Amethi started asking their leaders who would help them if they voted for Rahul Gandhi. Where and how could they approach Rahul Gandhi for official matters? During the 2019 parliamentary elections, people related to the Samajwadi Party and BSP started telling their leaders that Irani was a leader who was accessible to all. She was always available and on call for the people. They also demanded from their leaders that they should be given the freedom to choose their candidates. As a result, the RSS was able to convince them that their leadership was ready to sell them off in the market and they were ready to be sold. The people voted, but deals were struck by somebody else. This fact got so ingrained in the minds of the Samajwadi Party and BSP supporters that people from the Bahujan community raised their voices in many places and secretly started working for the BJP. Many leaders of the Samajwadi party changed sides and joined the BJP.

During elections, three groups influenced major voting in Amethi: ration dealers, past or present gram pradhans (village heads) and members of the kshetra panchayat (panchayat samiti), known as the BDC in common parlance. These three wielded a tremendous nexus in Amethi that had given rise to anarchic and corrupt practices. All of Amethi was divided into blocks; within these blocks gram pradhans would be identified. The next link was the ration dealer. It was through them that the game of money was played. A tradition of contractors was prevalent here during voting. More money meant more votes. The contractors and agents controlled elections here. The biggest challenge for Irani was to end this nexus. For that, it was imperative to reach out and talk to all the contractors. It was important to reason with them.

When Sanjeev Balyan arrived in Amethi to assist Irani in the 2019 elections, she informed him about this alliance. Balyan was tasked with breaking this coalition. To do so, Balyan started meeting zila panchayat representatives and tried to take them into confidence. Seen from the perspective of elections, two ministries were extremely important in Amethi—the first was panchayati raj and the other was food. To boost the efforts of breaking the nexus of the local ration dealers, gram pradhans/ex-gram pradhans and kshetra panchayat member, the Uttar Pradesh panchayati raj minister Bhupendra Singh was called to Amethi. Through him, the panchayat members and gram pradhans were asked to uphold democracy. The food minister of the state Atul Garg was also brought on a trip to the Amethi Lok Sabha constituency so that a clear message could be sent to the ration dealers that they should stay away from the old system of contractors and stop enticing people towards the Congress and let them vote according to their wish. Two trips each by Bhupendra Singh and Atul Garg were organised and their meetings were arranged with the concerned people. These people used to come on tours and then return, they didn't need to meet Irani. Irani was busy interacting with the voters and holding small meetings. In this way, the contractors who used to distribute money were brought under control.

The Samajwadi Party was in power in Uttar Pradesh during the Lok Sabha elections in 2014 and Akhilesh Yadav was the state's chief minister. Even though he was head of the state, it was the Congress that ruled in Amethi. Rajesh Masala says, 'The local officers were as if instructed to work according to the directions of the Congress candidate and his representatives. During the election, the entire local administration would do their bidding, at the behest of Lucknow. For that reason, BJP supporters were prevented from voting during that election in some cases, not even allowed to go to the polling station. When in one of the booths, Irani questioned the presence of an assistant of Priyanka Gandhi Vadra, the latter was allowed to leave, instead of being stopped and arrested. The police did not say anything to that personal assistant of Mrs Vadra. On the contrary, a policeman continued to argue with Irani with considerable arrogance, asking her to mind her business and let him do his work.'

8

Making Sense of the Numbers

In theory, parliamentary democracy in the Indian political system is governed by people-centric policies, people's strength and people's autonomy. But in reality, it is a slave of neoliberalism and neo-capitalism, which are nurtured by subjective faith. In terms of the new version of democracy, the land of India has been very fertile in this form because of its civilisation, tradition, philosophy, belief and culture. Personality-based cults and following is not surprising behaviour in a country that has faith in trees, mountains and rivers, but even within this, people like Irani not only emerge on the lines of alternative systems but write new history with their hard work.

A detailed description of the reasons why Irani was successful in checkmating Rahul Gandhi in the 2019 Lok Sabha elections, thereby composing a new chapter in Indian politics, has been provided elsewhere in this book. In this chapter, we will look at electoral statistics from the Amethi parliamentary constituency and the assembly seats that fall under it, which, to a large extent, reflect the political winds of the country and Uttar Pradesh.

On 22 September 2018, Navika Kumar, political editor of news channel Times Now asked Irani that she had been quiet for a long time. There is a lull before every storm, so was a storm expected in 2019, Kumar asked. Irani replied that she felt that she was assigned because she is one who always clashed with a few elements in Lutyens' Delhi. As far as Rahul Gandhi was concerned, he was not the battle for her, she said, adding that she had taken an ideological and political stand in Amethi and for her, Rahul Gandhi not only represented a political dynasty but also what was wrong in the Indian political system. Irani revealed that she had taken an oath in 2014 that she would keep coming back to Amethi, and by her presence, keep compelling Rahul Gandhi to return too.

The result of this was that every time Rahul Gandhi went to Amethi, it was as if a press release was going to Amethi. If you visit the Uttar Pradesh government's website in 2020, the information that you get is that Amethi district comes under the Ayodhya division of Uttar Pradesh. On 1 July 2010, Amethi became the 72nd district of Uttar Pradesh by merging the Amethi, Gauriganj and Musafirkhana tehsils of Sultanpur district with the Tiloi and Salon tehsils of Raebareli districts. Initially, it was called Chhatrapati Shahuji Maharaj Nagar. Later, the name was changed back to Amethi. There are four assembly constituencies in the district—Tiloi, Gauriganj, Amethi and Jagdishpur (reserved). Gauriganj town is the headquarters of the Amethi district. There are two municipal councils—Gauriganj and Jais. As a parliamentary constituency, it is Lok Sabha constituency number 37. While the Amethi district comprises four assembly segments, the parliamentary constituency includes under its ambit five Assembly segments, which extend over Sultanpur and Raebareli districts apart from Amethi.

A special thing about Amethi is that it did not become a parliamentary constituency immediately after Independence. When the election to the Lok Sabha was held for the first time in 1951-52, the Amethi Lok Sabha constituency did not exist. At the time, this area came under the Sultanpur-South Lok Sabha seat. Balakrishna Vishwanath Keskar of the Congress won that first election. In 1957, the Musafirkhana Lok Sabha seat was created. Musafirkhana is currently a tehsil of Amethi district. That time too, the Congress gave the ticket to Balakrishna Vishwanath Keskar and he was re-elected as an MP. In the 1962 election, the party fielded the king of Amethi, Raja Rananjaya Singh from the Musafirkhana.

It was not until the 1967 general elections that Amethi came into existence as a Lok Sabha constituency in the truest sense. There is another misconception regarding Amethi—that it is a Nehru-Gandhi bastion. The truth, however, is that despite all efforts by this family, it could not be made into its bastion. The opposition has always been strong here. It is another matter that this family has taken advantage of the opposition's votes getting divided. The Congress's Vidyadhar Bajpai achieved the distinction of being the first MP from the newly formed constituency. However, the Bharatiya Jana Sangh's Gokul Prasad had made it considerably tough for him.

In the 1967 Lok Sabha election, Vidyadhar Bajpai got 35.81 per cent of the total votes, that is 63,231 votes, while Gokul Prasad got 33.74 per cent, that is 59,566 votes. Bajpai won this election by a slender margin of 3,665 votes. Extraordinarily, in this election, independent candidate A Wahid was also able to garner 12.65 per cent of the votes. He polled 22,333 votes. You would be surprised to know that even at that time the number of voters in the Amethi parliamentary constituency stood at 5,05,259, but of them only 1,88,666 people voted, and the voting percentage was a mere 37.34 per cent.

Remarkably, this also had an impact on the results of the five assembly seats that fall under this parliamentary constituency, elections to which were held simultaneously as the Lok Sabha polls.

In the assembly elections, the Congress and the Bharatiya Jana Sangh bagged two seats each. One seat went to the independents. It may be noted that the voting percentage in the assembly elections was higher than that in the Lok Sabha polls. Out of the 92,577 registered voters in the Tiloi Assembly constituency, 46.95 per cent, that is, 43,469 exercised their franchise and W Naqvi of the Congress won by garnering 11,614 votes, which amounted to 28.87 per cent of the total votes. His nearest rival was Bharatiya Jana Sangh's RK Awasthi. He got 8,080 votes, which was 20.09 per cent of the total votes. The Congress also carried the day in Salon. The number of electorates in this constituency was 97,837, with 56.48 per cent of the people, which is 55,263, exercising their franchise. The winning candidate here was the Congress's DB Singh, who got 43.16 per cent of the total votes polled, which amounted to 22,160 votes. His nearest rival, SP Pandiya of the Samajwadi Socialist Party polled 12,386 votes, that is 24.12 per cent of the vote cast. The Bharatiya Jana Sangh finished third. Its candidate got 14.17 per cent of the votes, which is 7,277 votes.

In the Jagdishpur reserved seat, there were 1,03,505 voters during the election in that year. Of them, only 26.78 per cent, that is, 27,719 voters, exercised their franchise. Ram Sevak of the Bharatiya Jana Sangh won the election by garnering 9,899 or 38.46 per cent of the votes. The Congress's I Pal could get 6,276 votes or 24.39 per cent of the total votes. The Samajwadi Socialist Party candidate secured 14.99 per cent of the votes, which is 3,858 votes, and ended up third. The figures from Gauriganj were even more startling. Here, G Singh won after he managed to get 18,758 votes, which is 49.57 per cent of the total votes even while contesting as an independent candidate. While KRP Singh of the Congress was the runner-up with 11,109 votes, that is, 29.36 per cent votes, Vijay Bahadur of the Bharatiya Jana Sangh finished third, with only 2,773, votes, which translated to 7.33 per cent of the total votes cast. There were a total of 1,15,728 voters in the Gauriganj constituency that year, of whom 42,105, or 36.38 per cent, exercised their franchise.

In Amethi, the Bharatiya Jan Sangh candidate RP Singh triumphed. Out of a total of 43,052, or 42 per cent votes, he collected 22,022, which is 55.55 per cent votes, and trounced the Congress's BNS Vaidya. Vaidya got 12,791 votes, which is 32.27 per cent of the total votes. At the third position was an Independent candidate, who polled 3,527, or 8.9 per cent of the votes. The Amethi Assembly constituency had a voter strength of 1,02,508 that year.

The results of the Amethi parliamentary seat and those of its constituent assembly segments in the 1967 general elections reflect the historical political atmosphere of the country at the time. This was the first election in the country after Independence that did not have the shadow of Pandit Jawaharlal Nehru. The major newspapers of the time carried numerous reports on the military and political upheavals in the country. From the military point of view, the country had faced two wars one after the other, and Pandit Nehru's aura was also on the wane. The country was dealing with war and corruption. A few months after the general elections of 1962, a war between India and China broke out in October, and it was nearly a one-sided affair. China betrayed India even amid chants of 'Hindi-Chini Bhai Bhai' (Indians and Chinese are brothers). The country was shocked and downcast. Pandit Nehru continued to be cornered not only by the opposition but also by his own party members. It left Nehru struggling for words.

In the war, fought from 20 October to 21 November 1962, the Indian Army, lacking adequate military equipment, had to cede territory and retreat; the people of the country were in grief, while Nehru was embarrassed and in shock. Pandit Nehru never seemed to recover from this shock and, within a year and a half of the India-China war, on 27 May 1964, he passed away. After his death, Gulzarilal Nanda became the acting Prime Minister. Within a few days, the reins of the country were taken up by Nehru's successor, Lal Bahadur Shastri. With the slogan of 'Jai Jawan, Jai Kisan' (Hail the Soldier, hail the Farmer), Shastri had just started his efforts to revive the emotionally and militarily shattered country when Pakistan imposed another war on India.

In 1965, Pakistani ruler General Ayub Khan misjudged Prime Minister Lal Bahadur Shastri to be weak and overestimated his own power. Pakistan was under the impression that the Indian leadership and Army, saddened by the loss to China and the death of Nehru, would not be in a position to deal with a war with Pakistan. In this way, the Pakistani rulers, counting on the Kashmiri masses to be on their side, very cleverly laid the board. In April 1965, Pakistan started the war by launching 'Operation Desert Hawk' in the Rann of Kutch and claiming a large portion of Kutch. Russel Brines's book, *The Indo-Pakistani Conflict*, also mentions how 'Operation Desert Hawk' was the first stage of the war plotted by Pakistan against India. He mentions that although a ceasefire was declared on 30 June 1965, Pakistan resorted to its nefarious ways again with 'Operation Gibraltar'. In response, India occupied Haji Pir on 28 August. Pakistan retaliated with its third offensive—'Operation Grand Slam', and on 1 September entered India from the direction of Chamb and reached as far as the Akhnoor Bridge. In a counter-attack, an angry India opened the Punjab front on 6 September and the Indian Army reached Barki—Lahore was now not far away.

On 7 September, the Indian forces started taking a lead in the Sialkot sector, while Pakistan attacked Khemkaran to occupy Amritsar and on 8 September had reached Asal Uttar. But in the battle of tanks fought there, Pakistan suffered a massive setback and had to stop in its tracks. Till then, India had won Sialkot, Lahore and some fertile areas in Kashmir from Pakistan, but the latter occupied Indian territories like Chamb and Sindh. Still, from a military and geographical point of view, India held the advantage. On 23 September, following pressure from the United Nations and intervention by the Soviet Union, the two countries declared a ceasefire. Under the Tashkent Declaration of 10 January 1966, the two countries returned each other's territories. But after the ceasefire, Lal Bahadur Shastri died under mysterious circumstances in Tashkent on 11 January 1966, soon after the declaration was signed. Gulzarilal Nanda once again became the acting Prime Minister. On 24 January 1966, Indira Gandhi succeeded him as the Prime Minister.

It is important to note here that the then Congress president, K Kamaraj, played a big role in Indira Gandhi becoming the Prime Minister, despite opposition from many old leaders of the Congress. Morarji Desai was a strong voice of this opposing faction. Still, Indira Gandhi became the Prime Minister. But if properly analysed, this was not a good time for the country and the Congress. The country's ruling party was struggling with internal crises and the country itself was recovering from the aftermath of two wars. Corruption was rearing its head and the economy was on the verge of collapse. The morale of the army and the citizens had plummeted. Against this scenario, some other issues that shook the Lok Sabha were the Mizo tribal revolt, famine, the labour movement, devaluation of the rupee and poverty. During this time, along with the south, separatist movements along linguistic and religious lines had started to surface in Punjab too.

If we turn our attention towards some of the other political developments at that time, in 1963, socialist veteran Ram Manohar Lohia won the bypoll from the Uttar Pradesh's Farrukhabad parliamentary seat and reached the Lok Sabha for the first time. Similarly, Swatantra Party ideologist Minoo Masani won Gujarat's Rajkot seat and knocked open the doors of Parliament. In 1964, socialist leader Madhu Limaye had also reached the Lok Sabha after winning the bypoll from Bihar's Munger. During this time, the Communist Party of India split up because of ideological differences. After parting ways with the CPI, leaders like AK Gopalan, EMS

Namboodiripad, BT Ranadive and others formed the Communist Party of India (Marxist). In this way, regional satraps and leaders had started to make their presence felt not just in Parliament, but also at the level of state assemblies. In the election that took place in the dark transition period that had witnessed two wars and the deaths of two Prime Ministers, the seats and votes of the Congress shrunk despite the best efforts of Indira Gandhi.

In the election of 1967, the total number of seats in the Lok Sabha was raised from 494 to 520. Nearly 25 crore people, including around 13 crore men and 12 crore women, were witness to this election as voters. About 61 per cent or 15,27,00,000 people cast their ballots. The result of this election was astonishing. Although the Congress got a clear majority, its numbers in the Lok Sabha were greatly diminished. In the three previous general elections, the Congress had won three-fourths of the seats, or 364 seats in the first Lok Sabha elections of 1951-52, 371 seats in 1957 and 361 seats in 1962. In comparison to these, in 1967, it could bag only 283 seats. In other words, only 22 seats more than the cut-off. Its vote percentage also fell by about 5 per cent. While the Congress got 44.87 per cent, 47.78 per cent and 44.72 per cent votes in 1952, 1957 and 1962 respectively, in 1967 its vote percentage was reduced to 40.78 per cent. Extraordinarily, in this election, the Swatantra Party garnered 44 seats with a vote share of 8.67 per cent, while the Bharatiya Jana Sangh won 35 seats with 9.31 per cent vote share. While the Swatantra Party dented the Congress in Gujarat, Rajasthan and Odisha, the Bharatiya Jana Sangh did so in Uttar Pradesh, Madhya Pradesh and Delhi. In West Bengal and Kerala, the communists posed a stiff challenge. In the earlier elections, the Congress had never won less than 73 per cent of the seats, and even in assembly elections, it had never won less than 60 per cent of the seats. Its future was going to be even darker.

Author Ramachandra Guha believes that the disenchantment of the minorities with the Congress was one of the biggest reasons for its weakness. Whereas according to historian Bipan Chandra, since the general elections of 1967, the middle class and rich farmers of India took the plunge in politics. They formed several coalitions and started bargaining with political parties, keeping their own benefit in mind, Chandra points out.

It was the last time in 1967 that elections to the Lok Sabha and all assemblies in the country took place simultaneously. In those elections, the Congress was wiped out from six states. Even in Kerala, where during the lifetime of Pandit Jawaharlal Nehru itself Indira Gandhi had deemed the communist government to be unconstitutional and imposed president's rule, the Congress faced crushing defeat.

Ramachandra Guha has written in his book, *India After Nehru*, that the Congress's biggest loss was in Tamil Nadu, which was known as the Madras province at the time, considered to be a Congress bastion. Here, the Dravida Munnetra Kazhagam hammered the Congress by bagging 138 out of 234 Assembly seats. Such was the situation that the national president of the Congress and the former Madras chief minister K Kamaraj lost too. The Congress was beaten in West Bengal as well. The same thing happened in Odisha. Gujarat also slipped out of the Congress's hands.

In such an atmosphere, to calm disgruntled voices, Indira Gandhi appointed Morarji Desai as the deputy Prime Minister and also the finance minister, but it did little to alleviate the discontent in the party. The Congress's disappointing performance in the Lok Sabha and assembly elections gave rise to disagreements within the party.

The political situation of Uttar Pradesh was different. When politics focused on a non-Congress discourse started in the country, Chaudhary Charan Singh was also involved in it. Charan Singh was unhappy with his position in the Congress. He believed that the Congress had been taken over by the Brahmin-Bania-Thakur leadership. He had cold relations with chief minister Chandra

Bhanu Gupta over issues like age relaxation for OBC candidates for entry into the police department and a 50 per cent increase in the tax levied on the farmers. It was the era when, as a result of the Green Revolution, the backward and agricultural castes were getting economically stronger, and Lohia's slogan of 'Pichhra pave sau mein sath' (Backwards will get sixty out of hundred) gave wings to their high political ambitions. So in the end, Charan Singh decided to move away from the Congress and planned to capture the throne on the back of the political power of the backward sections and farmers.

In the fourth assembly elections held in 1967, the Congress somehow managed to struggle to win a majority, but after Chndra Bhanu Gupta became the chief minister on 14 March 1967, Charan Singh raked up some other issues and broke the party. Sixteen Congress MLAs followed Charan Singh and the Gupta government turned minority. This time around, Gupta had to relinquish his post after being the chief minister for just nineteen days. Charan Singh left the Congress on 1 April 1967 and after two days, on 3 April 1967, took oath as the chief minister of Uttar Pradesh in place of Gupta. Under his leadership, amazingly, the first non-Congress government was formed in Uttar Pradesh. The multi-party government of non-Congress parties is still known in the country as the SVD (Samyukta Vidhayak Dal) government. Among the parties involved were the Bharatiya Jana Sangh, socialists, praja socialists, communists, Ambedkarites and the Swatantra Party. However, because of high personal ambitions and ideological contradictions, this government could not run for even a year. Charan Singh could stay as the chief minister of the state only till 17 February 1968, and after that president's rule was imposed in Uttar Pradesh.

In the political history of Uttar Pradesh, it was the first Assembly that could not complete its term. In the fifth Assembly election in 1969, out of the total 425 seats, the Congress won 211, while the Jana Sangh got 49, communist parties got 5, the Samyukta Socialist

Party got 33 and Charan Singh's Bharatiya Kranti Dal got 98 seats. Once again, the Congress failed to get a full majority on its own. With some patchwork, Chandra Bhanu Gupta of the Congress once again became the chief minister but his government could not survive long. The moment he sensed an opportunity, Charan Singh turned the tables and became the chief minister again on 18 February 1970. However, in that period of ups and downs, he managed to stay in the post for a very short time and his government collapsed in eight months.

The political instability that had started in Uttar Pradesh during the previous election continued unabated. This assembly created a record in terms of the number of chief ministers. President's rule was imposed again on 2 October 1970. The Congress somehow formed the government once more and on 18 October 1970, Tribhuvan Narain Singh took oath as the chief minister. But in just five months, he was replaced by Kamalapati Tripathi. Pandit Kamalapati Tripathi became the chief minister on 4 April 1971 but had to leave his post after two years and two months. On 12 June 1973, president's rule was imposed in the state again. It was lifted only after Hemwati Nandan Bahuguna became the chief minister on 8 November 1973. Within just one assembly term, Uttar Pradesh saw five chief ministers and faced president's rule twice.

If we look at the political atmosphere of Amethi during this period, in the assembly elections of 1969, out of the five seats, the Congress and Samyukta Socialist Party got one seat each, while three seats went to the Bharatiya Jana Sangh. That year, there were 1,03,468 voters in Tiloi, of whom 52,284, that is, 50.53 per cent participated. Mohan Singh of the Bharatiya Jana Sangh defeated the Congress's W Naqvi by getting 39.8 per cent of the total votes, which is 19,960 votes. Naqvi got 17,698 votes, which is 35.29 per cent of the votes. Ram Bahadur of the Samyukta Socialist Party also managed to get 12.83 per cent or 6,433 votes.

Salon had 1,05,380 voters, of whom 52.07 per cent, that is 54,876 participated. Here, Sheo Prasad Pandia of the Samyukta Socialist Party defeated the Congress's Dal Bahadur Singh by getting 26,164, that is 49.36 per cent votes. Dal Bahadur Singh got 33.77 per cent or 17,902 votes. At number three was Manbodh, a candidate of the Charan Singh-led Bharatiya Kranti Dal. He too secured 11.78 per cent or 6,244 votes.

In Jagdishpur, there were 1,06,611 voters, of whom only 29.16 per cent, that is 31,086 participated. In this election, Ram Sevak of the Bharatiya Jana Sangh secured 46.38 per cent of the total votes. He got 13,812 votes, while Inder Pal of the Congress finished second with 32.82 per cent, which is 9,774 votes. The Communist Party's Ram Nath, stood third and got 3,107 votes, but it was 10.43 per cent of the total votes cast as well.

Talking about Gauriganj, 45,549 or 38.39 per cent of the 1,18,651 voters took part in the election process. Congress candidate Rajpati Devi defeated Ravindra Pratap Singh of the Bharatiya Jana Sangh by getting 19,024 votes, which is 44.06 per cent of the total votes cast. Singh was second with 33.02 per cent, which is 14,256 votes. Indian Revolutionary Party candidate Anand Prakash got only 6.67 per cent, which is 2,881 votes.

In the Amethi Assembly constituency, only 49,536 out of the 1,06,982 voters cast their votes. The polling percentage here was 46.30 per cent. The victorious candidate here was Raja Rananjaya Singh of the Bharatiya Jana Sangh. He defeated Baij Nath Singh Vaidya of the Congress by getting 47.16 per cent, or 22,372 votes. Vaidya got 17,689 votes. His vote percentage was 37.29 per cent. Surya Narayan Singh of the Bhartiya Kranti Dal, who stood third, got 6,555, which is 13.82 per cent votes.

Surprisingly, the opposition parties could not hold on to their success against the Congress in the assembly elections till the 1971

Lok Sabha polls. The fifth Lok Sabha elections of independent India, it was also the first mid-term elections in the country. The chaos within the Congress had become clear even before this. In 1969, so many incidents happened in the country, especially in political circles, that they need to be mentioned here. Indira Gandhi, the 'Goongi Gudiya' (dumb doll) of before, had emerged in a different incarnation. She had built a distinct identity and a class of supporters for herself. These supporters had transformed from colleagues equal in status in the Nehru era to subordinate supporters. Such was the situation that Indira Gandhi did not include the prominent leader of the Congress from Andhra Pradesh Neelam Sanjiva Reddy in her council of ministers, even after he was elected from Hindupur in the 1967 Lok Sabha polls and despite that fact that he had handled the ministry of steel and mines in Lal Bahadur Shastri's cabinet. After Shastri's death, when Indira Gandhi became the Prime Minister, Reddy had served as in-charge of the ministries of transport, shipping, civil aviation and tourism. He was the Congress president as well between 1960 and 1962. Indira Gandhi played another tactic to clip Reddy's political wings and made him the speaker of the Lok Sabha. But it did not work.

Senior Congress leaders, who by that time had come to be seen as part of syndicate, opened a front against Indira Gandhi. When the election for the post of president of India was held, K Kamaraj and the rest of the leaders of the syndicate decided to make Reddy a candidate. On 19 July 1969, Reddy resigned from the post of Lok Sabha speaker and became the official Congress candidate for the presidential election. Indira Gandhi did not like this. Affronted by this behaviour of the senior Congress leaders, Indira Gandhi went to Vice President VV Giri and convinced him to fight the presidential election. The seventy-five-year-old Giri then publicly announced that even if the Congress did not make him their official candidate, he would contest the presidential poll as an independent candidate, and that is what happened.

To ensure Reddy's victory, the syndicate leaders then contacted the Bharatiya Jana Sangh, which by that time had come to be known as a right-wing party, and the Swatantra Party. Without directly opposing Reddy, Indira Gandhi approached all chief ministers and appealed in favour of Giri. These included chief ministers of states where her party was not in power. Indira Gandhi appealed to the Congress leaders to vote according to their 'conscience'. The election took place on 16 August and the counting of votes started on 20 August. Sometimes Giri would be ahead and sometimes Reddy. When no one got the majority after the first round, the second-choice votes were counted, in which the Indira-Gandhi-supported candidate Giri pipped the Congress's official candidate Reddy by a slim margin of 14,650 votes. As a result of Indira Gandhi's efforts, Giri received the support of the Communist Party, Akali Dal, independents and DMK. The senior Congress leaders saw this behaviour by Indira Gandhi as rebellion, and on 12 November 1969, she was expelled from the party even while she was the Prime Minister. However, Indira Gandhi had become more popular and powerful than the other senior Congress leaders. The people of her group expelled Morarji Desai from the Congress on charges of 'indiscipline', and the Congress split into two parts— Congress (O) and Congress (R).

Indira Gandhi could still hold on to power because of her political prowess and popularity among the public. Till December 1970, she ran a minority government with the support of the CPI(M). However, she did not want to continue with a minority government, so she dissolved the Lok Sabha fourteen months before elections were due and announced a mid-term election. She decided to fight this election in her name. Her confidence was quite high despite the split in the party because of many reasons. Immediately after becoming the Prime

Minister, she started to nationalise the banks. Not just that, she also put an end to the privy purse of the princes. Although the Supreme Court put a stay on these measures by the government, Indira Gandhi was difficult to dissuade. Historian Ramachandra Guha writes in *India After Gandhi* that Indira Gandhi stirred the memory of the nearly forgotten princely states in a way that the common people started to hold them responsible to an extent for the ills afflicting the country.

Indira Gandhi worked day and night while campaigning for this election. She travelled 58,000 km and addressed 300 rallies. When the Election Commission froze the Congress's election symbol of a pair of oxen, the Indira-Gandhi-led Congress (R) made a cow nursing a calf as its symbol. Her efforts bore fruit. The poor, landless and Muslims voted overwhelmingly for Indira's Congress. It is a fact that even without television coverage, in that era, nearly two crore people saw and heard her. This election was fought solely in the name of Indira Gandhi. Indira Gandhi gave the slogan of 'Garibi Hatao' (Eradicate poverty) during this election. Not only that, in all her rallies, she would not forget to mention, 'Woh kehte hain Indira hatao, main kehti hoon garibi hatao' (They say get rid of Indira, I say get rid of poverty).

In the 1971 elections, a total of 520 Lok Sabha seats went to polls, out of which the Congress won 352. In all, 54 parties tried their luck in these elections. The Congress formed the government for the fifth consecutive time. A total of 15.15 crore votes were cast and 55.3 per cent of the total voters exercised their franchise. The vote percentage of the victorious Congress was 43.68 per cent. The Amethi Lok Sabha constituency was also not exempt from Indira Gandhi's charisma. There were a total of 5,33,697 voters in Amethi, of whom 30.05 per cent, or 1,60,395 participated. Congress candidate Vidyadhar Bajpai got 62.13 per cent of the total votes polled. He defeated Gokul Prasad Pathak of the Bharatiya Jana Sangh by getting 96,312 votes. Pathak got 21,335, or 13.76 per cent votes, while the third-ranked Wast Nabvi was also able to get 19,051, or 12.29 per cent votes.

As discussed before, this was a time when the Lok Sabha and assembly elections started to take place separately. Meanwhile, on 4 March 1974, the sixth assembly was formed in Uttar Pradesh. But even after this election, the political instability in the state could not be done away with. Despite best efforts, the Bharatiya Kranti Dal and socialist parties could not put up a joint alternative against the Congress. In the assembly elections of 1974 as well, the Congress, with 215 seats, was able to maintain its status as the single biggest party. President's rule and the use of new chief ministers continued but this assembly witnessed only two chief ministers—Hemwati Nandan Bahuguna and Narayan Datt Tiwari.

The result of the split in the opposition could be seen in Amethi as well and in the assembly elections of 1974, the Congress was able to capture four out of five seats in this parliamentary constituency. The remaining seat went to the Bharatiya Kranti Dal. Tiloi had a total of 1,26,276 voters in 1974, of whom 66,540, or a total of 52.69 per cent participated. Mohan Singh of the Congress won the election with 44.54 per cent of the total votes polled. He got 28,463 votes in this election, while his nearest rival, Ram Gopal Tripathi of the Bharatiya Jana Sangh, got 14,904 votes or 23.32 per cent of the total votes polled. W Naqvi of the NCO finished third with 17.67 per cent or 11,296 votes.

The Scheduled Caste seat of Salon had a total of 1,19,425 voters till this election, of whom only 45,039 exercised their franchise. The polling percentage in this election was 37.71 per cent. Dina Nath of the Bharatiya Kranti Dal secured 16,832, or 38.79 per cent votes, which helped him defeat Ram Pher of the Congress. The Congress candidate got 14,192 votes or 32.70 per cent of the total votes. Independent candidate Sheo Balak got 4,376 votes, or 10.08 per cent of the total votes and ended up third. In Jagdishpur, which was also a seat reserved for Scheduled Castes, Ram Sevak Dhobi of the Congress defeated Ram Ther of the Bharatiya Jana Sangh by securing 13,679, or 37.16 per cent votes. The BJS candidate got 10,809, or 29.36 per cent votes. Independent contestant Ram Nath also managed to get 20.13 per cent or 7,412 votes. In the election, there were 1,09,234 voters in Jagdishpur, but out of them, only 38,339, or 35.10 per cent participated in the voting.

Gauriganj had 1,20,143 voters in the 1974 Assembly election, of whom 52,493 cast their votes. The polling percentage here was 43.69 per cent. Congress candidate Rajpati Devi was successful in defeating Jamuna Prasad Shukla of the Bharatiya Jana Sangh by securing 22,785, or 45.49 per cent votes. The BJS candidate got 11,058, or 22.08 per cent votes, while Ram Naresh Singh of the NCO, who finished third, could get 4,223, or 8.43 per cent votes.

Similarly, if we look at the Amethi Assembly constituency, 54,929 out of 1,16,827 voters took part. The polling percentage was 47.02 per cent. Congress's Raja Rananjaya Singh won by bagging 20,464 votes, or 39.18 per cent of the total votes cast. Ravindra Pratap Singh of the Bharatiya Jana Sangh, who was second, managed to get 16,882, or 32.32 per cent votes. Har Charan Yadav of the Bharatiya Kranti Dal was third with 7,946, or 15.21 per cent votes.

Defeat in the Lok Sabha elections earlier and subsequently in the assembly elections in the state directly affected the opposition's politics in Uttar Pradesh. The regional satraps took stock of their position and in the urge to put up a strong resistance to the Congress, formed a new party as a strong alternative. This new party included Raj Narain's Samyukta Socialist Party and Chaudhary Charan Singh's Bharatiya Kranti Dal. It is through their merger that the Bharatiya Lok Dal came into being.

Senior fellow of the Vivekananda International Foundation RNP Singh has drawn a detailed picture of that period in an article titled 'Dawn of the Coalition Era in Indian Politics', which, considering the diversity of the Indian society and complexity of problems, has given rise to many parties at the national, regional and local levels. He writes, 'The period from 1967 to 1977 witnessed the passage from one-party dominance to multi-party politics. Several states had moved towards a two-party system, though it varies from state to state. Two factors have contributed to the multiplication of parties: One has been the growing power of regionalism and regional parties; and the other, intensified pursuit of political power rather than disagreement over principle. When the Emergency was lifted and Indira Gandhi announced the general elections in 1977, all the opposition parties came together against Mrs Gandhi to form Janta Party.

The atrocities during Emergency became the core election issue. The Indira Gandhi government had abolished civil liberties from 25 June 1975 to 21 March 1977, and extensive powers of the government were concentrated in the hands of the Prime Minister. Consequently, the public uproar against Indira Gandhi's dictatorship ensured that the Congress was wiped out from both the Centre and Uttar Pradesh. Under the banner of Jai Prakash Narayan's non-political campaign of 'Sampoorna Kranti', the Janata Party notched up record victories in 85 seats of Uttar Pradesh and 54 seats of Bihar. In 1977, Ravindra Pratap Singh—a resident of Amethi—defeated Sanjay Gandhi. Meanwhile, Raj Narain vanquished Indira Gandhi in Raebareli and recorded a historic win, which has already been mentioned in this book. While the Janata Party coalition won 345 seats in the Lok Sabha with 51.89 per cent votes, the Congress alliance got only 40.98 per cent votes and could win 189 seats".

As for Uttar Pradesh, elections to the state assembly were held on 23 June 1977. This was the seventh assembly elections in the state, in which the Janata Party captured 352 out of 425 seats, while the Congress ended with 47 seats. For the sake of a strong alternative, Raj Narain's Samyukta Socialist Party and Chaudhary Charan Singh's Bharatiya Kranti Dal had merged to form the Bharatiya Lok Dal in 1974. Later, when the entire opposition joined hands in the wake of the Emergency imposed by Indira Gandhi, the Bharatiya Lok Dal became a part of the Janata Party. For this reason, the credit for the win in Uttar Pradesh has been given to the alliance of backward castes apart from opposition unity, and for the first time, a person from a backward caste, Ram Naresh Yadav, occupied the highest position in a state in the form of the chief minister.

For the Amethi parliamentary constituency, this election was historic. It has been mentioned earlier that this was the time the powerful family of national politics arrived in the extremely backward Khairahana village through shramdaan. There were a total of 6,30,123 voters in this Lok Sabha constituency during the elections, of whom 2,94,363 exercised their franchise. The voting percentage here was 46.72 per cent. Ravindra Pratap Singh, who contested on a Janata Party ticket, won by getting 1,76,410 votes or 60.47 per cent of the total votes, while Sanjay Gandhi of the Congress got 1,00,566, or 34.47 per cent votes. The third place was insignificant in this election. Independent candidate Abdul Wahid got only 8,450 votes or only 2.9 per cent of the total votes polled.

The results of the assembly elections was also similar. The Congress, however, was not finished. In 1977, out of the five seats in Amethi, the Congress got one and the Janata Party got four. There were 1,32,241 voters in Tiloi, of whom 53,464 cast their votes. The voting percentage here was 40.43 per cent. Mohan Singh was the Congress candidate in this election. He got 30.74 per cent, or 15,988 votes. Surprisingly, the second place was won by independent contestant Ram Gopal Tripathi. He was able to get 13,688 votes and had a vote share of 26.32 per cent, while Janata Party candidate Assad Husain finished third with 12,956 votes. His vote percentage was 24.91 per cent. The Congress was able to win this seat due to a split in opposition votes.

Salon, a seat reserved for the scheduled castes, had a total of 1,24,612 voters, of whom only 34.17 per cent, or 42,579, participated. Here, Janata Party candidate Deena Nath Sevak won by securing 21,381 votes. Though he got 51.78 per cent of the total votes cast,

Sheo Balak of the Congress was not far behind. He also managed to get 48.22 per cent or 19,913 votes. This apathy of the voters was strange. The condition of the Jagdishpur scheduled caste seat was even worse. Only 21,615 of the 1,17,277 voters exercised their right. The voting percentage here was just 18.43 per cent. Rampher Kori of the Janata Party won by getting 11,396 votes, which was 53.76 per cent of the total votes cast, while the second-ranked Ram Sevak Dhobi of the Congress got 5,464 votes. His vote share was 25.78 per cent. Independent contestant Nand Lal was not far behind. He also managed to get 4,336, or 20.46 per cent votes.

Gauriganj had a total of 1,26,426 electorates in this election, of whom only 35,879 cast their votes. The voting percentage here was 28.38 per cent. Here too, the Janata Party was successful, with its candidate Tej Bhan Singh defeating Rajpati Devi of the Congress by getting 15,947, or 45.43 per cent votes. Rajpati Devi got 13,188 votes and her vote share was 37.57 per cent. Independent candidate Jagdamba Prasad Tripathi could get only 1,608 votes, but that was also 4.58 per cent of the total votes.

The Amethi Assembly constituency had a total of 1,23,421 voters in this election, of whom 42,354 exercised their franchise. The voting percentage here was 34.32 per cent. The Janata Party carried the day here too, with its candidate Haricharan Yadav securing 44.19 per cent of the total votes polled. He got 18,304 votes, while Congress candidate Baij Nath Singh Vaidya was second with 13,983 votes. His vote share was 33.76 per cent. Independent candidate Shiv Prasad, who finished third, received only 1,524, or 3.68 per cent votes.

However, the Indian political history records that the Janata-Party-led government at the Centre collapsed as a result of internal discord. While the Congress was swept away in the 1977 Lok Sabha elections, in the polls that took place after just three years, the Congress was able to regain its reputation to a large extent. This time, both the frontline national parties, the Congress and Janata Party were split into two parts each. The Congress fought under the banner of Congress (I) and Congress (U), the Janata Party fought under the banner of Janata Party, or JNP and Janata Party-Secular, or Janata Party (S).

It has been mentioned before that the Lok Sabha elections of 1980 marked Indira Gandhi's comeback. The Congress occupied 353 seats in the Lok Sabha. The Janata Party (Secular) won 41 seats, while CPI(M) bagged 36, CPI 11 and DMK 16 seats. The effect of the national trend could also be seen in the Amethi Lok Sabha constituency. With this election, the Congress, while staging a return to power, also wrested back this seat. Indira Gandhi's younger son Sanjay Gandhi won from this seat and became an MP. It was for the first time that a member of the Nehru-Gandhi family had won from this seat. The Amethi parliamentary constituency had a total of 6,75,683 voters during the 1980 Lok Sabha election. The voting percentage improved a bit that year. Here, 50.1 per cent or 3,38,531 people took part in the voting, of whom 57.11 per cent voted for Sanjay Gandhi. Ravindra Pratap Singh of the Janata Party could get only 58,445 votes as against 1,86,990 votes received by Sanjay Gandhi. His vote share was only 17.85 per cent. The condition of Mohd Isa of the Janata Party (Secular), who ended up at number three, was worse. He could get only 41,734, or 12.75 per cent votes.

At that time, the political situation of Uttar Pradesh was not very different either. In the wake of the mutual discord among the constituent parties, the first backward caste chief minister of the state, Ram Naresh Yadav could stay at his post for a mere one year and two hundred forty-nine days. Things came to such a pass that on 28 February 1979, he was removed and Banarasi Das was made the head of the Janata Party government, but internal conflicts did not end even then and ultimately the state's Janata government fell flat on its face. On 17 February 1980, president's rule was imposed in the state again. In this way, the seventh assembly could not complete its terms also and was dissolved after just 969 days. After the resignation of Banarasi Das, president's rule was enforced for 113 days. The eighth assembly was formed on 9 June 1980. In these elections, the Congress made an explosive comeback on the lines of that at the Centre. Out of the 425 seats, it triumphed in 309 seats, while the opposition was in tatters. Communist parties, including the CPI(M) and RPI, folded up for zero.

The Congress recorded victories in all five assembly seats falling under the Amethi parliamentary constituency. Tiloi had 1,37,315 voters during this election, of whom 62,505 took part in the voting. The voting percentage here was 45.52 per cent. Haji Mohammed Wasim of the Congress got 44.13 per cent of those votes. He managed to defeat Bharatiya Janata Party candidate Ram Gopal Tripathi by securing 26,939 votes. Tripathi got 23,285, or 38.14 per cent votes. While Jwala Prasad of the Janata Party (Secular-Chaudhary Charan Singh) or the JNP(SC) got only 3.72 per cent or 2,273 votes.

In Salon, out of the 1,30,291 voters, 41,701 cast their votes. At 32.01 per cent, the polling percentage here was extremely poor. Sheo Balak of the Congress (I) won by getting 19,479 votes. This was 48.01 per cent of the total votes cast. Vishwanath Prasad of Congress(U) managed to get 16.44 per cent votes. His vote tally was 6,671, while that of Ram Narayan of the CPI, who came in third, was 3,829, or 9.44 per cent of the total votes polled.

The condition of Jagdishpur was even worse in terms of voter turnout. The voting percentage here was just 18.56 per cent. Jagdishpur had 1,28,559 voters in this election, of whom only 23,857 cast their votes. Ram Sevak of the Congress managed to win even after getting just 14,211 votes. Nand Lal of the Janata Party (Secular-Raj Narain), or the JNP(SR), got 4,509 votes, which was 19.26 per cent of the total votes cast, while the BJP's Ram Pher got 2,444, or 10.44 per cent votes.

The Gauriganj constituency had a total of 1,39,474 voters during this Assembly election, of which 47,936 cast their votes. The voting percentage here was 34.37 per cent. Rajpati Devi of the Congress(I) won by getting 24,655 votes. She received 52.56 per cent votes. Tejbhan Singh of the BJP was in the second position. He managed to get 13,245 votes, and his vote share was 28.24 per cent. The JNP-SC's Harihar Prasad Shukla finished third with just 2,084 votes. He could get only 4.44 per cent of the votes.

Interestingly, while Amethi chose Sanjay Gandhi in the parliamentary elections in 1980, the assembly seat went to the local royal family. The Amethi assembly constituency had a total of 1,43,617 voters, of whom 72,082 voted. The polling percentage here was 50.19 per cent, which was much better than the other four assembly seats falling under the Amethi parliamentary constituency. Congress candidate Sanjay Singh won the elections. He managed to get 65.88 per cent of the total votes polled. He secured 46,603 votes and easily defeated Haricharan of JNP-SC. Haricharan received only 13,959 votes, which was just 19.73 per cent of the total votes polled. The third place went to Jamuna Prasad of the BJP. He got 4,162, or 5.88 per cent votes.

It is worth noting that while the scattering of opposition votes benefited the Congress in every seat in this election, the BJP, which was established only a few days ago, on 6 April 1980, left a deep impression during assembly polls in Amethi.

This process would have got stronger, but on 23 June 1980, local MP Sanjay Gandhi died in a plane crash in New Delhi. After a lot of thought, the Congress decided to field Indira Gandhi's elder son Rajiv Gandhi from Amethi in the bypoll of 1981. It is a known fact that Rajiv Gandhi was unwilling to join politics, but pressure from his mother and the youth quartet associated with Sanjay Gandhi ultimately convinced him to contest the elections. Rajiv Gandhi won from Amethi and reached Parliament for the first time, and became permanent there. In 1981, Sharad Yadav of the Lok Dal had challenged Rajiv Gandhi. The people of Amethi doted on Rajiv Gandhi and voted for him in huge numbers. Rajiv Gandhi got 84.18 per cent of the total votes cast. He managed to get 2,58,884 votes, while his opponent Sharad Yadav got only 6.89 per cent or 21,188 votes. It can be said about Rajiv Gandhi that he did not forget this affection bestowed on him by the people of Amethi throughout his life, even when he was in trouble. He became an MP for the first time in 1981 from Amethi and went on to represent the constituency in the Lok Sabha till he breathed his last on 21 May 1991.

The year 1984 was very turbulent for the country. On 31 October 1984, Prime Minister Indira Gandhi was assassinated by members of her own security force at her house. After that, the Congress leaders handed over the reins of the country to Rajiv Gandhi. He was quite inexperienced at that time. He had not yet settled into his parliamentary role when the responsibility of running the country as the Prime Minister was thrust upon him. He was the youngest Prime Minister the country has had. Rajiv Gandhi announced mid-term polls for December 1984, In the eighth Lok Sabha elections, the Congress notched up a momentous victory. Under Rajiv Gandhi, it benefited from the sympathy for Indira Gandhi to such an unimaginable extent. Political pundits held that a deceased Indira Gandhi turned out to be more powerful than a living Indira Gandhi. The Congress bagged 415 seats in this election and, in a way, wiped out the entire opposition. The Telugu Desam Party finished second with 28 seats. The CPI(M) got 22, CPI six, Janata Party 10 seats and BJP could win only two seats.

Rajiv Gandhi fought from Amethi again and bagged a famous win. This election was also significant because the opposition surrendered to Rajiv Gandhi without a fight. But Rajiv Gandhi's path was not secure. He had to face one of his own family members: Maneka Gandhi, the widow of his younger brother Sanjay Gandhi, who had parted ways in the wake of a family dispute with mother-in-law Indira Gandhi, and laid claim to Amethi's legacy on behalf of her husband. Maneka Gandhi took the field as an independent candidate from Amethi. But she could not pose even a semblance of a challenge to the young Prime Minister Rajiv Gandhi, who was riding the wave of sympathy.

The Amethi Lok Sabha constituency had a total of 7,40,782 voters in 1984, of whom 4,46,289 took part. Amethi had a polling percentage of 60.25 per cent in this election. Rajiv Gandhi secured 83.67 per cent of the total votes, bagging 3,65,041 votes, while Maneka Gandhi could get only 11.50 per cent votes. Her vote tally was 50,163. At number three was another independent candidate Atam Prakash. His vote share was 0.68 per cent and the total number of votes that he got was 2,975.

The eighth assembly of Uttar Pradesh completed its tenure. It ran for 1,735 days from 9 June 1980 to 10 March 1985, but during this phase, the Congress's internal factionalism was at its peak. The state witnessed three chief ministers. Vishwanath Pratap Singh was the chief minister for two years and thirty-nine days, from 9 June 1980 to 18 July 1982, while Sripati Mishra was at the helm for two years and fourteen days, from 19 July 1982 to 2 August 1984. Narayan Datt Tiwari was made the chief minister on 3 August 1984 and under him, the Congress fought the ninth assembly elections. This assembly came into being on 10 March 1985. The Congress, with 269 seats, got a clear majority. The BJP could muster only 16 seats. After this victory, Congress continued with Tiwari as the chief minister, but the factionalism did not cease. He could remain the chief minister for one year and fifty-two days and had to relinquish his post on 24 September 1985.

In the eighth assembly elections in 1985, all the five seats in Amethi sided with the Congress once again. The reason was that MP Rajiv Gandhi was the local leader cum Prime Minister. By that time, he had come to be known as 'Mr Clean' among the youth. In 1985 assembly election, there were 1,55,173 voters in all in Tiloi, of whom 69,869 participated in the voting process. The Congress candidate Md Wasim won by getting 32,877 votes. His tally was 47.73 per cent of the total votes cast. Significantly, the second-ranked BJP candidate Ram Gopal Tripathi was also not far behind. In this straight fight, he managed to get 29,265, or 42.48 per cent votes. Independent candidate Piyare, managed only 1,890 votes. His vote share was 2.74 per cent.

Salon had 1,51,407 voters, of whom 57,330 participated. The voting percentage here was 37.86 per cent. The Congress candidate Sheo Balak won by getting 35,736, or 63.49 per cent votes. Ram Lal of the LKD, who finished second, got 13,841, or 24.59 per cent votes, while CPI's Ram Aasare finished third with 3,492, or 6.2 per cent votes.

Similarly, there were a total of 1,33,939 voters in the Jagdishpur seat, but only 40,173 voters cast their ballots. The voting percentage here was 29.99 per cent. Ram Sevak of the Congress got 32,565, or 81.92 per cent of votes. Second-ranked LKD candidate Nand Lal could get only 2,234 votes, only 5.62 per cent of the total votes cast, while Sheo Karan of the BJP finished third with only 1,453, or 3.66 per cent votes.

Rajpati Devi of the Congress won the Gauriganj seat by winning 26,808, or 48.89 per cent votes. There were a total of 1,56,834 voters in this constituency, of whom 55,545 participated. The voting percentage here was 35.42 per cent. Tejbhan Singh of the BJP finished second with as many as 23,556, or 42.96 per cent votes. In the third spot was Ramdular Maurya of the LKD, who got only 1,215, or 2.22 per cent votes.

In the Amethi constituency, Sanjay Singh of the Amethi royal family once again managed to win as a Congress candidate. Out of 1,60,788 voters in this constituency, 1,26,649 turned out to vote. At 78.77 per cent, the voting percentage here was the highest in the entire parliamentary constituency. Sanjay Singh got 1,24,017, or 98.29 per cent votes. The BJP's BC Mishra got only 1,665, that is 1.32 per cent votes, while independent candidate Jagat Pal, finished at number three, with only 178, or 0.14 per cent votes.

By the time the ninth Lok Sabha election was upon the country in 1989, it had passed through a period of terrible turmoil. The coterie that surrounded Rajiv Gandhi conflicted with the other leaders of the party. Vishwanath Pratap Singh, who was finance minister in the Congress government, started to corner the Congress on the issue of corruption. Not just that, VP Singh initiated probes into several allegations of tax fraud by corporate houses, and a great ruckus was created when he started raiding their establishments. Under duress, Prime Minister Rajiv Gandhi removed him from the finance ministry and placed him in charge of the defence ministry. There too, VP Singh did not stay silent. He opened a front against his own government, alleging kickbacks in the deal to purchase Bofors cannons for the Indian Army. This was a very uncomfortable situation for Rajiv Gandhi. When it became annoying for him, Rajiv Gandhi gave VP Singh marching orders. When VP Singh was expelled from the party, he left the Congress. This led to him losing his Lok Sabha membership. He took to the streets. It was alleged that Rajiv Gandhi and his associates were paid a brokerage of Rs 64 crore for the Bofors deal. The name of Amitabh Bachchan's brother Ajitabh Bachchan also came up in this case. In the wake of this controversy, Amitabh Bachchan withdrew from active politics. It was alleged that under Rajiv Gandhi's influence, the Swedish cannon maker Bofors was preferred over French cannons in this defence deal. A Swedish radio channel revealed this deal in 1987. VP Singh grabbed this issue.

Ramachandra Guha writes in *India After Gandhi* that the people snatched the crown of 'Mr Clean' from Rajiv Gandhi and handed it to VP Singh. According to Guha, in the eyes of the people, VP Singh was a victim of the pro-corruption lobby and emerged as a messiah fighting against it.

Now the Congress was under pressure from VP Singh on one hand and the BJP on the other. The BJP started attacking the Rajiv government's initiative against the Supreme Court verdict in the case of a woman named Shah Bano, calling it appeasement of the Muslims. To recover from this allegation, the Rajiv Gandhi government opened the doors of the Babri Masjid and delivered to the Hindus the right to worship the idol of Ram Lalla kept there. The BJP, under the leadership of Lal Krishna Advani, immediately lapped up this issue. Slogans like 'Ramlala hum aayenge, mandir wahin banayenge' (Ramlala, we will come and build the temple there) and 'Yeh toh sirf jhanki hain, Mathura, Kashi baaki hain' (This is just the trailer, Mathura, Kashi are still left) started echoing all across north India. Ashutosh Varshney writes in his book *Adhoori Jeet* that secularism for the country's first Prime Minister Jawaharlal Nehru meant 'equal distance from every religion', but in the eyes of Indira and Rajiv Gandhi, secularism involved 'establishing equal proximity to every religion'. It was a result of this policy that Rajiv Gandhi's government started to get cornered on various issues, one after the other. The Ram Mandir issue had started to heat up. The Vishwa Hindu Parishad announced the worship of the Ram Shila and the BJP supported it. The clash of secular nationalism and Hindu nationalism was a serious challenge to the administrative principles and intellectual structure of independent India. A riot broke out in Bihar's Bhagalpur in October 1989 and it stretched for a long time. Rajiv Gandhi was hemmed in by the rise of corruption and religious bigotry and had no keen sense of handling these issues. He neither had the aggression of Indira Gandhi nor her hold over the people. He was not a diplomat like his grandfather Pandit Nehru either. As a result, when pressure increased, he took many wrong decisions. To curb news being published against him, he introduced a Defamation Bill looking to end press freedom. In reply, the media turned even more against him. Journalists, under the leadership of Ramnath Goenka of the *Indian Express*, joined hands in protest. Defeated, the government withdrew the bill.

But in the 1989 election, all these became big issues. The entire opposition was united against the Rajiv-Gandhi-led Congress. Rajiv Gandhi, albeit, acknowledged the existence of corruption in the system. He used to say that if the Centre sends one rupee to the states, only 15 paisa remains by the time it reaches the people. The public appreciated what he said, but he could not find an antidote for the toxic atmosphere that was engulfing him. VP Singh was going across the country, opposing the Congress. During that time, there was a slogan for him, 'Raja nahi fakir hain, Bharat ki takdeer hain' (He is not a king, but a saint, he is India's destiny). Not only that, anti-Congress parties like DMK in Tamil Nadu, NT Rama Rao's Telugu Desam in Andhra Pradesh, CPM in West Bengal and the Akali Dal in Punjab were also quite strong.

VP Singh started to tour the country after the election dates were announced. In every rally, he would bring out a piece of paper from his pocket and claim that it contained the names of those who had accepted brokerages in the Bofors deal. They had put the money into Swiss accounts that were codenamed 'Lotus', 'Tulip' and 'Mont Blanc', and he said the moment he came to power he would disclose the entire episode. Not only that, VP Singh, along with Vidya Charan Shukla, Ramdhan, Satpal Malik and other disgruntled Congressmen, formed a separate front on 2 October 1987. Later the BJP also joined this front. The Left parties also announced their support for this front. In this way, a seven-party front was set up on 6 August 1988, and on 11 October 1988, the National Front formally came into being. Consequently, the result of the 1989 Lok Sabha elections was totally different. The Congress could not secure a majority and had to sit on the opposition benches. VP Singh's National Front bagged 146 seats. The BJP had 86 MPs and the Left had 52. In this manner, the National Front received the support of 248 members. Since this election was fought under VP Singh's leadership, he positioned himself as the natural candidate for prime ministership. He claimed that it was because of him that Rajiv Gandhi and the Congress could be defeated. However, Devi Lal and Chandrasekhar too were in the race to become Prime Minister.

After several meetings, VP Singh became the Prime Minister and Chaudhary Devi Lal the deputy Prime Minister, but this government could not last for long either.

The anti-Rajiv Gandhi wave across the country did not have much effect in Amethi, though the constituency saw three stalwarts sparring that year. The Amethi parliamentary constituency had a total of 9,10,177 voters during the 1989 Lok Sabha election, of whom 4,25,746 took part. The polling percentage here was 46.78 per cent. Congress candidate Rajiv Gandhi, who was also the Prime Minister of India, got a total of 2,71,407 votes, which was 67.43 per cent of the total votes cast. Janata Dal candidate Rajmohan Gandhi finished as runner-up. Rajmohan Gandhi, the grandson of Mahatma Gandhi, could get only 69,269 votes despite all the efforts and slogans of 'real' versus 'fake' Gandhi. He received just 17.21 per cent of the votes. Kanshi Ram of the Bahujan Samaj Party, who wrote a new story of Dalit politics in the country and Uttar Pradesh, ended up third. He got only 25,400, or 6.31 per cent votes.

As has been mentioned earlier, the politics of Uttar Pradesh continued to be full of ups and downs. Although the ninth assembly completed its term of 1,725 days and was dissolved on 29 November 1989, during this time it also saw a struggle for dominance between Brahmin and Rajput satraps. Narayan Datt Tiwari, despite taking oath twice, could stay chief minister for only one year and fifty-two days. He was replaced by Vir Bahadur Singh, but the latter too remained chief minister for only two years and two hundred and seventy-four days from 24 September 1985 to 24 June 1988. During his reign, riots broke out in more than half of the districts of the state. The riot in Meerut was so violent that 181 people were killed. The Ayodhya dispute also moved to its height during this time. Sixteen lakh government employees went on strike, and so did twenty-nine private organisations, including cinema halls. There was a drought in the state and the farmers were distressed, peasant leader Mahendra Singh Tikait even threatened to take up arms. As a result, Vir Bahadur Singh was replaced once more by Narayan Datt Tiwari. On 25 June 1988, Tiwari took command of Uttar Pradesh for the third time, and under his leadership, the Congress fought the 10th assembly elections, in which the Congress was shown the door and has not been able to return even to this day.

In the 10th assembly elections of Uttar Pradesh in 1989, the Congress could muster only 94 seats. Although its vote share was 27.9 per cent, it had contested in 410 seats, which was the highest. In comparison, the Janata Dal put up candidates on 356 seats and won 208 of them, and its share of votes was 29.71 per cent. The BJP contested in 275 seats and won 57 of them with a vote share of 11.67 per cent. In that changed political atmosphere, Mulayam Singh Yadav took up the post of the chief minister with the BJP's support. He became chief minister on 5 December 1989. The assembly seats in Amethi continued to stay by the Congress's side even amidst such an adverse wave.

There were 1,88,810 voters at the time of the 1989 Assembly election in Tiloi, of whom 96,027 cast their votes. The polling percentage in this election here was 50.86 per cent. Haji Mohammad Wasim of the Congress got 36,444, or 40.98 per cent votes. The second place went to BJP candidate Ram Gopal Tripathi, who got 27,366 votes, with a vote share of 30.77 per cent. In third place was Jahoor Ahmad of the BSP, who got 15,057, or 16.93 per cent votes.

Salon had 1,88,492 voters during this election, of whom 92,574 participated. The voting percentage here was 49.11 per cent. Congress candidate Sheo Balak defeated Janata Dal's Ramnath Amalkar by securing 42,423 i.e. 49.08 per cent votes. Amalkar got 26,083, or 30.18 per cent votes. Independent candidate Brij Mohan was at number three. He got only 4,945, that is 5.72 per cent.

In Jagdishpur, the Congress candidate walked away with a one-sided victory. During this election, this constituency had 1,69,091 voters, of whom 67,172 cast their votes. The polling percentage was 39.73 per cent. Congress candidate Ram Sevak got 49,956, or 78.13 per cent votes. Ram Kripal of Janata Dal, who finished second, got 6,399, or just 10.01 per cent votes. In the third place was BSP's Saroj Kumari, who was voted by only 6,154 people. Her vote share was 9.62 per cent.

In Gauriganj, there were 1,82,407 voters, of whom only 83,247 cast their ballots. The winning candidate here was the Congress's Rajpati Devi, who got 39,716 votes, or in other words, 52.57 per cent of the total votes polled. Tejbhan Singh of the BJP was in the second place and got 24,504, or 32.44 per cent votes. BSP's Ahmad, who finished third, received only 5,664 votes, with a vote share of 7.5 per cent.

There was a big somersault in the Amethi assembly constituency during this election. The heir of the local royal family, Sanjay Singh, left the Congress and joined VP Singh. There were 1,81,377 voters here during this election, of whom 86,308 took part in voting. The voting percentage was 47.58 per cent. Congress candidate Haricharan Yadav polled 53,197, or 65.14 per cent votes and defeated Janata Dal candidate Sanjay Singh badly. The latter could get only 20,949, or 25.65 per cent votes. Shri Ram of the BSP, who ended up third, was in a worse position. He got only 2,025, or 2.48 per cent votes.

The VP Singh government could not last for long. VP Singh, under political pressure from his colleagues, made several false steps. The morale of terrorists in Kashmir rose markedly during his tenure. He also played the Mandal Commission gamble in the name of providing reservation to the backward classes. But this broke apart the society. Political experts feel that it was VP Singh's brahmastra to tackle the increasing influence of the BJP. However, this decision by him was opposed all over the country. Especially by the youth, who engaged in demonstrations, arson and even suicides. The political turmoil was affecting everyone, and eventually, Chandrasekhar became the Prime Minister with Congress support. But the Congress did not want to see a stable government formed by the opposition. One day, it withdrew support on a very small pretext. After going through one more phase of instability, the country moved towards another election, for the 10th Lok Sabha, which happened in May-June 1991. The first phase of voting was over. The campaign was on. On 21 May 1991, Rajiv Gandhi had gone to Tamil Nadu, where he was brutally murdered in a bomb blast at an election rally in Sriperumbudur. This was a major setback for the Congress and the Nehru-Gandhi family. Sonia Gandhi was alone. Her two children, Rahul and Priyanka Gandhi, were quite young. In the final phases of polling, the Congress again benefited from public sympathy and it returned to power. Although it did not get a clear majority, it had many more MPs than the other parties. The Congress got 232 seats in his election. The BJP got 119, Janata Dal 59, CPM 35, CPI 13 and TDP 13 seats. Senior Congress leader PV Narasimha Rao became the Prime Minister.

In the Amethi Lok Sabha constituency, Rajiv Gandhi was victorious as the Congress candidate. Although the voters in the Amethi Lok Sabha constituency at that time were 9,18,257, only 3,76,202 people participated in the voting process. The voting percentage here was 40.97 per cent. When the result was declared,

Rajiv Gandhi was the winner. However, he was not alive to hear the result. He received 1,87,138 votes or 53.23 per cent of the total votes polled. In second place was Ravindra Pratap of the BJP, who got 75,053, or 21.35 per cent votes. Naeem of the Janata Dal got 54,680, or 15.55 per cent votes. But due to the assassination of Rajiv Gandhi, a by-election had to be held, and Captain Satish Sharma, a close associate of the Gandhi family, contested the election. Captain Sharma took care of Rajiv Gandhi's legacy.

The 10th assembly of Uttar Pradesh could not complete its term and after running for just 488 days, was dissolved on 4 April 1991. Mulayam Singh Yadav, who was governing with the support of the BJP, was chief minister for only one year and two hundred and one days till 24 June 1991. Election to the 11th assembly took place and the BJP formed the government with 221 seats. The Janata Dal got 92 seats, the Congress recorded 46 seats and Janata Party bagged 34 seats. Kalyan Singh was the first BJP leader to occupy the chief minister's chair. However, the instability in the state was far from over.

Despite this change, there was not a lot of difference in the results of the assembly seats in Amethi, but the BJP was able to make a considerable foray. It fought tooth and nail with the Congress on every seat, though in comparison to four candidates of the Congress, only one BJP candidate won.

In the assembly elections of 1991, Tiloi had 1,90,082 voters, of whom 87,730 participated. The voting percentage here was 46.15 per cent. Congress candidate Haji Mohammed Wasim got 28,598, or 34.84 per cent votes. However, the second-ranked BJP's Ram Gopal Tripathi was not far behind. He got 26,781 votes or 32.62 per cent. Zahoor Ahmad of the Janata Dal got 18,179, or 22.14 per cent votes.

Salon had 1,88,585 voters during this election, of whom 82,380 participated. The voting percentage here was 43.68 per cent. Congress candidate Shiv Bala Pasi won after getting 30,004, or 39.49 per cent votes. Here too, the BJP was the runner-up with its candidate Dal Bahadur getting 19,571 votes or 25.76 per cent of the total votes cast. Dina Nath Sevak of the Janata Party finished third with 13,019, or 17.14 per cent votes.

The Jagdishpur seat had 1,69,732 electorates during this election, of whom 60,395 cast their votes. The voting percentage here was 35.58 per cent. Ram Sevak of the Congress won by securing 35.83 per cent votes. He received 19,874 votes. Here too, the BJP was in the second place. Its candidate Jagroop Deshbandhu secured 17,751 votes with a vote share of 32 per cent. Gaya Prasad of Janata Dal finished third after getting 6,956, or 12.54 per cent votes.

The number of voters in Gauriganj was 1,84,782, of whom 76,927 voted. The voting percentage here was 41.63 per cent. Here, BJP candidate Tejbhan Singh defeated Rajpati Devi of the Congress in a close contest. Tejbhan Singh polled 24,606 votes, which was 34.45 per cent of the total votes cast, while Rajpati Devi got 24,417, or 34.18 per cent votes. Shiv Prasad of the Janata Party ended up third with 6,617, or 9.26 per cent votes.

Similarly, the Amethi assembly constituency had 1,85,076 voters during this election, of whom 72,746 participated. The voting percentage here was 39.31 per cent. Hari Charan Yadav of the Congress was the winner with 33,176 votes, which was 48.68 per cent of the total votes cast. The BJP's Jamuna Prasad Mishra got 17,597, or 25.82 per cent votes, while Jaya Bahadur Singh of the Janata Dal finished third with 6,065 votes. His vote share was 8.9 per cent.

In the bypoll that happened after Rajiv Gandhi's assassination, Captain Satish Sharma won from Amethi as the Congress candidate. He received 1,78,996 votes. His nearest rival was BJP candidate MM Singh polled 79,687 votes. Satish Sharma was given a ticket to the next elections as well. He not only became a two-time MP but also the union petroleum minister.

These results make it clear that it was a time when the BJP was briskly moving ahead with its Hindutva agenda. The party never hid this either. It even lost its government after the demolition of the Babri Masjid in the wake of the Ayodhya conflict. The 11th assembly of Uttar Pradesh could continue for only 533 days from 22 June 1991 to 6 December 1992, and after the Babri Masjid was pulled down, Kalyan Singh had to relinquish his post as chief minister after one year and one hundred and sixty-five days. Again president's rule was imposed in the state, which ended only after Mulayam Singh Yadav became the chief minister on 4 December 1993. The 12th assembly elections of Uttar Pradesh in 1993 produced several startling results. Such was the effect of the Mandal versus Kamandal conflict at the Centre on this state that instead of the national parties, the reins of power and politics passed into the hands of regional parties. The leadership of Kanshi Ram, Mayawati and Mulayam Singh Yadav emerged during this election. Although a national party, BJP was not close to power. It got 177 seats, while among the other national parties, the Congress and Janata Dal got 28 and 27 respectively. In comparison, the Bahujan Samaj Party, which was listed as a regional party, won 67 seats, while the Samajwadi Party, which was unrecognised despite being registered, bagged 109 seats under the leadership of Mulayam Singh Yadav. With the support of BSP, Yadav became the chief minister for the second time.

In this election, for the first time, the Congress was uprooted from all five assembly seats in Amethi. While the BJP won four seats, the Samajwadi Party got one.

There were 2,11,965 voters in Tiloi during the Assembly election of 1993, of whom 1,24,881 took part. The voting percentage here was 58.92 per cent. Mayankeshwar Sharan Singh of the BJP won by getting 55,911, or 45.88 per cent votes. Mohammad Muslim Siddiqui of the Samajwadi Party who stood against him polled 46,795, or 38.4 per cent votes, while Haji Mohammad Wasin of the Congress got

12,573 votes, or only 10.32 per cent of the total votes polled and had to settle for the third place.

Similarly, BJP's Dal Bahadur Kori secured the Salon seat with 37,402 votes. This was 38 per cent of the total turnout. There were 2,05,374 voters in this constituency, of whom 1,01,660 participated. The voting percentage here was 49.5 per cent. In the second place was Bindeshwari Prasad of the Samajwadi Party with 29,860 votes. This was 30.33 per cent of the total votes polled. Sheo Balak Pasi of the Congress got 21,815 votes, thereby finishing third with 22.16 per cent of the total votes.

The Jagdishpur seat was the only seat from where the Samajwadi Party won. Its candidate Nand Lal got 37,511 votes. This was 45.58 per cent of the total votes cast. During this election, this constituency had a total of 1,90,117 voters, of whom 84,463 voted. The voting percentage here was 44.43 per cent. The BJP stood second with 37.86 per cent votes. Its candidate Daulat Ram polled a total of 31,161 votes. The Congress ended up third with 12.8 per cent of the total votes cast. Its candidate Ram Sevak received 10,537 votes.

The Gauriganj constituency, on the other hand, consisted of 2,04,594 voters, of whom 93,184 cast their ballots. The polling percentage was 45.55 per cent. The BJP candidate Tejbhan Singh beat the Samajwadi Party's Sheo Hari Vijay by polling 35,028, or 38.41 per cent votes. The Samajwadi Party candidate got 23,750, or 26.04 per cent votes, while the Congress's Rajpati Devi was third with 20,659, or 22.66 per cent votes.

The condition of the Amethi constituency was similar. Out of the 1,97,373 voters here, 95,661 cast their votes. The voting percentage here was 48.47 per cent. BJP candidate Jamuna Mishra won with 23,270, or 24.94 per cent votes. The second-placed Samajwadi Party candidate Radhe Shyam Yadav received 19,503 votes, which was only 20.9 per cent of the total votes cast. Surprisingly, the third-placed candidate here was the Independent Karmaraj Singh. He got 17,616, or 18.88 per cent votes. Congress candidate Hari Charan had to settle for the fourth place with 17,406, or 18.65 per cent votes.

However, Mulayam Singh Yadav and Mayawati could not get along for too long, and Mayawati withdrew support. Consequently, Yadav had to leave his post of chief minister after one year and one hundred and eighty-one days itself. Meanwhile, the BJP came forward and extended support to Mayawati, who became the chief minister. But her tenure could also last for just 137 days, from 3 June 1995 to 18 October 1995, and the state was again placed under president's rule. The result was that when the elections for the 11th Lok Sabha were being held in 1996, Uttar Pradesh had to hold polls for its 13th assembly.

The result of the 11th Lok Sabha was quite strange. It was a hung parliament in which no party mustered a clear majority. It was the first election in which the BJP emerged as the largest party of the country. It registered victories in 161 constituencies, while the Congress stopped at 140. The Janata Dal got 46, CPM 32, Samajwadi Party 17, TDP 16, CPI 12, and BSP 11 seats. It was a period of an odd kind of instability. On 16 May 1996, a BJP government was formed at the Centre under the leadership of Atal Bihari Vajpayee. However, having failed to assemble an adequate number of MPs for a majority in the Lok Sabha, Vajpayee resigned on 1 June 1996.

In the 1996 Lok Sabha elections too, Amethi stayed with the Congress. The Amethi Lok Sabha constituency had 11,02,927 voters in this election, of whom only 4,26,913 cast their votes. The polling percentage here was 38.71 per cent. Congress candidate Captain Satish Sharma bagged 1,57,868 votes, with 38.81 per cent of the voters siding with him. His nearest candidate Raja Mohan Singh of the BJP had to finish second with 1,17,725, or 28.94 per cent of the votes. BSP's Choudary Mohammad Isa was third with 79,285, or 19.49 per cent votes.

The result of the Uttar Pradesh assembly elections was not too different either. Among the national parties, only the BJP's results were respectable, but still, the party was quite far from the majority. It got 174 seats, while the Congress wound up for 33. The Janata Dal could get merely seven seats. On the other hand, the BSP—registered as a regional party—got 67 and Samajwadi Party got 110 seats. No government could immediately be formed in the state and president's rule continued.

The results of the five asembly seats in Amethi was not entirely different either. The BJP was ahead of the others, bagging three of the five seats. The Samajwadi Party and Congress picked up one seat each.

In the assembly elections of 1996, the total number of voters in Tiloi was 2,29,305, out of which 1,32,521 took part in the voting. The voting percentage here was 57.79 per cent, in which Samajwadi Party candidate Muslim won by getting 56,896, or 43.90 per cent votes. Mayankeshwar Sharan Singh of the BJP got 42,308 votes. His vote share was 32.65 per cent. Vinod Kumar of the Congress was third with 27,579, or 21.28 per cent votes.

The number of voters in the Salon constituency was 2,22,245, of whom 1,07,089 cast their votes. The voting percentage here was 48.19 per cent. BJP candidate Dal Bahadur Kori won by getting 39,423, or 37.72 per cent votes. Congress candidate Sheo Balak Pasi was second with 34,713 votes. The percentage of votes he received was 33.22 per cent. In the third place was the Janata Dal candidate Suresh Kumar Chaudhari. He got 25,129 votes with a vote share of 24.04 per cent.

The number of voters in the Jagdishpur constituency was 2,07,705, of whom 93,913 cast their ballots. The polling percentage here was 45.21 per cent. Here too, the BJP won with its candidate Ram Lakhan getting 33,757 votes. His vote percentage was 36.75 per cent. In the second place was Nandlal of Samajwadi Party. He got a total of 32,141, or 34.99 per cent votes. Babu Lal of Congress was third. He could get only 22,098 votes or 24.06 per cent.

There was a fierce fight in the Gauriganj constituency, in which the BJP won again. Its candidate Tej Bhan Singh defeated Noor Mohammad of the Congress by securing 35,706, or 32.39 per cent votes. However, the difference between the two was very less. The Congress candidate got 35,104, or 31.84 per cent votes. The number of electorates in the Gauriganj constituency was 2,17,986 in this election, of whom 1,12,501 exercised their franchise. The voting percentage here was 51.61 per cent. Samajwadi Party candidate Shivhari Vijay finished third with 27,428, or 24.88 per cent votes.

The number of voters in the Amethi constituency was 2,25,346, of whom 1,08,063 people took part. The voting percentage here was 47.95 per cent. Congress candidate Ram Harsh Singh won with 36,069 votes and a vote share of 34.01 per cent. The BJP's Jamuna Prasad Mishra got 31,870, or 30.05 per cent votes, while Samajwadi Party's Gayatri Prasad got 25,112, or 23.68 per cent votes.

Owing to these election results and in the absence of a clear majority for any party, the president's rule that was imposed in Uttar Pradesh on 18 October 1995 stretched for one year and one hundred and fifty-four days, or till 21 March 1997. The then governor Romesh Bhandari was a seasoned player in politics. He did not dissolve the assembly and recommended that president's rule be extended for another six months. This created a legal dispute. The Allahabad High Court stayed the decision, but the Supreme Court put a stay order on the high court's verdict.

During this time, political equations in the state continued to quickly form and deteriorate, and in the end, the BJP and BSP struck an agreement to run the government for six months each, and on 21 March 1997, the BSP's Mayawati became the chief minister and stayed in the post for 184 days, till 21 September 1997. On the same day, Kalyan Singh was again crowned as the chief minister. The moment he came to power, he started to overturn those decisions of the Mayawati government that he deemed to be anti-people. On the other hand, after tasting power, Mayawati's ambitions were going through the roof. The difference between the ruling parties came out in the open and the conflict grew so much that on 19 October 1997, within a month itself, Mayawati withdrew support from the Kalyan Singh government. Governor Bhandari, who was keeping a close eye on the proceedings gave no opportunity and asked Kalyan Singh to prove his majority on the floor of the Assembly within two days, by 21 October. However, for the BJP two days were enough. In these two days, several MLAs of the BSP, Congress and Janata Dal broke ranks and joined the BJP. As a result, there were scuffles between the MLAs in the assembly. Microphones were thrown, there were fisticuffs, shoes were hurled, but even amidst this pandemonium, Kalyan Singh proved his majority. He had the support of 222 MLAs in all.

On the pretext of this violence, Governor Bhandari once again sought to realise his desire to exert direct rule over the state and recommended president's rule. The Centre immediately sent this recommendation to President KR Narayanan. However, President KR Narayanan refused to accept this recommendation and sent it back for reconsideration by the Centre. The Centre did not wish to get involved in a dispute with President Narayanan, who had been an educationist and was a constitutional expert. To provide stability to the government, Kalyan Singh gave ministerial berths to all those who had defected from other parties. For the first time in the history of India, a council of ministers with 93 ministers took the oath.

In the meantime, the Centre saw two Prime Ministers of the United Front, which was a mismatch coalition. HD Deve Gowda was the Prime Minister from 1 June 1996 to 21 April 1997, and Inder Kumar Gujral from 21 April 1997 to 18 March 1998. Eventually, the country had to deal with another mid-term election. As has been mentioned earlier, political ups and downs at the Centre had a lot of impact on the politics of Uttar Pradesh. All the highly ambitious leaders of the state were consumed by a desire to become chief minister, by hook or crook. Soon 21 MLAs broke away from the Congress to form the Loktantrik Congress. These MLAs extended support to Kalyan Singh.

On 21 February 1998, Governor Bhandari sacked Kalyan Singh and administered the oath to Jagdambika Pal at 10.30 p.m. for the post of the chief minister. BJP leader and former Prime Minister Atal Bihari Vajpayee started a fast unto death against this decision. This decision by the governor was challenged in the high court that very night, and the high court stayed the order the next day and reinstated the Kalyan Singh government. Jagdambika Pal parted from the chief minister's chair with great difficulty. However, the high court's verdict was challenged at the Supreme Court. Later, on the direction of the apex court, there was a floor test again on 26 February, in which Kalyan Singh emerged as the winner.

There was a mid-term election to the 12th Lok Sabha in 1998. The age of a single party getting a majority at the Centre was over. When the results were declared, the BJP emerged as the single largest party with 182 seats. The Congress got 141 seats, CPM 32, Samajwadi Party 20, TDP 12, CPI 9 and BSP 5. Again, no one party had a clear majority. The 12th Lok Sabha was formed on 10 March 1998 and after nine days, the National Democratic Alliance government under the leadership of veteran BJP leader Atal Bihari Vajpayee was administered the oath.

In this election, the result of the Amethi Lok Sabha constituency changed too. The BJP fielded Sanjay Singh, the heir of the Amethi royal family, who had come from the Congress. Sanjay Singh won and Satish Sharma lost. This was the second occasion that the Congress lost from this seat after the entry of the Nehru-Gandhis. Amethi had 11,12,191 voters during the 12th Lok Sabha elections, of whom 5,97,556 participated. The voting percentage here was 53.73 per cent. BJP candidate Sanjay Singh won by getting 2,05,025 votes with a vote share of 35.08 per cent. Congress's Captain Satish Sharma got 1,81,755, or 31.1 per cent votes. In the third place was Mohammad Naim of the BSP. He got 1,51,096, or 25.85 per cent votes. Shiv Prasad of the Samajwadi Party could get only 29,888 votes. His vote percentage was 5.11 per cent.

However, the 12th Lok Sabha could run for only 413 days, and on 17 April 1999, the BJP-led government of Atal Bihari Vajpayee was evicted by only one vote. This was the fifth time the Lok Sabha had been dissolved before completing its term. After this thirteen-month Vajpayee-led government, the country was once inching towards a mid-term election. By the time the elections arrived, Sonia Gandhi was chosen as the Congress president. Following this, Sharad Pawar left the Congress on the question of Sonia Gandhi's foreign origin. The BJP not only effectively made Sonia Gandhi's Italian origin an electoral issue, but it also made the Vajpayee government's positive outlook during the Kargil War an issue. Furthermore, as a result of economic liberalisation and financial reforms under Vajpayee, India was able to reduce the rates of inflation and increase industrial growth. Perhaps the people had now understood the importance of coalition governments. Therefore, when the results were declared on 6 October, the BJP's seats may not have increased, but the Vajpayee-led NDA bagged 298 seats. The Congress and its partners won only 136 seats. Vajpayee took oath as the Prime Minister on 13 October.

Meanwhile, Sonia Gandhi contested from Amethi and notched up a largely one-sided victory. Amethi had 11,10,623 voters in the 1999 Lok Sabha election, of whom 6,38,178 exercised their franchise. The voting percentage was 57.46 per cent. Congress candidate Sonia Gandhi secured 67.12 per cent of the total votes cast, which translated into 4,18,960 votes. In comparison, Sanjay Singh could get only 1,18,948 votes with a vote share of 19.06 per cent. The BSP's Paras Nath Maurya finished third with 33,658 votes. He received 5.39 per cent of the votes polled.

Amidst all this, the 13th assembly of Uttar Pradesh completed its term despite witnessing four chief ministers. It was active for 1,967 days from 17 October 1996 to 7 March 2002. After Kalyan Singh, Ram Prakash Gupta ruled for 351 days, from 12 November 1999 to 28 October 2000. After him, Rajnath Singh became the chief minister, and stayed in this post for one year and one hundred and thirty-one days, from 28 October 2000 to 8 March 2002. When the 14th assembly was formed in the state on 26 February 2002, again no party got a majority. The state was again staring at a hung house. The BSP had gained recognition as a national party by this election. While the BSP won 98 seats, the BJP stopped at 88. The Congress got 25 seats, while the Samajwadi Party emerged the winner with 143 seats. No party could form the government immediately after this result. President's rule was in place for fifty-six days and after that Mayawati took oath as the chief minister on 3 May 2002 with the support of the BJP and Rashtriya Lok Dal. This was the third time that she was at the helm of the country's most populous state.

The results of the five Assembly seats in Amethi were similar. The BJP and Congress shared two seats each in this election and the Samajwadi Party won a seat too. Tiloi had 2,35,957 voters, of whom 1,35,709 took part. The voting percentage was 57.51 per cent. There was a tough fight between the Congress and the BJP here, in which the BJP's Mayankeshwar Sharan Singh defeated the Congress's Muslim by getting 33,579, or 24.74 per cent votes. The Congress candidate got 32,593, which was 24.02 per cent of the total votes polled. The BSP's Mohammad Naeem got 26,170, or 19.28 per cent votes.

In the Salon seat that was reserved for scheduled castes, the Samajwadi Party's Asha Kishor defeated the Congress's Sheo Balak Pasi by securing 36,536, or 28.29 per cent votes. The Congress candidate got 32,509, or 25.17 per cent votes. Out of 2,29,140 electorates in this constituency, 1,29,148 exercised their franchise.

The voting percentage here was 56.36 per cent. The BJP was in third place. Its candidate Dal Bahadur Kori got 23,897, or 18.50 per cent votes. The BSP finished fourth. Its candidate Jagjiwan Ram Vadle got 15,325, or 11.87 per cent votes.

In the Jagdishpur scheduled caste seat, there were 2,14,142 voters, of whom 1,10,945 cast their ballots. The voting percentage here was 51.81 per cent. Congress candidate Ram Sewak won with 3,66,40, or 33.04 per cent votes. Samajwadi Party's Nand Lal was the runner-up with 28,221, or 25.45 per cent votes. BJP candidate Ram Lakhan was third with 21,239, or 19.15 per cent votes.

The Gauriganj constituency had 2,29,276 voters during this election, of whom 1,31,863 took part. The voting percentage here was 57.51 per cent. Here also there was a fierce competition between the Congress and BJP. Congress candidate Noor Mohammad won by getting 29,944, or 22.71 per cent votes, while Tej Bhan Singh of the BJP got 29,677 votes, which was 22.51 per cent of the total votes polled. Jang Bahadur of the BSP was not far behind either. He got 29,527, or 22.4 per cent votes. Samajwadi Party candidate Priyank Hari Vijay got 28,143, or 21.35 per cent votes.

In the Amethi constituency, Amita Singh, the second daughter-in-law of the Amethi royal family, won on a BJP ticket. There were 2,37,053 voters during this election, of whom 1,32,510 cast their votes. The vote percentage here was 55.9 per cent. Amita Singh secured 55,949, or 42.23 per cent votes. The second place went to Ashish of the Congress, who got 37,184, or 28.06 per cent votes. Gayatri Prashad of the Samajwadi Party recorded 21,764, or 16.43 per cent votes, and BSP's Tej Pratap was reduced to 7,023 or 5.3 per cent votes.

Fearing president's rule, Mayawati's government was formed in the state all right, but it could not hold on to power for long. The dispute between the BJP and BSP increased over independent

MLA Raghuraj Pratap Singh alias Raj Bhaiya being charged under the Prevention of Terrorism Act (POTA) and the construction of the Taj Heritage Corridor. Eventually, Mayawati called a meeting of her cabinet on 26 August 2003 and submitted her resignation to the governor, and recommended the dissolution of the Assembly. But Governor Vishnu Kant Shastri did not accept her resignation. There were many reasons for this. The BJP had already submitted the letter of withdrawal of support from the Mayawati government to the governor. Not just that, the same day, Mulayam Singh Yadav had staked claim to form the government in the state. After considering all political permutations and combinations, Mulayam Singh Yadav was sworn in as the chief minister on 29 August 2003, and was given two weeks to prove his majority; which, through his practical skills, Mulayam Singh Yadav was able to demonstrate. The Rashtriya Lok Dal, Kalyan Singh's Rashtriya Kranti Party, independents and nineteen MLAs from smaller parties were part of this Mulayam government. Apart from this, the Congress and CPM also supported him from the outside. While reporting these interesting political developments in Uttar Pradesh, *Frontline* magazine pointed out that the BJP, which did not let Mulayam Singh from becoming the chief minister in February 2002, had now helped him form the government. Ajit Singh, who indulged in anti-Mulayam politics for fourteen years, now supported him; Kalyan Singh, who used to call Mulayam the 'Ravan' who had killed Ram sevaks, helped Mulayam attain majority; and Sonia Gandhi, whom Mulayam had prevented from becoming the Prime Minister in 1999, supported the Mulayam government, the report said.

After this incident, the BSP broke up. Its rebel MLAs first arranged for recognition as the Loktantrik Bahujan Dal and later merged with the Samajwadi Party. In spite of this, to strengthen his government, Mulayam had to form the largest council of ministers in the legislative history of Uttar Pradesh; even with the Congress and CPM supporting him from the outside.

Meanwhile, the political situation at the Centre had moved to a large extent into the BJP's grasp. At least that was the impression from the outside. Under Prime Minister Atal Bihari Vajpayee, the BJP-led NDA government created a spectacular atmosphere with the 'Shining India' and 'Feel Good Factor' slogans and advertisements. Owing to constant growth in the economy, disinvestment of public sector undertakings, and so on, India's foreign exchange reserves went over a $100 billion, which was the world's seventh-biggest pool. As a result, in 2004, Vajpayee, at the suggestion of his special advisers, especially Pramod Mahajan and Brajesh Mishra, recommended the dissolution of the Lok Sabha, a few months before the end of his five-year tenure. Elections to the 14th Lok Sabha took place in the country in four phases from 20 April to 10 May 2004.

While the BJP contested as a part of the NDA, it fought alongside parties like the Telugu Desam Party (TDP) in Andhra Pradesh and All India Anna Dravida Munnetra Kazhagam (AIADMK) in Tamil Nadu. Meanwhile, the Congress did not form any pre-poll alliance but did join hands with regional parties. Hence, the result was completely different. The voters were swayed by local issues instead of national ones. Farmer issues, health, water shortage, drought, and so on ensured that the NDA was shown the door. On 13 May, the BJP conceded defeat. While the Congress had emerged as the single largest party with 145 seats, the BJP was relegated to second place, with 138 seats. Regional parties won 159 seats.

Under the guidance of Sonia Gandhi, the Congress, with the help of its allies, staked claim to form the government. It had the support of 335 MPs out of 543. BSP, Samajwadi Party, MDMK and the Left Front supported it from outside. This post-poll coalition was called the United Progressive Alliance (UPA). Just as it seemed that Sonia

Gandhi would become the next Prime Minister, several incidents occurred to shake this belief. Sonia's Gandhi Italian ancestry was raked up again. BJP leader Sushma Swaraj said something that made the entire country think. She said, 'If I go and sit in Parliament, I would have to address Sonia Gandhi as Honourable Prime Minister at all costs, which is not acceptable to me. My national pride shakes me. I will not be a part of this national shame.' She also warned that if Sonia Gandhi became the Prime Minister, she would shave her head, wear a white saree, sleep on the floor and eat dried gram. None of this came to pass, of course, and Sonia Gandhi herself came forward and declared she would not take up the Prime Minister's post.

Many years later, in 2013, when Swaraj was the leader of opposition in the Lok Sabha, she shared the reason behind her strong reaction at the time, at a programme in Delhi. She clarified, 'I have always said that Sonia Gandhi came to our country as the daughter-in-law of Indira Gandhi and wife of Rajiv Gandhi, and so she is entitled to our love and affection. As the president of the Congress, she is entitled to our respect, but if she wants to become the Prime Minister, I would still say "no". The reason for this is that our country had been under foreign rule for over 150 years and many people sacrificed their lives for independence. If after 60 years of Independence, we place a foreigner at the topmost post, it would mean that 100 crore people are unworthy…this would hurt the sensitivity of the people. For this reason, I fought against Sonia Gandhi in Bellary in 1999. This was a mission for me. In Bellary, I lost the battle, but won the war.'

Whatever be the reason, Sonia Gandhi stepped back and proposed Dr Manmohan Singh as the Prime Minister, and in this way, on 22 May 2204, the UPA government was formed under Dr Manmohan Singh. Sonia Gandhi left the Amethi seat for her son Rahul Gandhi. The Samajwadi Party did not field a candidate here. As the Congress president, Sonia Gandhi chose the neighbouring seat of Raebareli for herself. Rakesh Pandey writes in his book, *Jananayak Rahul Gandhi*, 'Sonia and Priyanka Gandhi had already prepared the electoral ground in Amethi, in which Rahul Gandhi had to build his possibilities while earning the confidence of the people.'

In his book, Pandey describes how Sonia Gandhi kept politics at arm's length for a long time after Rajiv Gandhi's untimely death, and chose Amethi when she decided to end her silence. 'On 23 August 1995, when her convoy arrived in Amethi, the enthusiasm among the people and the reception they gave her was historic.' On 24 August, at the Ramlila Maidan of Amethi, Sonia Gandhi attacked the Narasimha Rao government of that time.'

The figures also confirm this. The voter strength of Amethi in the Lok Sabha elections of 2004 was 13,24,443, of whom 5,89,634 people participated. The number of valid votes was 5,89,596, of which 3,90,179 went to Rahul Gandhi. He defeated the BSP's Chandra Parkash Mishra Matiyari by 2,90,853 votes. The BSP candidate got only 99,326 votes, while the BJP's Ram Vilashdas Vedanti finished third with 55,422 votes.

While the 14th Lok Sabha result gave rise to an era of coalition governments at the Centre, the 14th assembly of Uttar Pradesh completed its terms despite getting caught in legal tangles. The BSP, however, had filed a petition at/with the Lucknow bench of the Allahabad High Court challenging Assembly Speaker Keshari Nath Tripathi's decision regarding the breakdown of the party. The high court delivered its verdict on the petition on 12 March 2006, but both parties challenged it at the Supreme Court. When after a long time, the Supreme Court upheld the BSP's plea and reversed the speaker's decision, it was so late that the verdict's significance could only be as an example for the times to come. This was because the Uttar Pradesh Assembly had already completed its term, running for 1,902 days. During this period, Mulayam Singh Yadav was the chief minister for three years and two hundred and fifty-seven days.

In April-May 2007, elections were held to the 15th assembly of Uttar Pradesh. The result was startling. The BSP, which had secured recognition as a national party, scooped up 206 seats. While the BJP got 51 seats, the Congress could manage only 22. Among the regional parties, the ruling Samajwadi Party got 97. Ajit Singh's Rashtriya Lok Dal got only 10 seats. The BSP formed the government with a majority and Mayawati became the chief minister of Uttar Pradesh for the fourth time.

The Congress strengthened its position a bit, by bagging three assembly seats in Amethi. The BSP and Samajwadi Party got a seat each. A total of 1,40,582 people exercised their franchise in Tiloi during this election. Samajwadi Party candidate Mayankeshwar Sharan Singh won with 44,513 votes, while Dr Mohammad Muslim of the Congress finished second with 44,056 votes. Dinesh Pratap Singh of the BSP was third with 31,257 votes. Dharmesh Kumar of the BJP stood fourth with 6,810 votes.

In Salon, 1,21,369 people voted. Congress candidate Shiv Bal Pasi won 45,078 votes. He defeated Samajwadi Party's Asha Kishor, who got 31,969 votes. Dalbahadur of the BSP finished third with 26,589 votes.

In Jagdishpur— another scheduled castes seat—91,912 people exercised their franchise. Congress candidate Ram Sewak won by getting 34,563 votes. Shri Ram of the BSP was second with 21,356 votes, while Vijay Kumar of the Samajwadi Party was third with 14,875 votes. BJP's Rajendra Kumar finished fourth with 10,800 votes.

In Gauriganj, 1,15,650 people cast their votes. BSP candidate Chandra Prakash was the winner with 34,386 votes. Congress candidate Mohd. Naeem received 28,398 votes and finished second. The BJP was in third place. Its candidate Tejbhan Singh got 27,115 votes, while Samajwadi Party's Jang Bahadur Singh finished fourth with 17,231 votes.

In the Amethi assembly constituency, 1,18,516 votes were cast. Congress candidate Amita Singh won with 48,108 votes. The BSP's Ashish was second with 35,684 votes. Rajesh Kumar of the Samajwadi Party was third with 20,804 votes, while Govind Narayan of the BJP was fourth with 6,340 votes.

The 15th assembly of Uttar Pradesh ran for 1,762 days from 13 May 2007 to 7 March 2012. Mayawati, a member of the state legislative council, served as the chief minister for four years and three hundred and sixty days. During this time, the country also voted for the 15th Lok Sabha in May 2009. The people once again reposed their faith in the Sonia-Gandhi-led coalition. The UPA, which was anchored by the Congress, received a clear majority. The Congress bagged 206 seats, while the BJP could get no more than 116. The Rashtriya Janata Dal got 4, Samajwadi Party 23, BSP 21, CPM 16, Shiv Sena 11, TDP 6 and CPI 4. The UPA came back to power under Manmohan Singh. He served as the Prime Minister from 22 May 2004 to 26 May 2014.

In Amethi, Rahul Gandhi romped to victory with no opposition in sight. If we look at the figures, there were 14,31,787 voters in the Amethi Lok Sabha constituency in 2009, of whom 6,46,650 took part. Rahul Gandhi got 71.78 per cent or 4,64,195 votes in this election. BSP candidate Asheesh Shukla was second with 93,997 votes and a vote share of 14.54 per cent. The BJP's Pradeep Kumar Singh was third with 37,570 votes. His vote percentage was just 5.81 per cent. What we see, therefore, is that in the election immediately before Irani stepped in Amethi, the presence of the BJP was next to nil. Whatever votes it managed at the assembly level, was a function of its candidates' aura, public relations and behaviour rather than a credit to the party per se.

Elections to the 16th assembly of Uttar Pradesh took place in 2012. When the Assembly was formed on 8 March 2012, the Samajwadi Party, under Mulayam Singh Yadav and Akhilesh Yadav's leadership, had already got a full majority. The Samajwadi Party won 224 seats. The BSP was reduced to 80 seats, while the BJP could get only 47. The Congress won 28 and Chaudhary Ajit Singh's Rashtriya Lok Dal could manage nine. Although it was he who had won, Mulayam Singh Yadav made his son Akhilesh the chief minister, keeping his legacy in mind.

The Samajwadi Party, by and large, destroyed the aura of the Congress, and especially the Nehru-Gandhi dynasty in Amethi. The Samajwadi Party scooped up three out of the five seats here, while the Congress got two.

Tiloi had 3,12,629 voters in the 2012 Assembly elections, of whom 1,84,949 exercised their franchise. The voting percentage here was 59.16 per cent. The Congress's Dr Mohd Muslim won from here, getting 61, 249 votes, which was 33.12 per cent of the total votes polled. Samajwadi Party's Mayankeshwar Sharan Singh stood second with 58,539, or 31.65 per cent votes. BSP candidate Nadeem Ashraf was third with 24,027 votes and a vote share of 12.99 per cent. The BJP finished fourth. Its candidate Mahendra Singh got 21,990 votes. His vote percentage was 11.84 per cent.

The Salon scheduled caste constituency had 3,09,713 registered voters, of whom 1,71,350 participated. The voting percentage here was 55.33 per cent. Samajwadi Party candidate Asha Kishore won by winning 69,020 votes and a vote share of 40.28 per cent votes, while Congress's Sheo Balak Pasi got 48,443 votes. His vote percentage was 28.27 per cent. BSP's Vijay Ambedkar was third with 23,069, that is 13.46 per cent votes, while BJP candidate Dal Bahadur Kori got 18,959 votes. His vote percentage was 11.06 per cent.

In Jagdishpur, there were 3,21,645 voters, of whom 1,72,982 cast their ballots. The voting percentage here was 53.78 per cent. Congress candidate Radhe Shyam was the winner with 56,309 votes. His vote percentage was 32.55 per cent. In the second place was Vijay Kumar of the Samajwadi Party who got 50,912, or 29.43

per cent votes. The BSP's Shri Ram Krantikari secured 32,665 votes, with a vote share of 18.88 per cent, while BJP candidate Ramlakhan was fourth with 24,330, which is 14.07 per cent votes.

The Gauriganj constituency had 3,09,472 registered voters during this election, of which 1,81,832 participated. The voting percentage here was 58.76 per cent. Samajwadi Party candidate Rakesh Pratap Singh won by getting 44,287, or 24.36 per cent votes. Mohammad Nayeem of the Congress was second with 43,784, or 24.08 per cent votes. Tejbhan Singh of the BJP was third with 34,840 votes and a vote share of 19.19 per cent. The BSP's Chandra Prakash got 31,021 votes, and a vote share of 17.08 per cent.

The Amethi assembly constituency had 2,96,160 voters, of whom 1,63,038 cast their ballots. The voting percentage here was 55.05 per cent. Here too Samajwadi Party was successful, with its candidate Gayatri Prasad defeating the Congress's Amita Singh by getting 58,434, or 35.84 per cent votes. Amita Singh received 49,674 votes, with a vote share of 30.47 per cent. Ashish Shukla of the BSP was third with 35,374, or 21.70 per cent votes and Rashmi Singh of the BJP was fourth with 8,605 votes. His vote percentage was 5.28 per cent.

The statistics may seem too academic to some readers, but it was necessary to explain why Irani's win in Amethi is so important and what its significance is. Another part of this book discusses in detail Irani's strategies that led to the Amethi triumph. That is why figures have been discussed here—as statements of fact. The Lok Sabha elections of 2014 was a big symbol of change for the Amethi constituency. The country was changing, and there was a restlessness in Amethi as well.

From the time the then chief minister of Gujarat Narendra Modi was nominated as the prime ministerial candidate, there was enthusiasm of a different kind among the youth, especially the workers connected to the BJP and RSS. Modi helped the dreams of the common man to take flight. He came to the electoral battle with the development model of Gujarat, where he had been the chief minister for four consecutive terms, from 2001 to 2014. Modi had with him a group of young, enthusiastic and dedicated workers who had complete faith in him and would do anything for him, and the ideology of the BJP and the Sangh. Irani was one among them.

Significantly, while Modi now had rich administrative experience, when he first got attached to the RSS it was at an age when an ordinary adolescent would not think about their surroundings, leave alone the country. After completing high school in 1967, he left home at the age of seventeen and took up formal membership of the RSS. Since then, he has never looked back. In 1975, the Sangh, impressed with his presence of mind during the Emergency imposed by Indira Gandhi, made him a divisional pracharak at the age of thirty. In 1985, he became directly involved with mainstream politics.

Such was the BJP and RSS's faith in Modi that when in 1990, party stalwart Lal Krishna Advani took out the Somnath-Ayodhya 'Rath Yatra', it was Modi who was made the sarathi (charioteer). Likewise, when in 1991 Murli Manohar Joshi brought out an 'Ekta Yatra' from Kanniyakumari to Srinagar with the dream of Akhand Bharat (undivided India), Modi was one of the active managers. Modi's stature in the party continued to increase as a result of his successful discharge of duties, tact and dedication to the organisation. In 1995, he arrived in Delhi after being made the national secretary, and after just three years, in 1998, he was given a big responsibility and made general secretary, 'organisation'. Modi held this post till October 2001, during which he developed personal relations with party workers and leaders from all over the country.

In 2001, when Gujarat experienced a terrible natural calamity in the form of the earthquake, Chief Minister Keshubhai Patel could not handle the situation in the manner that was required. Modi was sent from Delhi to Ahmedabad to stop the factionalism within the BJP, and in October 2001, he became chief minister of the state, though he had not contested any election. His tenure in Gujarat, in the time that was to follow, is an important part of Indian political history. For that reason, in an important session of the BJP in Goa in September 2013, Modi was chosen as the prime ministerial candidate for the 2014 Lok Sabha election. The then president of the party, Rajnath Singh, announced Modi's candidature. Although Lal Krishna Advani and a few other veteran leaders were opposed to announcing a prime ministerial candidate before the Lok Sabha election result, the Sangh brass was in favour of the move.

The country was fed up with Manmohan Singh's silence and the arrogance of the Congress leaders. Inflation and corruption were peaking. The group circumambulating 10 Janpath had lost its appeal with the technology-loving, social media savvy youth of the twenty-first century. Consequently, when the result of the 2014 Lok Sabha elections was declared, the Modi-led BJP had garnered 282 seats and galloped past the majority mark. After a long time, a party had mustered a clear majority in the Lok Sabha. The youth had turned Modi's slogan of 'Achche din aayenge' (Good days will come) into their dream and happily put their votes into the kitty of the BJP. This time, while the Congress stopped at 44, a party like BSP didn't get a single seat. Also, the two prominent Left parties, CPI and CPM, could barely get 10 seats.

The BJP had sent Irani to Amethi with high hopes and she perfectly lived up to the expectations of the organisation. In 2014, there were 16,69,843 registered voters in Amethi, of whom 8,74,625 participated. The voting percentage here was 52.38 per cent. Rahul Gandhi got 4,08,651 votes, with a vote share of 46.71 per cent, while Irani secured 3,00,748 votes, with a vote share of 34.38 per cent. Dharmendra Pratap Singh of the BSP got 57,716, or 6.6 per cent votes. He was third. The worst was in store for the Aam Aadmi Party's Kumar Vishvas, who before the election, had tried to create an atmosphere in the media that it was he who would present the real challenge to Rahul Gandhi. Vishwas could manage only 25,527 votes, a mere 2.92 per cent of the total votes polled.

Now let us look at the result of the 17th assembly elections of Uttar Pradesh in 2017. When the BJP went to this election under the spectacular leadership of Modi and the guidance of party president Amit Shah, it was a bit concerned. In spite of all its efforts, it had lost in Bihar and Delhi, and so, the Sangh took over command this time. Despite supporting this top pair of the BJP, it had made up its mind on Yogi Adityanath as the chief ministerial face of Uttar Pradesh. The frontline leaders of the RSS never hid this, and in the chintan (contemplation) session of the Bharatiya Sant Sabha held at the Gorakhnath Temple in March 2016, the RSS vowed to make Yogi Adityanath the chief minister.

The monks said, 'When we joined hands in 1992, the "structure" was demolished. We have our own government at the Centre now. Even if the Supreme Court rules in our favour, the temple at Ramjanmabhoomi will not be able to be built as long as there is Mulayam Singh Yadav or Mayawati's government in the state. For that, we have to make Yogi Adityanath the chief minister.' These words of the monks found favour with the Sangh leaders present. Modi and Shah were already in Delhi, now the party workers and Sangh pracharaks gave their all to crown Yogi in Lucknow. The result was evident as well. Amazingly, out of six parties registered as national parties, only three could open their accounts. While the BJP captured 312 seats by itself, the BSP and Congress got 19 and 7 seats respectively. The Samajwadi Party, registered as a state party, managed 47 seats, while Rashtriya Lok Dal got only one.

Even if Rahul Gandhi had paid heed to the warning contained in the Congress's misery in the five assembly seats of Amethi in the

2017 state elections, and done something, the result of 2019 wouldn't probably have been what it turned out to be. In the 2017 elections, the BJP won four seats here, while the remaining seat went to the Samajwadi Party.

In Tiloi, out of 3,39,401 registered voters, 1,95,746 exercised their franchise. The voting percentage was 57.67 per cent. BJP candidate Mayankeshwar Sharan Singh won with 96,119 votes and a vote share of 49.76 per cent. BSP candidate Mohd. Saood received 52,072 votes. His vote percentage was 26.96 per cent. The Congress finished third. Its candidate Vinod Kumar Mishra could manage only 35,709 votes. This was only 18.55 per cent of the total votes cast.

The Salon constituency had 3,39,963 registered voters, of whom 1,92,964 took part in the election. The voting percentage was 56.76 per cent. BJP candidate Dal Bahadur Kori won 78,028 votes, with a vote share of 41.19 per cent. Suresh Chaudhary of the Congress was second with 61,973, or 32.72 per cent votes, while Braj Lal Pasi of the BSP got 39,851, or 21.04 per cent votes.

The Jagdishpur constituency had 3,61,697 voters, and 1,92,972 voters exercised their franchise. The voting percentage was 53.35 per cent. BJP candidate Suresh Kumar won by getting 84,219 votes, with a vote share of 44.36 per cent. Congress candidate Radhe Shyam was second with 67,619, or 35.61 per cent votes. BSP candidate Jagdatt finished third with 31,338, or 16.51 per cent votes.

Gauriganj had 3,35,745 voters during this election, of whom 2,01,048 participated. The voting percentage was 59.88 per cent. Samajwadi Party candidate Rakesh Pratap Singh was the winner with 77,915 votes and a vote share of 38.98 per cent. Congress's Mohammad Nayeem got 51,496, or 25.76 per cent votes, while Vijay Kishor of the BSP got 33,848 votes, which was 16.93 per cent of the total votes cast. BJP candidate Uma Shankar Pandey got 23,642, or 11.83 per cent votes.

BJP candidate Garima Singh was the winner in the Amethi assembly seat. The constituency had 3,34,587 registered voters during this election, of whom 1,87,717 participated. The voting percentage was 56.1 per cent. Garima Singh, the former daughter-in-law of the Amethi royal family, was engaged in a family dispute, but when the result was declared, she emerged as the winner. Garima Singh received 64,226 votes, with a vote share of 34.34 per cent. Gaytri Prasad of the Samajwadi Party received 59,161, or 31.63 per cent votes. The BSP's Ramji was third with 30,175, or 16.1 per cent votes. The Congress's Amita Singh finished fourth. Despite all efforts of husband Sanjay Singh, she could manage only 20,291, or 10.85 per cent votes. The discord in the old royal family of Amethi came to the surface during this election. Sanjay Singh's current wife and his ex-wife both contested from Amethi. While Amita Singh represented the Congress, Garima Singh contested in favour of the BJP.

If you look at statistics, while in 1980 Sanjay Gandhi won by a margin of 1,28,545 votes, Rajiv Gandhi won by 2,37,696 votes in the bypoll of 1981. In 1984, in the wake of a wave of sympathy after Indira Gandhi's assassination, Rajiv Gandhi won by 3,14,878 votes. Rajiv Gandhi's margins of victory in 1989 and 1991 were 2,02,138 and 1,12,085 votes respectively. Sonia Gandhi entered active politics and contested the 13th Lok Sabha elections in 1999 simultaneously from Amethi and Karnataka's Bellary. While in Bellary she could win against Sushma Swaraj by a margin of 56,000 votes, in Amethi, she received 4,18,960 votes and won by a huge margin of 3,00,012 votes. After that, she left this seat for her son Rahul Gandhi in the 14th Lok Sabha elections of 2004.

In 2004, Rahul Gandhi won by a margin of 2,90,853 votes, and by a record 3,70,198 votes in 2009. But in 2014, this margin shrunk to 1,07,903 votes. That too when it was his opponent Irani's first time in Amethi. For her, the place was new, the time was less and the people were unknown. Her fight was with an individual who had a legacy behind him, but if legacies could achieve anything in a democracy, then members of the royalty would not have travelled the length and breadth of the country to rise in the eyes of the people and become their representatives.

The general elections to the 17th Lok Sabha was held over seven phases from 11 April to 19 May 2019, and when the result was declared on 23 May, the BJP under Modi emerged victorious in 303 seats. The BJP bettered its clear majority with an increased share of Lok Sabha seats, and the coalition it led had 353 seats. While Modi was applauded for this spectacular electoral success, analysts also underlined the strategies of BJP president Amit Shah that had contributed to the historic win. However, the biggest upset of this election was in Amethi.

When Rahul Gandhi took the field in Amethi for the 2019 Lok Sabha elections, having won the 2004, 2009 and 2014 elections from there, he became a victim of complacency. Irani, on the other hand, fought from Amethi—and she fought tooth and nail.

Bechu Khan, a businessman from Jagdishpur, told the media, 'A generational change is being noticed in Amethi. The new generation gives little room to emotions and is more concerned about its future, which they have seen in Irani and the BJP...' He clarified, 'The new generation has not seen Rajiv Gandhi's attachment with the local people. It has not seen how Sanjay Gandhi made Amethi significant. For that reason, they do not have an emotional bond with the Gandhi family.' The youth of Amethi wanted development along with change. Their problems were more with the contractors of the Nehru-Gandhi dynasty than the dynasty per se.

Anyway, this book aims to consider the factors behind Irani's victory from Amethi and so there has been a lot of discussion on it in the other chapters. But what stands out is Irani staying put in Amethi despite losing the seat by more than one lakh votes in 2014.

She continued to tour the constituency regularly and point towards Rahul Gandhi's conspicuous absence. The people of Amethi were able to contact her easily even when she was in Delhi. She would herself and at times ensure help was forthcoming from the other ministers.

Ranu Solanki, who runs a tea stall in the Salon bus stand, feels Rahul Gandhi's relation with the voters was superficial. He said, 'It was his team of advisers that spoiled his opportunities.' Comparing Rahul Gandhi's style of work to Irani's, he said, 'The programmes of the Nehru-Gandhi family used to be around key areas and highways and couldn't focus on rural areas. Whereas Irani reached villages and households to establish direct communication with the people, seek votes for development and change and take her message to the people benefiting from these measures.'

The local people also believe that the condition of the Congress had become so bad in Amethi that even the presence of Priyanka Gandhi could not make any difference. Khilawan Raj, a member of the local community, added sarcastically, 'You don't get votes just by waving hands and travelling on the streets in big vehicles.'

However, staunch Congress supporter Kishori Lal does not concur with the others. He believes that the new generation of Amethi is not aware of the developmental work undertaken by the Congress, and the BJP lured those people away from the Congress by selling its schemes full of razzle-dazzle. He commented that the younger generations in Amethi do not know that the place used to be a wasteland, which was treated during Rajiv Gandhi's tenure. The BJP successfully sold the programmes of the Centre and these people moved away from the Congress.

There were 1,431,787 voters in Amethi in the 2019 Lok Sabha elections, of which 9,42,453 participated. The result of this constituency came late due to counting in three districts, but when it came, BJP candidate Smriti Irani was the winner with 4,68,514 votes. She received 49.71 per cent of the total votes cast. In second place was Rahul Gandhi, who received 4,13,394 votes, and vote share of 43.86 per cent. The rest of the candidates had to forfeit their security deposits.

With her victory, Irani wrote such a script that the Congress is still searching for the reason behind its loss, while political scientists and researchers are searching the reasons for Irani's triumph.

Amethi has moved ahead from the historic elections of 2019. With new dreams, hopes and beliefs.

Appendix

**Work done at Smriti Irani's initiative in Amethi
between 2014 and 2019:**

(Based on the booklet distributed during the elections.)

1. Gauriganj: Provision of manure racks at Gauriganj.
2. Gauriganj: Construction of soil testing laboratory in progress in Amethi district.
3. Jagdishpur: Construction of Krishi Vigyan Kendra for Amethi district in progress.
4. Gauriganj: Separate arrangements for reservation counter, ticket house, enquiry office for the convenience of passengers at Gauriganj railway station.
5. Amethi: Better passenger facilities provided at Amethi railway station.
6. Amethi: Approval for railway under bridge in Amethi-Mahaso.
7. Gauriganj: Approval for high-level platform at Gauriganj railway station.
8. Salon: Budget approval for Dih, Chhatoh, Amethi-Sultanpur to Amethi-Unchahar railway line.

9. Gauriganj: Rail Neer project launched.

10. Bahadurpur, Gauriganj, Amethi, Sangrampur: Approval for doubling of railway line from Bachhrawan to Pratapgarh.

11. Bahadurpur, Gauriganj, Amethi Sangrampur: Electrification of railway line from Bachhrawan to Pratapgarh started.

12. All blocks: Purchase of crop affected by hailstorms from farmers of Amethi.

13. Haliyapur: Dam construction completed by the National Flood Disaster Management to stop the erosion by the Gomti River at Haliyapur, Pipri.

14. Bahadurpur, Gauriganj, Amethi, Sangrampur: Funds allocated from the Budget for the doubling and electrification of -Utretia Varanasi via Raebareli-Amethi line. Work is in progress.

15. Bahadurpur, Gauriganj, Amethi, Sangrampur: Ambedkar Nagar via Fatehpur, Lalganj and Raebareli line to connect Raebareli and Amethi with the national highway network. The Amethi-Sultanpur road was declared a national highway and the budget was allotted with instructions to complete work in a year.

16. Amethi: Kendriya Vidyalaya inaugurated in Tala and the process of temporary school operation completed.

17. All blocks: Under the Pradhan Mantri Mahila Suraksha Bima Yojana, 25,000 women of the Amethi district were given women safety insurance.

18. All blocks: Under Pradhan Mantri Suraksha Bima Yojana, 25,000 people of the Amethi district were insured.

19. All blocks: Distribution of one lakh fruit-bearing trees in Gauriganj, Tiloi, Amethi and Jagdishpur through the Khushali Foundation, Bareilly.

20. All blocks: Kisan panchayat with the Minister of State for Agriculture, Dr Sanjeev Kumar Balyan, and distribution of Rs 25,000 to the families of affected farmers in Amethi district.

21. Singhpur, Jagdishpur, Jamo, Musafirkhana: Instructions for six-laning of National Highway 56 for traffic movement from Lucknow to Varanasi.

22. Jagdishpur: Mr Abhishek of Matiyari Kala and many other people of the Amethi parliamentary constituency repatriated.

23. All blocks: Support provided with proper efforts for the treatment of people suffering from cancer, coronary and other serious ailments.

24. All blocks: Following an appeal by the local people of Amethi, admission to Kendriya Vidyalayas was provided in various places of the country including Amethi district.

25. Shahgarh: All possible assistance to the farmers displaced by the Samrat cycle project.

26. Jamo: A 200-bed hospital for women in Jamo block approved by the central and state governments.

27. Jagdishpur: A girls' college approved in Kathora-Jagdishpur-Amethi.

28. All blocks: Approval to purchase and install about 250 IndiaMark hand pumps across Amethi parliamentary constituency with the help of CSR.

29. Salon, Dih, Chhatoh, Amethi, Musafirkhana, Gauriganj, Jagdishpur, Singhpur: Passenger rest houses provided at all major pilgrimage sites, railway stations, bus stations of the Amethi parliamentary constituency.

30. Amethi: Distribution of e-rickshaws in the entire constituency.

31. Bahadurpur: The Rajiv Gandhi Institute of Petroleum Technology, Jais was completed at the cost of Rs 360 crore by the NDA government and handed over to the public.

32. Bhadar: A satellite branch of the Baba Saheb Bhimrao Ambedkar University, Lucknow established at Tikermafi in Amethi.

33. All blocks: Distribution of thousands of tricycles to the differently-abled people of Amethi to help them sustain their livelihood.

34. Amethi: Eye treatment for the welfare of thousands of elderly people and women of the Amethi parliamentary constituency, eye surgery done on 1,134 people and eyeglasses distributed.

35. Musafirkhana: The body of a person of the Amethi parliamentary constituency brought home after sudden demise abroad.

36. Amethi, Bhadar: A branch of IGNOU and NIOS for the working women and men, youth, students of the Amethi constituency.

37. Amethi: Approval for multipurpose master building at Amethi railway station and allocation of funds. Work is in progress.

38. Bahadurpur, Amethi, Gauriganj, Bhetua: National Highway 232 (Tanda-Banda) completed by the NDA government and dedicated to the nation.

39. Tiloi: The construction of a 200-bed hospital almost complete.

40. Jamo, Bahadurpur, Gauriganj: Bani, Gauriganj and Jais railway stations of Amethi accorded the status of a model railway station.

41. Jamo: Pradhan Mantri Kaushal Kendra opened.

42. Shahgarh: After getting approval for a Sainik School in Amethi, work started with an investment of Rs 121 crore.

43. Bahadurpur: Struggle to free the Vocational Training Centre, Jais from illegal occupation.

44. All blocks: Distribution of 25,000 sarees among the women of the Amethi parliamentary constituency.

45. All blocks: Housing provided to 2,500 people under the Pradhan Mantri Awas Yojana-Gramin.

46. All blocks: 400 families were benefited under the Family Benefit Scheme.

47. All blocks: Government funding provided to 66 people belonging to the Scheduled Castes and Tribes in Amethi district.

48. All blocks: Distribution of tricycles to 25 beneficiaries of mass empowerment.

49. All blocks: Distribution of labour registration cards to 2,000 people.

50. All blocks: Distribution of 100 infant beneficiary cards to mothers.

51. All blocks: 10 people got sanction certificates for loans.

52. All blocks: Distribution of certificates to 34 meritorious students.

53. Jagdishpur: Distribution of rotavators, soil health cards.

54. All blocks: Distribution of cards to 400 malnourished women and children.

55. All blocks: Distribution of cards to the beneficiaries of 1,500 personal toilets under the Swachh Bharat Abhiyan scheme.
56. Gauriganj: Distribution of acceptance letters to six people under the Maharani Laxmibai Samman Kosh Yojana.
57. All blocks: Distribution of acceptance letter of ex-gratia amount of Rs 4 lakh for natural disasters.
58. Gauriganj: TB unit under District Hospital Amethi handed over to the public.
59. Gauriganj: Inauguration of Chief Medical Officer's office and residential, non-residential buildings.
60. Tiloi: Primary Health Centre, Odari-Tiloi handed over to the public.
61. Shukul Bazar: Community Health Centre, Shukul Bazar handed over to the public.
62. Amethi: Bhumipujan of CHC Centre.
63. All blocks: 200 villagers of the Amethi constituency were taken on a pilgrimage to Hardwar and Rishikesh.
64. Gauriganj: Inauguration of a cancer centre on behalf of the Bhaurao Deoras Institute at CHC Amethi.
65. Jagdishpur: Bhoomipujan of Krishi Vigyan Kendra at Kathora.
66. Shahgarh: Inauguration of free Wi-Fi at the BSNL office.
67. Sangrampur: Bhoomipujan of community toilet.
68. Sangrampur: Inauguration of BSNL Wi-Fi.
69. Amethi: Inauguration of marriage hall in Ward No 1.
70. All blocks: Under the neem project, 580 metric tonnes of nimboli was procured.
71. Musafirkhana: DG village in Pindara Musafirkhana, Gauriganj handed over to the public.
72. Amethi: Inauguration of India Post Payment Bank at Amethi post office.
73. Bahadurpur, Jagdishpur, Sangrampur, Gauriganj: Approval of public facilities at major pilgrimage sites of Amethi constituency by the state government.
74. All blocks: Distribution of relief materials to families suffering from fire each year.

75. All blocks: Distribution of PWD (persons with disabilities) equipment to 1,492 differently-abled people.
76. Gauriganj: Employment fair organised by Pradhan Mantri Kaushal Vikas Kendra. Employment given to 3,000 youths.
77. Gauriganj: Primary health centres, Sentha, Jethi, Mavai handed over to the public.
78. Jagdishpur: Newly built power plant in Jagdishpur Assembly constituency handed over to the public.
79. Gauriganj: Vikas Bhawan handed over to the public.
80. All blocks: Inauguration of 49 new connectivity routes in Amethi district.
81. Jagdishpur: Inauguration of approved harmony pavilion Kathoura cillage in the Jagdishpur development block.
82. Shukul Bazar, Bahadurpur, Jagdishpur, Singhpur: Foundation stones laid for four new approved ITIs at Santhin, Tendua, Kathora and Inhauna in Amethi district.
83. Gauriganj: CT scan at District Hospital Gauriganj handed over to the public. Free CT scan facility available to patients.
84. All blocks: Cleaning and painting of major temples of Amethi constituency.
85. All blocks: Free screening of the film *Uri: The Surgical Strike* through Picture Time for the local people at all major places in the Amethi constituency.
86. All blocks: Kamal Mela organised in every Assembly segment of the Amethi parliamentary constituency to spread awareness on welfare works undertaken by Prime Minister Narendra Modi.
87. All blocks: Free electric potter's wheel distributed to 300 potter families of Amethi after training, and plans to provide them to a further 200 families soon.
88. Sangrampur, Bhetua, Chhatoh, Amethi, Dih, Jamo: To provide self-reliance and employment to the people of Amethi, 50 families were trained in bee-keeping and 500 bee boxes were distributed.
89. Amethi and Bhadar: Distribution of mass blazer machines for economically benefiting the potter families of Amethi.

90. All blocks: PMEGP workshop organised in Salon's Chhatoh intending to employ the youth.

91. Salon: Lijjat-papad-making centre started in Salon under the scheme to employ women.

92. Jagdishpur: Halt of train number 2417/18 *Mahamana Express* at Nihalgarh railway station.

93. Musafirkhana: Halt of train number 221419/20 *Suhaildev Express* at Musafirkhana railway station.

94. Bahadurpur: Halt of train number 12183/84 *Pratapgarh-Bhopal Express* at Jais railway station.

95. All blocks: Distribution of 50,000 fruit-bearing trees in Amethi through the Utthan Sewa Sansthan.

96. All blocks: 200 senior functionaries of the Amethi constituency taken on a pilgrimage to Hardwar and Rishikesh.

97. All blocks: Distribution of 25,000 vegetable seed packets to women of Amethi through the Khushali Foundation, Bareilly.

98. All blocks: State roadways buses begin operating from each Assembly constituency to Amethi-Gauriganj.

99. All blocks: 20,000 common people of Amethi provided with facilities for taking a holy dip at Kumbh and returning to their homes after meals.

100. All blocks: Through the joint efforts of GNFC and Utthan Seva Sansthan, free speller machines distributed to provide self-reliance and employment to the families associated with the neem project.

101. All blocks: Distribution of seeds of different vegetables of the kitchen garden to 10,000 families of the Amethi constituency.

102. All blocks: Cricket Mahakumbh organised in 2018-19 for the promotion of sports among the youth of Amethi.

103. Amethi: Beautification of Amethi Ramlila Maidan approved.

104. Amethi: Nagar Panchayat of Amethi recognised as model nagar panchayat.

105. Amethi: Sultanpur-Amethi railway line approved, funds approved.

106. All blocks: Free health camp organised for the common people through the Bhaurao Deoras Sewa Trust.

107. Musafirkhana: Allotment of buildings to the 67 fire-ravaged families in Barulia on full funding.

108. Jamo: Barulia completely developed as a model village.

109. Shahgarh: Hariharpur completely developed under the Sansad Adarsh Gram Yojana.

110. Jagdishpur: Inauguration of a trauma centre.

111. Jagdishpur: Establishment of a blood bank.

112. Shukul Bazar, Haliyapur: Start of Purvanchal Expressway.

113. Bahadurpur: Beautification of the stairway of the Sri Tapeshwardham Temple.

114. Tiloi: Drinking water tank approved in Semrauta.

115. Amethi: Amethi Bypass inaugurated.

116. Tiloi: A 132/33 KV power substation inaugurated.

117. Musafirkhana: Large cow protection centre inaugurated at Newada, Musafirkhana.

118. laid the foundation of malre pure Gajrala link road in Aryanwana

119. Amethi: Renovation and coating of the link road from Ondih to Pure Bhoop and Chhichha on the Amethi-Rae-Bareli-Ayodhya road.

120. Singhpur: Inauguration of Sadbhav Mandap at Jaipur.

121. Salon: 400 KV power station in Sirsira under Salon Assembly inaugurated.

122. Amethi: Amethi bus station upgraded and Amethi depot workshop reconstructed and handed over to the public.

123. Amethi: Rest houses and shops constructed and handed over to the public at Amethi bus station.

124. Musafirkhana: Pandit Deendayal Upadhyay Rajkiya Model Inter College Chharauli, Musafirkhana handed over to the public.

125. Jamo: The main building of the primary health centre, Dakhinwara, Amethi handed over to the public.

126. Gauriganj: Buildings of the chief medical officer and subordinate workshop handed over to the public.

127. Sangrampur: 33/11 KV power substation built under Pandit Deendayal Upadhyaya Grameen Jyoti Yojana handed over to the public.

128. Amethi: 33/11 KV power substation built under the IPDS scheme handed over to the public.

129. Jagdishpur: Steel processing unit of SAIL handed over to the public.

130. Amethi: Medical camp organised in Ramganj, Amethi.

131. Shukul Bazar, Jagdishpur, Singhpur, Tiloi, Gauriganj municipality, Musafirkhana, Shahgarh: An attempt was made to interlock various roads with the help of the then Finance Minister Honourable Shri Arun Jaitley's MP fund.

132. Shukul Bazar, Jagdishpur, Singhpur, Tiloi, Gauriganj municipality, Musafirkhana, Shahgarh, Amethi: An attempt was made to interlock various roads with the help of the MP fund of Rajya Sabha MP Anil Agarwal.

133. Chhatoh: An attempt was made to interlock various roads in the Chhatoh block with the help of Rajya Sabha MP Ashok Bajpai's MP fund.

134. Shukul Bazar, Jagdishpur, Singhpur, Tiloi, Gauriganj municipality, Musafirkhana, Shahgarh, Amethi: An attempt was made to interlock various roads with the help of Rajya Sabha MP Sonal Mansingh's MP fund.

References

1. Ajoy Bose and John Dayal, *The Shah Commission Begins*.

2. Amartya Sen, *Development As Freedom*.

3. Anand Vaidya, Alf Gunvald Nilsen, Kenneth Bo Nielsen, *Indian Democracy: Origins, Trajectories, Contestations*.

4. Arthur Cotterell, *Origins of European Civilization*.

5. Atul Kohli, *The Success of India's Democracy*.

6. Coomi Kapoor, *The Emergency: A Personal History*.

7. D.L. Sheth, *At Home with Democracy: A Theory of Indian Politics*.

8. Emma Tarlo, *Unsettling Memories*.

9. Frank M Bryan, *The Vermont Papers*.

10. Fritz W. Scharpf, *Governing in Europe: Effective and Democratic*.

11. Gerard Alexander, *The Sources of Democratic Consolidation*.

12. Gyan Prakash, *Emergency Chronicles: Indira Gandhi and Democracy's Turning Point*.

13. Harry Redner, *The Tragedy of European Civilization: Towards an Intellectual History of the Twentieth Century*.

14. J. Benjamin Hurlbut, *Experiments in Democracy: Human Embryo Research and the Politics of Bioethics.*

15. Jan van Deth and Kenneth Newton, *Foundations of Comparative Politics.*

16. John Dayal, *For Reasons of State: Delhi Under Emergency.*

17. Khushwant Singh, *Why I Supported the Emergency: Essays and Profiles.*

18. Lal Krishna Advani, *A Prisoner's Scrap Book.*

19. Martha Nussbaum, *The Clash Within: Democracy, Religious Violence, and India's Future.*

20. Meghnad Desai, Baron Desai, *The Raisina Model: Indian Democracy at 70.*

21. Milan Vaishnav, *When Crime Pays: Money and Muscle in Indian Politics.*

22. Nancy Goldstone, *The Maid and the Queen: The Secret History of Joan of Arc.*

23. P.N. Dhar, *Indira Gandhi, the 'Emergency', and Indian Democracy.*

24. Peter Kellner, *Democracy: 1,000 Years in Pursuit of British Liberty.*

25. Peter Ronald de Souza, *In the Hall of Mirrors: Reflections on Indian Democracy.*

26. Prashant Bhushan, *The Case that Shook India.*

27. Rajdeep Sardesai, *How Modi Won India*, 2019.

28. Rajdeep Sardesai, *The Election That Changed India*, 2014.

29. Ramachandra Guha, *Gandhi: The Years That Changed the World: 1914-1948.*

30. Ramachandra Guha, *India after Gandhi.*

31. Robert Crowcroft, SJD Green, Robert Whiting *the Philosophy, Politics and Religion of British Democracy: Maurice Cowling and Conservatism* (International Library of Political Studies).

32. Robert W. Stern, *Democracy and Dictatorship in South Asia.*

33. Ruchir Sharma, *Democracy on the Road.*

34. Sagarika Ghose, *Indira: India's Most Powerful Prime Minister.*

35. S.Y. Quraishi, *The Great March of Democracy: Seven Decades of India's Elections.*

36. Stephanie Hemphill, *Language of Fire: Joan of Arc Reimagined.*

37. T.V. Rajeswar, *India: The Crucial Years.*

38. Taruvai Subayya Krishnamurthy, *Miracle of Democracy: India's Amazing Journey.*

39. Tavleen Singh, *Durbar.*

40. Thomas Blom Hansen, *The Saffron Wave: Democracy and Hindu Nationalism in Modern India.*

41. Todd Landman, Human Rights and Democracy: The Precarious Triumph of Ideals.

42. Vinod Mehta, The Sanjay Story: From Anand Bhavan To Amethi.

43. Will Durant, The Reformation.

44. Ashutosh Varshney, *Adhoori Jeet.*

45. Rakesh Pandey, *Jannayak Rahul Gandhi.*

46. R.P.N. Singh, *Bharat me Gathbandhan Kaal.*

47. Outlook (Hindi).

Acknowledgements

I met dozens of people while writing about the Amethi struggle. I conversed with them for hours—travelled from Amethi to Goa. During many of my Amethi visits, I used to simply roam around to get a sense of the mood of the people there. I would stop anywhere and chat with people to collect information that would be useful for this book. In Lucknow, I met the leaders of different political parties. Now that the book is in your hands, the credit for that should go to these people who helped me understand Amethi and its grassroots politics. At the outset, I would like to express my gratitude towards Smriti Iraniji who shared her thoughts about Amethi with me. She never avoided my questions and answered them with considerable clarity—many thanks to Smritiji. Union minister Dr Sanjeev Balyan narrated his experiences of the Amethi election for several hours. My heartfelt thanks to Balyanji. I would also like to thank the Chief Minister of Goa Pramod Sawantji. I was allotted an hour by the chief minister's office, but when we sat down at his residence, we continued to chat on the Amethi election for nearly two-and-a-half hours. During the conversation, the name of the former chief minister of Goa, the late

Manohar Parrikar came up. Today I remember him with reverence as well because this book mentions a meeting with him when he was the defence minister. Parmeshwarji and Satendraji helped a lot in understanding the functioning of the Rashtriya Swayamsevak Sangh. I thank both of them from the core of my heart. I express my gratitude also towards Smriti Irani's election-in-charge Rajesh Masalaji, the BJP's district president Durgesh Pathakji, Pragya Tripathiji, who was with Smritiji as her aide during the 2014 and 2019 elections, Vijay Guptaji and the Mayor of Ranchi Asha Lakdaji, who helped me with their stories. Thanks also to Devanshi Shah. I am also grateful to the dozens of residents of Amethi whom I had met during my tours.

Indian National Congress leaders had represented the Amethi Lok Sabha seat for a long time. I felt it was imperative to talk to the local Congress leaders to understand the politics of the Gandhi family. I did speak to them. I am thankful towards Nadim Ashraf Jaisi, Kishori Lal Sharma and others. A number of Congress leaders spoke but requested anonymity. I thank them all.

I also thank my editor-in-chief Sanjay Guptaji for his encouragement. I am extremely indebted towards my executive editor Vishnu Prakash Tripathiji. He has a repository of authentic memories on Uttar Pradesh politics. Listening to him, you get transported to that day and age. Through his words, I was able to understand the politics of Uttar Pradesh, the leaders of the various parties and their politics. Thanks also to my friend Manoj Rajan Tripathi—I would call him up even at odd hours for information and he would readily oblige. Thanks to my journalist friends Rohan Dua, Pankaj Jha and Vasudha Venugopal. How to thank Jai Prakash Pandey, my friend from the early days of journalism, on whom I have a right? Thanks to my friends Sundeep Bhutoria and Yatindra Mishra. I am beholden to all those, whose interviews and statements I have quoted.

I am grateful to the translator of the book Debdutta Bhattacharjee. He offered crucial advice apart from translating the book. Sanjeev Jha provided the research material for this book. I express my gratitude to him. Minakshi Thakur lent patient support during the making of this book—thanks to her. I am grateful to Pallavi Singh for sharp editing of the original Hindi text. My wife Vandana helped me a lot during the entire process of writing the book. Without her cooperation, perhaps it wouldn't have been possible for the book to assume the form that it has.

9 789357 769952